Subjective quality of life and social work

Otger Autrata · Bringfriede Scheu

Subjective quality of life and social work

Social Widerspiegelung as a basis

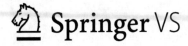

Otger Autrata
Forschungsinstitut Riss
Feldkirchen, Austria

Bringfriede Scheu
Studiengang Soziale Arbeit
Fachhochschule Kärnten
Feldkirchen, Austria

ISBN 978-3-658-40399-7   ISBN 978-3-658-40400-0   (eBook)
https://doi.org/10.1007/978-3-658-40400-0

© The Editor(s) (if applicable) and The Author(s), under exclusive licence to Springer Fachmedien Wiesbaden GmbH, part of Springer Nature 2023
This book is a translation of the original German edition „Subjektive Lebensqualität und Soziale Arbeit" by Autrata, Otger, published by Springer Fachmedien Wiesbaden GmbH in 2021. The translation was done with the help of artificial intelligence (machine translation by the service DeepL.com). A subsequent human revision was done primarily in terms of content, so that the book will read stylistically differently from a conventional translation. Springer Nature works continuously to further the development of tools for the production of books and on the related technologies to support the authors.
This work is subject to copyright. All rights are solely and exclusively licensed by the Publisher, whether the whole or part of the material is concerned, specifically the rights of translation, reprinting, reuse of illustrations, recitation, broadcasting, reproduction on microfilms or in any other physical way, and transmission or information storage and retrieval, electronic adaptation, computer software, or by similar or dissimilar methodology now known or hereafter developed.
The use of general descriptive names, registered names, trademarks, service marks, etc. in this publication does not imply, even in the absence of a specific statement, that such names are exempt from the relevant protective laws and regulations and therefore free for general use.
The publisher, the authors, and the editors are safe to assume that the advice and information in this book are believed to be true and accurate at the date of publication. Neither the publisher nor the authors or the editors give a warranty, expressed or implied, with respect to the material contained herein or for any errors or omissions that may have been made. The publisher remains neutral with regard to jurisdictional claims in published maps and institutional affiliations.

This Springer VS imprint is published by the registered company Springer Fachmedien Wiesbaden GmbH, part of Springer Nature.
The registered company address is: Abraham-Lincoln-Str. 46, 65189 Wiesbaden, Germany

Contents

1   Starting Point 1

2   Widerspiegelung: An Approach 11
    2.1   Widerspiegelung and Philosophy of Science 13
    2.2   Principles of Widerspiegelung 20
    2.3   Hominization... 32
    2.4   Widerspiegelung in Humans.............................. 38
    2.5   Subjective Quality of Life................................ 43

3   Social Widerspiegelung in Humans: Fundamentals 57
    3.1   Contrast: Existing Research Findings....................... 59
    3.2   The Social as Framing................................... 82
    3.3   Social Widerspiegelung as a Unique Process 96
    3.4   Cognition, Personalised Cognition and Recognition 101
    3.5   Social Widerspiegelung and Individuality 108
    3.6   Social Widerspiegelung from the Subject Standpoint...........116

4   Social Widerspiegelung in Humans: Shaping 121
    4.1   Social Widerspiegelung and Social Action...................123
    4.2   Social Widerspiegelung and Social Relations.................133

5   Social Widerspiegelung in Humans: Perspectives.................149
    5.1   Reciprocity 150
    5.2   Understanding...164
    5.3   Directional Provisions...................................182

6 Social Widerspiegelung and Social Work 195
6.1 Social Widerspiegelung in the Context of the Discipline 196
6.2 Social Widerspiegelung as Framing for the Profession 206

7 Outlook 221

References 225

Introduction

This publication focuses on the question of how humans' quality of life can be achieved and what is beneficial or detrimental to this goal. By way of explanation, it should be added that quality of life is always subjective, i.e. it depends on the subject's point of view on what he or she considers important for his or her quality of life.

Although the subjective quality of life of humans is subjective and thus differs from person to person, it always has an essential basis in the social and especially in social Widerspiegelung. It is therefore important to clarify the relationship between social Widerspiegelung and subjective quality of life: Social Widerspiegelung can contribute to achieving or even increasing subjective quality of life, but it can also – quite the opposite – prevent the realization of subjective quality of life.

It is therefore a matter of presenting social Widerspiegelung in its fundamentals and establishing the connection to subjective quality of life. On the one hand, this project can be classified as fundamental research. On the other hand, however, the application of the results must also be considered: How can problems resulting from social Widerspiegelung be remedied; how can – unrecognized – potentials of social Widerspiegelung be exploited? Both – the fundamental research and the application – are the task of social work: for the fundamental research, it is responsible as a discipline, for the application as a profession. The course of the argumentation in this regard is outlined in the following.

It is also worth mentioning that the present publication follows some unusual paths in the process of gaining knowledge. Social Widerspiegelung and subjective quality of life are something that occupies the scientific literature. However, social Widerspiegelung and subjective quality of life are also essential components in humans' lives: To illustrate where and how phenomena such as recognition, which is itself a core part of social Widerspiegelung, occur, we occasionally look at the life and adventures of a legendary hero from ancient Greece. Social Widerspiegelung plays a role in the present, it should be made clear, but it was also present in the past.

The first chapter outlines the starting point for this publication. The topic does not originate from a momentary idea of the authors but continues earlier debates and publications: on the one hand, the theory of social work developed by the authors, on the other hand, the social as the object of this theory of social work is deepened. It is noted that social Widerspiegelung – and its contribution to subjective quality of life – needs to be defined more precisely.

An analytical separation becomes necessary, which will be undertaken in Chap. 2: Before clarifying social Widerspiegelung, an approach to Widerspiegelung in general must first be undertaken. For this purpose, Widerspiegelung is classified in terms of the theory of science in historical-dialectical materialism as a grasp of objective reality. Through the further scientific-theoretical deepening in the historical approach, principles can be identified that can be found in all living beings that are capable of Widerspiegelung. This is continued to the specificity of humans: Only humans are capable of specifically human Widerspiegelung through hominization, which is characterized by subjectivity.

In the third chapter, social Widerspiegelung, that is, Widerspiegelung directed at other humans, is considered. By contrast, existing research results are introduced, and their scope is illuminated. This is followed by the unfolding of social Widerspiegelung in humans on the basis of the theoretical derivation of the social that has been made. In this third chapter, foundations of social Widerspiegelung are subsequently introduced and explained. This includes the differentiation of cognition, personalizing cognition and recognition. Furthermore, it is necessary to clarify what individuality and individuals are in the context of social Widerspiegelung. This, in turn, is to be distinguished from subjectivity and the subject standpoint within social Widerspiegelung. The aim of this third chapter is to allow a basic understanding of social Widerspiegelung to emerge.

The fourth chapter follows on from this and explains the shaping of social Widerspiegelung in correspondence to social action and social relations: Social Widerspiegelung is not an end in itself but is closely related to what humans realize vis-à-vis other humans in individual actions or in consequences of actions. Social Widerspiegelung is, on the one hand, responsible for the preparation and selection of actions, but on the other hand, it is also responsible for evaluating the subjectively achieved success of actions.

In the fifth chapter, the interlocking of social Widerspiegelung is presented as well as the perspectives that result from it: Social Widerspiegelung is generally in a direct relationship to the social Widerspiegelung of other humans. This is reflected in reciprocity, which can be narrowing, but finds an important perspective in intersubjectivity. Social Widerspiegelung also includes understanding, through which other humans' subjective justifications for their social actions can be grasped. Social Widerspiegelung can further assume both a restrictive and a generalized directionality: This, too, needs to be broken down analytically in order to find bases for how support and accompaniment of social Widerspiegelung might be possible.

The considerations developed so far lead in the sixth chapter to the statement that social work should be responsible for supporting and accompanying social Widerspiegelung. Social Widerspiegelung is primarily the responsibility of the humans but can also be supported by scientific research as well as the application of these results in professional practice. This chapter explains how social work as a discipline and profession can achieve this.

In a brief outlook, the seventh chapter expresses the hope that social work can help to deal with the problems and challenges of social Widerspiegelung and to promote its potential.

Starting Point 1

The authors of the present publication have been working on the foundation of social work theory for a long time, provided basic information on theory formation in 2011 and presented their own theory of social work in 2018.[1] An important station on the way to this theory building was the formulation of a paradigm on the subject and task of professional social work in 2008. Explained in the publication at that time was the "Verständnis eines erweiterten Paradigmas der Sozialen Arbeit".[2] It was argued that social work should expand its traditional orientation towards the elimination of problem situations to the effect that it should also take into account the shaping of the social. For the development of the understanding of shaping the social as an extended paradigm of social work, which was developed in 2008, the scientific debate on social work as well as model projects in practice were evaluated.[3]

It turned out that in the scientific debate on social work, one can certainly find considerations that critically comment on the common paradigmatic orientation of professional social work towards help in problem situations. Nohl, for example, said as early as 1928 that "(…) Jugendfürsorge (…) heute vor allem damit beschäftigt [sei, d. Verf.), Wagen, die aus dem Gleis gesprungen sind, wieder auf die Schienen zu bringen. Aber das Schienensystem selbst ist eben heute vollständig zerstört. (…) Alle entscheidende Arbeit unserer Jugendhilfe müßte darauf gerichtet sein, dem Kinde wieder ein solches Schienensystem, auf dem es relativ gefahrlos

---

[1] cf. Scheu and Autrata (2011 u. 2018).
[2] Autrata and Scheu (2018, p. 9).
[3] cf. Autrata and Scheu (2018).

© The Author(s), under exclusive license to Springer Fachmedien Wiesbaden GmbH, part of Springer Nature 2023
O. Autrata, B. Scheu, *Subjective quality of life and social work*,
https://doi.org/10.1007/978-3-658-40400-0_1

vorwärtskommt, zu schaffen".[4] Such demands for a paradigmatic reorientation of social work – at the time of Nohl still: social pedagogy – existed already in historically early publications.

In dealing with the question of whether and how a paradigmatic expansion of social work could be feasible, another question came to the fore for the authors. The paradigmatic expansion of social work should result from the shaping of the social, so was the earlier consideration of the authorship. But what exactly is the social that is to be shaped? If one wants to design something, so the simple train of thought, one must first know what is to be designed. This, of course, revealed a glaring scientific as well as professional deficiency in social work – and not only there: In social work, which bears the compound of the social in its denomination, the social is often spoken or written about; however, a sustainable definition of the social is not found. This applies equally to disciplines such as sociology, which – as was summarised in the 2011 publication – does not provide any secure knowledge about the social.[5] The fact that they do not provide secure knowledge about the social also applies to psychology or educational science. Sociology deserves special mention here because – translating its Latin-Greek denomination – it is the science of the social, i.e. the scientific study of the social is programmatically included in its name.

The authorship statement in 2011 had two peaks: First, it outlined that "(…) dass die Soziale Arbeit und ihre Vorläufer theoretisch inkonsistent sind, die Theoriebildung oft als Rechtfertigung der bestehenden professionellen Praxis konzipiert wird und theoretische Überlegungen ungeprüft aus Bezugsdisziplinen übernommen wurden (…)."[6] The dignity of what passes for social work theory is thus, on the whole, highly questionable, was one finding. This critical assessment can be sharpened even further: It is distinctly doubtful for many publications from scientific social work whether they are a theory at all. A theory must meet the criteria of scientific work that apply to theory building.[7] The second result was that in – until then existing – theories of social work the social was not determined. What the social actually is was not clarified.

The authors have filled the two gaps mentioned above: First, the social was scientifically derived and determined. The scientific determination of the social was further integrated into the formulation of the theory of social work, which was able to close the second gap: Social work theory now has a designated and clarified

---

[4] Nohl (1965, p. 48 f.), first publication: 1928; cf. also: Autrata and Scheu (2018, p. 13 ff.).

[5] cf. Scheu and Autrata (2011, esp. p. 45 ff.).

[6] Scheu and Autrata (2011, p. 107).

[7] cf. Autrata and Scheu in: Krieger and Kraus (2018, p. 236 ff.).

1 Starting Point

object. This object of social work theory is the social. The denomination of *social work* is subsequently to be understood in this way: Social work is *work on the social*. Both the social as an object and the associated theory of social work were explicated in detail in a 2018 publication[8]: The social – according to the definition introduced at that time – are Widerspiegelungen and activities towards living beings of the same kind.

The social, however, includes an area that has not yet received sufficient attention in previous publications by the authors, namely social Widerspiegelung. This is now to be made up for. In order to illustrate the starting point of the present publication in this respect, it is necessary – for the time being far removed from any theorizing – to take up an incident from a legendary past, which is described by an equally legendary poet – namely Homer[9]: Odysseus returned to Ithaca after his participation in the Trojan War and his adventurous journey home. In the meantime, men had gathered at the court of Ithaca who assumed that Odysseus had fallen in battle or at least would not return home. These men pressed Odysseus' wife, Penelope, as a suitor and wanted to marry her. Odysseus did not want to reveal himself at first, so he came to the palace disguised as a beggar. Thus Odysseus was indeed not recognized, not even by his wife. The latter told Eurykleia, his former nurse, to wash Odysseus' feet. Eurykleia noticed a scar on Odysseus' thigh, the result of a wound once inflicted by a boar. By this feature she recognized her returned master. But the disguised Odysseus threateningly forbade her to tell this discovery to his wife or anyone else: He wants to drive the suitors from his court, and in doing so also to avenge himself for harassing his wife. Odysseus wants to prepare this undetected.[10]

Odysseus is thus recognized – as the short story describes it – after long years or even decades by his former nurse. At the first meetings with his wife and the aforementioned nurse, however, he was not recognized by them as Odysseus: He had disguised himself as a beggar, and apparently in the rest of his appearance he must no longer have resembled Odysseus as he had formerly been familiar to his wife and nurse. The changes that lead to his not being recognized as Ulysses at first glance, even by those very familiar with him, can be attributed to the experiences during the war and the long journey home, as well as to aging: Life leaves its traces,

---

[8] cf. Scheu and Autrata (2018).

[9] cf. Latacz (2003).

[10] On the *deeds and sufferings of* Odysseus, cf. Brommer (1983). Whether and to what extent the reports in the Iliad and Odyssey about the Trojan War as well as the adventures of Odysseus on his return are to be regarded as reports of historical events or rather as fiction is not of importance for the present publication.

as the proverb says. These traces obscure the fact that it is still Odysseus on whom these traces are to be found: After all, despite all the changes, it is still the same man.

So Odysseus is Odysseus, whether anyone recognizes him or not. But the very fact that he is called Odysseus points to the fact that recognition and the giving of a name are related. Odysseus can recognize himself – whether young or old – in a mirror or in polished metal plates, which had the function of a mirror during the presumable lifetime of the legendary Odysseus. He can therefore distinguish whether he himself is being reflected or someone else. But would he say to his own Widerspiegelung: I recognize myself, I am Odysseus? I do not think he would. Perhaps he would murmur: But I have grown old. The sequence that recognition is associated with a name, on the other hand, presupposes several humans: a person is recognized and the name of the person reappears from memory so that the name can be associated with the person.

The connection between humans and names can be provisionally summarized in this way: Humans usually have names, which are a feature by which humans can be recognized. Restrictively, one must mention that there are humans with the same name: In such cases the name, while remaining a feature, *may* contribute to recognition. For example, in the Trojan War on the Greek side there were two heroes with the name Ajax (Greek: Aias): For better distinction, one hero was called Ajax the Great, the other Ajax the Lokrian (after his origin from Lokris). In general, it can be said that features make an important contribution to recognition, but feature sameness or feature similarity can occur.

Apart from possible similarities of names, it is probable that if the nurse were to tell others – despite Odysseus' prohibition – whom she recognized at the court in Ithaca, she would probably not say: I have seen again the man with the scar from a boar's tusk on his thigh. She would say: I have seen Odysseus. This is because for other humans the feature of the scar on the thigh would not be recognizable: these other humans would not know of the existence of such a feature. In contrast, the message would be clear if the nurse said: Odysseus is back. The name as a feature that makes recognition possible would be more appropriate for the other humans at court.

It is known of Odysseus that he cleverly used the function of the name, thereby making a person recognizable, to confuse an overpowering opponent. To the violent one-eyed cyclops Polyphemus, who had already killed and eaten several of Odysseus' companions, he answered the question of what his name was: His name was *Nobody,* Odysseus informed him. Later Polyphemus was blinded by Odysseus in his locked cave. When other Cyclopes appeared in response to Polyphemus' cries of pain and wanted to know who was giving him such a hard time, he moaned:

1 Starting Point

No one has poked out my eye. The other Cyclopes then did not take Polyphemus' complaints seriously and went their separate ways without helping Polyphemus. Polyphemus, blinded and alone, could not catch Odysseus. Odysseus managed to escape from Polyphemus' cave through the confusion he had caused by mentioning the name *Nobody*. In the original text of the Odyssey, Odysseus' pun has another double bottom: In Greek, *Nobody is* called Outis; however, Outis also denotes a diminutive form of Odysseus, which could be – somewhat clumsily – rendered *Odysseuschen*. With his cunning conundrum, Odysseus demonstrates how one can speak the truth and yet provoke false perceptions in others. The mention of a name clouds the situation more than it illuminates it; recognition resembles a stay at a masked ball.

It suggests that being recognized has a universal importance that points beyond the life and fate of Odysseus. Odysseus, like every human being, has features that are more or less unique: The scar on his thigh after being injured by a boar or his name are such features. Likewise, Penelope, his wife, will later recognize Odysseus as Odysseus because he knows about the special construction of the marriage bed: Odysseus – and only he – knows this special construction because he made the bed himself. However, Odysseus also had all these features earlier, when he was in a foreign country. But these features only become significant when someone can recognize them and link them to knowledge about the person. The characteristics in themselves, if they cannot be linked to knowledge about the person in the course of recognition by other humans, are unique but of limited significance. Marx once wrote: "Ich weiß nichts vom Menschen, wenn ich weiß, daß ein Mensch Jacobus heißt".[11] Only when the name can be linked to knowledge about the person as a feature – perhaps not completely unique, but at least differentiating – does the process of recognition gain relevance. If Odysseus introduces himself to a stranger, his name remains a name like others. If someone who does not know him sees the scar on Odysseus' thigh, he might say: Oh, someone has an old scar.

Recognition and recognition of humans is therefore based on characteristics. Characteristics are – following the literal sense directly – to be understood as marks, i.e. clear signs or characteristics, which can be remembered. A scar or a burn mark can be such characteristics, but also a name or hair colour. Focusing on features, for example, allows for assured recognition: The disguised and aged Odysseus was recognizable to Eurykleia only because she found the distinctive feature of the scar on his leg. This makes it clear that humans have many characteristics: Not all of these traits are readily recognizable in the sense of characteristics, nor are they later recognizable. You can think of it this way: It is true that human

---

[11] Marx and Engels (1977, MEW 23, p. 115).

6   1   Starting Point

beings are so complex and differentiated in their nature that each person is unique, that is, different from all other humans. However, this uniqueness is in turn sometimes difficult to access: the scars on a person's body can be seen; what a person thinks, however, is not so easily ascertainable and retained in memory as an unmistakable characteristic.

The connection between the uniqueness and the recognition or recognition of a specific person can be summed up by a sentence that has been common since Aristotle: Genus proximum et differentia specifica.[12] To humans as *genus* belongs the determination that they are unique[13]: All men are men, that is, they belong to the *genus* of men; but in this every man is different. In order to be able to recognize or recognize a particular human being, his *differentia specifica* must be established: Since every human being is unique, he can be distinguished from other human beings. The determination of the *differentia specifica* is carried out by means of characteristics, i.e. by means of features and qualities that can be grasped as unambiguously as possible. The uniqueness of human beings thus exists on the one hand as the determination of the essence of human beings as *genus*. On the other hand, uniqueness is only constituted through recognition by others: Only when other humans recognize a person on the basis of characteristics can the uniqueness of that person be associated with knowledge about another person. Uniqueness, then, is first a determination for the *genus* of human beings. The proof that a human being is indeed to be distinguished from all other human beings and is accordingly unique is only furnished when the determination of the *differentia specifica of* this human being has succeeded via recognition. Thus the uniqueness of human beings gains a new quality: it is also bound to the determination of the *differentia specifica*, which is carried out by others. In the same way, for the recognized person, being recognized is a specific quality of life: one's own existence acquires this new quality through being related to other humans.

The incident surrounding Odysseus' return represents a particular form of recognition that often gives the plot a new twist in Greek dramas. Such a recognition, typical of dramas and usually surprising, is called anagnorisis. However, anagnorisis, or recognition, does not only occur in dramas and in the theatre; the recognition of another person on the basis of characteristics is also typical of humans's lives: Humans are unique humans in their own right, but recognizing other humans or being recognized by other humans creates a quality that cannot be achieved without

---

[12] cf. Buldt (2008) and Autrata and Scheu (2015). *Genus proximum et differentia specifica* is to be translated *as next higher genus and specific difference*.

[13] The uniqueness of human beings is only stated here. What the uniqueness of human beings is based on will be explained later: cf. Sect. 2.3 in this volume.

1 Starting Point

relating to other humans. That one can recognize oneself in a mirror is not as self-evident as one might think: most animals cannot do this, even small children are not yet able to do it.[14] The fact that one can recognise oneself is therefore definitely proof of a high level of recognising ability. The recognition of other humans and being recognized by other humans, however, opens the view for a dimension that is worth to be examined more closely. This dimension to be looked at more closely is the Widerspiegelung of other humans.

The starting point is thus outlined: Humans do things together, often against each other. But before they do something, they prepare themselves for it: They look at other humans and check, for example, whether they have seen these other humans before. Whether humans know each other or not usually has consequences on what they do towards these humans later. There is a broad and weighty area of humans's engagement with each other in which the situation and, above all, the so-ness of each other's humans is explored. This area is so important because it precedes what humans do towards other humans and forms the basis for this mutual doing. In the meantime, it is to be formulated as an assertion: What humans do towards other humans is essentially based on what they have grasped about other humans. We will return to this later.[15]

The capture of other humans is referred to as Widerspiegelung in the present publication. A central problem of Widerspiegelung is of central significance for determining the starting point for the following publication: one can see or hear what humans do with respect to other humans. But one can grasp the realm of Widerspiegelung only to a very limited extent with a sensory organ. Thus, a scientific elucidation of Widerspiegelung has to work partly with inferences: If a certain action towards other humans can be detected, it is plausible that this action is based on Widerspiegelung. It would not be plausible if humans made random choices about what they did. Thus, the assumption of the connection between the Widerspiegelung that precedes and the doing that follows is guiding for the further analytical breakdown of the Widerspiegelung between humans.

To recapitulate is the scientific starting point of the present publication. In the publication from 2018, the social as a whole, which has already been mentioned, was theoretically explicated and defined[16]: Following the given definition, the social is composed of Widerspiegelung and activities towards living beings of the same species. However, the authors have so far looked more closely at the part of

---

[14] cf. Sect. 3.1 in this volume.
[15] cf. Sect. 4.1 in this volume.
[16] See Scheu and Autrata (2018).

activities in the context of human social life.[17] However, the aspect of Widerspiegelung as a second component of the social needs to be examined in greater depth.

The present publication now aims to pursue and analytically elucidate this second component of the social. The work project can be outlined as follows: humans see each other, for example, they listen to each other; humans can also smell or feel other humans. From this, humans in turn draw conclusions that determine their activities. This needs to be defined more precisely. Widerspiegelung is to be used as a guiding concept for this: Admittedly, for the time being, this is only a concept that still needs to be clarified in terms of its content. What needs to be defined is that the concept of Widerspiegelung and its continuation into social Widerspiegelung should be used to break down what humans do in order to grasp other humans.

What happens between humans through social Widerspiegelung is of great importance: if recognition takes place, the event proceeds differently than if there had been no recognition. In the first case, humans may greet each other or even embrace each other; in the second case, humans carelessly move on. Recognition or non-recognition is only one example from the range of social Widerspiegelung: However, it should be made clear that the study of social Widerspiegelung is rewarding and fruitful when it comes to finding an approach to the dynamics and potentials of the social in humans.

This in turn results in necessities and perspectives for the disciplinary assignment: Which scientific discipline should and can take over this processing of social Widerspiegelung? The authors propose that this should be done by social work in the sense of its disciplinary location. In an earlier publication it was already postulated that the object of social work is the social.[18] Social work then, according to the denomination's explication, is work on the social. This continues to be true, but must now be differentiated: Social Widerspiegelung belongs to the object of social work, namely the social, as part of the social. It is therefore the task of social work as a discipline to research social Widerspiegelung in such a way that it can also be worked on professionally. This raises questions for scientific social work: The design of social work as a scientific discipline must be clarified if social Widerspiegelung is to be brought to bear as an essential part of the subject matter of this discipline. Firstly, it is necessary to analyse what social Widerspiegelung is and constitutes. Secondly, it must be examined which necessities result from this for scientific as well as professional social work.

---

[17] cf. Scheu and Autrata (2011).

[18] See Scheu and Autrata (2018).

1 Starting Point

Finally, the analytical clarifications of Widerspiegelung and their specification into social Widerspiegelung lead to the question of whether, how and by whom the complexity of the social can be accompanied or shaped. For the legendary Odysseus, the developments that take place after his return appear – typical of Greek drama – inevitable and fateful; his revenge on the suitors, but also on collaborating servants, is bloody, but necessary and justified from Odysseus' point of view. Social Widerspiegelung obviously yielded the result for Odysseus that only with sword in hand could the social be shaped at his court in Ithaca. For the social between humans in the present, however, the question arises as to whether it might not be possible to shape it in a way that would be peaceful for all concerned? In this context, a bold mental leap from the time of the Odyssey to the present is proposed, in which a science and profession is socially anchored that was not even thought of in the time of Odysseus: Social Work. In view of the new situation, namely that social work exists, the potential of social work in contributing to a shaping of the social is to be explored.

Widerspiegelung: An Approach

So it is about how humans grasp other humans. This is to be achieved through and with the concept of social Widerspiegelung. In order to be able to do justice to this task, however, analytical decompositions are necessary. At the end of Chap. 1, the concept of Widerspiegelung was introduced, but not yet further defined. The discussion of this term is to begin. So this chapter is concerned with the determination of Widerspiegelung in general. This is done because there are some problems connected with the analytical comprehension of Widerspiegelung, which have to be worked through one after the other. Accordingly, in this chapter, an approach to Widerspiegelung will be undertaken, progressing step by step. Thus, in a first step, Widerspiegelung is unfolded on the basis of scientific theoretical foundations. In a second step, principles of Widerspiegelung are then extracted that are found in all living beings that have the possibility of Widerspiegelung. In order to grasp the specificity of Widerspiegelung in humans and to be able to distinguish it from that of other living beings that also possess Widerspiegelung, hominization is – briefly – outlined in the third step: Humans, and only humans, exhibit qualities that in turn give rise to new qualities of Widerspiegelung. In the fourth and last step of this chapter, specifically human Widerspiegelung is presented as Widerspiegelung from the subject standpoint. Widerspiegelung is first to be considered in general as Widerspiegelung of the world; the focusing of Widerspiegelung on other humans, i.e. a social Widerspiegelung, will only take place later.[1]

The above explanation of the work project makes it clear that the breakdown of Widerspiegelung – and later of social Widerspiegelung – is an approximation. This is due above all to the peculiarity of the subject matter. What constitutes that can be

---

[1] cf. Chap. 3 in this volume.

© The Author(s), under exclusive license to Springer Fachmedien Wiesbaden GmbH, part of Springer Nature 2023
O. Autrata, B. Scheu, *Subjective quality of life and social work*,
https://doi.org/10.1007/978-3-658-40400-0_2

characterized by recourse to the encounter between Eurykleia and Odysseus presented in Chap. 1. Eurykleia says to Odysseus: You are Odysseus, I recognize you! This is an activity that was mainly performed linguistically, perhaps punctuated with gestures. Both spoken words and gestures are easily accessible via sensory organs, one can hear or see it; if one has physical contact, movements are also tactilely detectable. Necessarily, before this activity, i.e. the linguistic determination of recognition, recognition must have taken place in the form of Widerspiegelung. But this, namely the reflecting itself, is less accessible: one can only hear what someone says; what someone sees or hears cannot be grasped directly. Detours are necessary, which then lead to conclusions.

It should be emphasized that this does not make the study of Widerspiegelung obsolete: it is of fundamental importance to break down what lies before the activities of humans. What are those processes that obviously form the basis of activities? That is the question that needs to be elucidated. Admittedly, one must also take note of the fact that in answering the question, a methodology based on empirical procedures is only of very limited use. For example, one cannot observe Widerspiegelung; at best, one can determine activities that take place after Widerspiegelung. But whether Widerspiegelung then took place in a certain way and how exactly the connection to the subsequent activity is, remains speculation rather than certain knowledge. There is also the question of which part of the given world was reflected and how the selection made in the process is incorporated into the result. Widerspiegelung is thus meant to elucidate what takes place in humans's receiving engagement with the world – not yet conceived in scientific terms.

These introductory and structuring considerations make it clear that the representation of Widerspiegelung represents an approach in the sense of the scientific advance from the known into the unknown.[2] Widerspiegelung is, on the one hand, something that is performed as a receptive engagement with the world by living beings, which in turn have the physiological and psychological conditions to do so. The inanimate world cannot reflect itself. How could it? On the other hand, Widerspiegelung is also the establishment of a connection between the world and the reflected. Thus, the approach to Widerspiegelung must also be made with respect to this second pole, that is, to raise and answer the question of what is to be said about the object of Widerspiegelung. What is it, then, that is reflected, and what general properties does it have?

Thus, one result of these methodological Widerspiegelungs on how an approach to Widerspiegelung might succeed is that the representation of what Widerspiegelung is must begin before Widerspiegelung. Thus, before Widerspiegelung as a process

---

[2] cf. Autrata and Scheu (2015).

2 Widerspiegelung: An Approach

can be explained, we need to look at the preconditions of Widerspiegelung. Before a physiological and psychological breakdown of what the concept of Widerspiegelung entails, its epistemological and scientific background must be explained. This will be done in the first section of this chapter.

2.1 Widerspiegelung and Philosophy of Science

Every theory is based on a scientific-theoretical framing. An earlier publication stated it this way: "Wissenschaftstheorie fasst die Formen und Voraussetzungen der Erkenntnisse, die zwischen Bekanntem und Unbekannten zu erreichen versucht werden. Wissenschaftstheorie beschäftigt sich mit Wissen und versucht, das wissenschaftlich abzusichern. (…) Wissenschaftstheorie beschäftigt sich mit der Frage, wie letztlich Wissen, also abgesicherte Einsichten, zustande kommt".[3]

Before theorizing about an individual object, the question arises whether and how this theorizing is framed in terms of scientific theory. Not every theory fulfils the requirement of being framed in terms of scientific theory. However, the identification of the scientific-theoretical framing is in turn the key to the comprehensibility and verifiability of a theory. Theory clarifies an object in its entirety: That is the goal of theory building. Whether the theory in turn provides an explanation that becomes adequate to the object is examined with the truth test: a theory can be true or false.[4]

Science-theoretical framing, when designated and used as a guide to theory building, makes transparent how a theory is obtained: Some, not all, philosophy of science framings operationalize how a theory is to be obtained. This also leads to the observation that there are different science-theoretical framings, which in turn can be assigned to particular schools. This has been discussed at length in previous publications.[5]

For the theorizing of Widerspiegelung here, it is that Widerspiegelung derives from historical-dialectical materialism. Historical-dialectical materialism has also been presented earlier.[6] From historical-dialectical materialism results an essential determination, which will have to be evaluated later from the point of view of Widerspiegelung: Matter is "(…) die objektive Realität, die außerhalb und unab-

---

[3] Autrata and Scheu (2015, p. 166 f.).
[4] cf. Autrata and Scheu (2015, p. 211 ff.).
[5] See Autrata and Scheu (2015) and Scheu and Autrata (2018, esp. p. 84 ff.).
[6] On historical-dialectical materialism, cf. Scheu and Autrata (2018, pp. 96 ff.).

hängig vom menschlichen Bewußtsein existiert."[7] Thus, according to the understanding of historical-dialectical materialism, there is the objective reality that exists first of all without the intervention or influence of human beings. The objective reality, which is grasped with the concept of matter, is thereby not limited to inanimate nature, but is the opposite concept to consciousness: "(…) Materie [is, author's note] die einzige objektive Realität außerhalb des Bewußtseins (…)".[8] Matter is therefore everything that is outside of consciousness, and is thereby independent of this consciousness in its thus-being. So whether someone knows about it, what exists around him, and whether someone is concerned with it, does not change the objective reality. On the background of historical-dialectical materialism, consciousness is not to be understood as a counter-concept to the unconscious, as is done from psychoanalysis. In historical-dialectical materialism, consciousness is rather the "(…) spezifisch menschliche ideelle Widerspiegelung der objektiven Realität vermittels des Zentralnervensystems".[9] Matter is thus opposed to consciousness, this is how historical-dialectical materialism is to be understood. It should be noted that consciousness can only be found in humans, whereas Widerspiegelung also exists in non-human living beings. This will be discussed later. In the meantime, however, for the presentation of the scientific-theoretical ideas of historical-dialectical materialism, it must be noted that the Widerspiegelung of objective reality in humans is reflected in consciousness.

The concept of matter, which grasps the totality of objective reality, still needs to be deepened. The concept of matter runs through the history of philosophy in various connotations. Already in Aristotle, for example, we find the view that matter is the substrate from which all things consist. Matter is therefore that from which something arises, according to Aristotle.[10]

In historical-dialectical materialism the determination of matter experiences an extension by the dimension of movement. "Die Bewegung ist die Daseinsweise der Materie. (…) Alle Ruhe, alles Gleichgewicht ist nur relativ, hat nur Sinn in Beziehung auf diese oder jene bestimmte Bewegungsform".[11] Matter is thus also subject to the historical-dialectical process of development and change, which never comes to a standstill. Matter is therefore not static, but always in motion. The determination that matter always includes movement and development has led to the adjectival extension of materialism to *historical-dialectical* materialism.

---

[7] Klaus and Buhr (1976b, vol. 2, p. 769).

[8] Klaus and Buhr (1976b, vol. 2, p. 769).

[9] Klaus and Buhr (1976a, vol. 1, p. 224).

[10] cf. Wieland (1970).

[11] Marx and Engels (1962a, MEW 20, p. 503).

2 Widerspiegelung: An Approach 15

The key point for understanding what historical-dialectical materialism says is the concept of matter. One might be inclined to assume that matter is something that can be grasped directly or grasped sensually by other means. But this is not possible, as Engels makes clear: "(…) Materie als solche und die Bewegung als solche hat noch niemand gesehn oder sonst erfahren, sondern nur die verschiednen, wirklich existierenden Stoffe und Bewegungsformen. Der Stoff, die Materie ist nichts andres als die Gesamtheit der Stoffe, aus der dieser Begriff abstrahiert, die Bewegung als solche nichts als die Gesamtheit aller sinnlich wahrnehmbaren Bewegungsformen; Worte wie Materie und Bewegung sind nichts als *Abkürzungen*, in die wir viele verschiedne sinnlich wahrnehmbare Dinge zusammenfassen nach ihren gemeinsamen Eigenschaften".[12] *Matter*, then, is meant to conceptualize objective reality as well as the sensory apprehension of this objective reality. On the one hand, there is objective reality, and on the other hand, there are the attempts to grasp this objective reality through processes of sensory reception: both are subsumed under the condensed formula of *matter.*

Elsewhere Engels continues: "Die Materie als solche ist eine reine Gedankenschöpfung und Abstraktion. Wir sehen von den qualitativen Verschiedenheiten der Dinge ab, indem wir sie als körperlich existierende unter dem Begriff Materie zusammenfassen. Materie als solche, im Unterschied von den bestimmten, existierenden Materien, ist also nichts Sinnlich-Existierendes."[13]

Thus, if one wants to speak of matter in the understanding of historical-dialectical materialism, one must bear in mind that matter does not exist in such a way that it can be directly grasped by the senses. Matter, as Engels explained, is an abstraction that summarily denotes what exists. Matter, then, being a designation, is the product of thought. Engels characterized this as an *abbreviation* or *creation of thought.*[14] One cannot, therefore, grasp matter – at least conclusively – by sight or touch: One needs, for the apprehension of matter, in addition to sight and touch – or still further sensuous efforts – thinking, that is, the forming of a mental abstraction. Matter is given as objective reality, but needs abstracting thinking to be grasped.

If one looks again at the distinction that matter grasps the objective reality outside of human consciousness, two things must be noted: First, there is a reality outside human consciousness that exists for itself, that is, objectively. This reality is – partially – sensually perceptible. If, of course, one adds that forms of movement and development are also added to this reality, the limits of sensual

---

[12] Marx and Engels (1962a, MEW 20, p. 503); Herv. i. Orig.
[13] Marx and Engels (1962a, MEW 20, p. 519).
[14] cf. Marx and Engels (1962a, MEW 20).

comprehensibility are reached: movements and developments may only result from the mental comparison of different forms of states. The sensual comprehensibility of objective reality is – partly – possible, but has to be completed by thinking. Secondly, if objective reality is subsumed under the concept of matter, this is in itself an abstraction, i.e. the result of thinking: when one speaks of matter, one subsumes impressions of the world that exists sensuously into a concept, namely matter.

So there is objective reality outside the consciousness of human beings. Whether humans grasp this reality or not, first of all, does not change anything about reality: it exists, it continues to exist and changes in the process. The existence of objective reality remains even without the intervention of humans. Simonow formulates this as follows: The starting point is "(…) die Anerkennung des Primats der Gegenstände und Erscheinungen der Realität, die außerhalb des sie widerspiegelnden Subjekts existieren (…)".[15]

Opposite to the objective reality, however, is the ability of humans to sensually grasp the world. Humans can grasp objective reality sensually and in turn condense this into thoughts about reality. At a very high level of abstraction, concepts such as matter or movement can be formed. Such concepts summarize properties and determinations of things and experiences with such things. The dimension of the sensual grasp of the world is not to be skipped: abstractions are not speculation, but the mental continuation of sensual grasps of the world. Sensual apprehensions of the world and experiences, which are to be seen as sensually experienceable results of the occupation with things, are summarized and mentally evaluated. Such processes of abstraction lead to results. These results, however, are no longer visible to the things. Engels' determination must be repeated: "(…) Materie als solche und die Bewegung als solche hat noch niemand gesehn oder sonst erfahren."[16]

Thus, the understanding of matter cannot be formed directly as a result of sensory apprehensions of the world: One cannot see matter, grasp it, or have experiences with it. However, since the understanding that matter exists has been formed, it can be concluded that sensual grasp of the world and experiences have been transferred via mental processes to the abstractions of matter and movement.

One can summarize like this: The objective reality of the world exists outside of human beings, that is, separate from their consciousness. But it is possible for humans to get impressions of the objective reality by sensual perception of the world and experiences. Furthermore, humans can make abstractions on the basis of such

---

[15] Simonow (1975, p. 9). The concept of the subject used by Simonow, but not explained further, will be returned to in detail later; cf. Sect. 3.6 in the volume.

[16] Marx and Engels (1962a, MEW 20, p. 503); Herv. i. Orig.

2 Widerspiegelung: An Approach

sensual processes and experiences and thus arrive at mental condensations about the so-being of the world. The objective reality of the world and abstractions about it are thus in a consistent relationship: the abstractions are based on sensual grasping of the world and experiences that have been processed for the purpose of gaining knowledge.

Matter as an abstraction does not only stand for what is present: since "(…) in der Geschichte der Gesellschaft (…) die Handelnden lauter mit Bewußtsein begabte, (…) auf bestimmte Zwecke hinarbeitende Menschen; nichts geschieht ohne Absicht, ohne gewolltes Ziel."[17] Matter, then, Holz characterizes as including what is past, present, and possible in the future; matter further includes not only what is objectively present, but also forms of thought such as memories or anticipations.

For the time being, the dimension that both humans can influence the objective reality of the world, i.e. change it, and that objective reality, often already influenced by humans, in turn influences humans, is excluded. The relationship of humans to the world as well as the relationship of the world – for humans to be understood essentially as society – to humans is thus also a relationship of interaction: humans shape the world. For historical-dialectical materialism, it is formulated thus: There are "(…) in der Geschichte der Gesellschaft (…) die Handelnden lauter mit Bewußtsein begabte, (…) auf bestimmte Zwecke hinarbeitende Menschen; nichts geschieht ohne Absicht, ohne gewolltes Ziel."[18] Equally, however, it is also the case that the – societal – world frames humans. The actions of humans and the societal world in which they live are mediated by each other: "Durch seine gesellschaftliche Praxis *vermittelt* sich der Mensch sowohl mit der Natur als auch mit der Gesellschaft; und dadurch, daß er immer wieder, um leben zu können, gezwungen ist, diese aktiven Beziehungen mit der Natur und der Gesellschaft herzustellen, schafft er zugleich auch, mag er dies wissen oder nicht, die grundlegenden Voraussetzungen, auf Grund deren sich sein Bewußtsein von der Natur sowie auch von der Gesellschaft bildet und entwickelt."[19] Only the mediation between man and matter, which occurs through the actions of men and the social framing of human life, evokes a mutual influence. We will come back to this later.[20]

For the time being, however, the main thing is that the world is given as objective reality and, as historical-dialectical materialism puts it, as matter in motion. Matter and its movements exist as such. Whether human consciousness takes cognizance of matter and its motions in any way or not, does not change the so-being

---

[17] Holz (2003, p. 46).
[18] Marx and Engels (1962b, MEW 21, p. 296).
[19] Klaus and Buhr (1976b, vol. 2, p. 750; orig. cit.
[20] cf. Sect. 2.3 in this volume.

of matter and motions. Matter together with its motions is therefore, from the point of view of cognition, independent of human consciousness. Matter remains as it is, whether human consciousness is concerned with it or not.

Cognition and knowledge of men about matter and its movements form themselves, that is the opposite pole to objective reality, about sensual grasping of the world and mental processing of these perceptions. Cognition and knowledge of men are therefore based on the apprehension of objective reality. Speculations or assertions do not have such a connection to objective reality: they are indeed also creations of thought, but they are not based on the grasping of objective reality.

In order to make clear what this means, the account of historical-dialectical materialism and the derivations that follow from it are to be contrasted with another school of philosophy of science: What is meant here is radical constructivism. Glasersfeld, an important representative of radical constructivism, assumes that knowledge about the world is merely a construct: "Niemand wird je imstande sein, die Wahrnehmung eines Gegenstands mit dem postulierten Gegenstand selbst, der die Wahrnehmung verursacht haben soll, zu vergleichen".[21] A grasp of the world, one can continue the thought, provides a construct, but it does not or cannot provide a breakdown of the world. Whether and what the result of the apprehension of an object has to do with the object must be left open, since there is no consistent connection between apprehension and object. If one follows radical constructivism, the world and the apprehension of the world exist in an unrelated coexistence. As summarized in an earlier publication, "der radikale Konstruktivismus meint, dass die Welt und das Bild, das man sich von der Welt macht, nicht direkt miteinander verbunden seien: Jegliche Erkenntnis über die Welt sei nur ein Konstrukt".[22] Subsequently, it must be said that on the scientific-theoretical background of radical constructivism, the formation of a theory of Widerspiegelung is not possible: the two views, that the comprehension of the world takes place via Widerspiegelung or that the comprehension of the world is a mere mental construct and stands in an unconnected relationship to the world, are diametrically opposed.

It should be noted, then, that the scientific-theoretical framing in historical-dialectical materialism makes it possible to outline the preconditions of Widerspiegelung. With historical-dialectical materialism as a scientific-theoretical framing, it is in turn also possible to derive from it the theorizing of Widerspiegelung that is yet to be done: How humans reflect the world and – what will be presented

---

[21] Glasersfeld in: Foerster et al. (1992, p. 12).
[22] Scheu and Autrata (2018, p. 103).

2 Widerspiegelung: An Approach

later[23] – other humans, can be explained in its premises from the fundamental provisions of historical-dialectical materialism.

As a preliminary endpoint of the reference to the scientific-theoretical framing in historical-dialectical materialism is to be fixed: The result of the apprehension of objective reality is a likeness. "Jedes Abbild ist eine Einheit von Objektivem und Subjektivem, da es die Gegenstände, Eigenschaften und Beziehungen der objektiven Realität vermittelt durch die Tätigkeit des Subjekts, die Beschaffenheit seines Erkenntnisapparates (…) widerspiegelt (…)".[24]

This establishes important cornerstones of Widerspiegelung: Widerspiegelung is always a mediation process between objective reality and the one who reflects it. Widerspiegelung is not a mirror image, but is influenced by the peculiarities of the reflector: these peculiarities include life activity and, above all, the nature of the possibilities of Widerspiegelung. At the end of Widerspiegelung, there is always an image that represents a section of objective reality with the peculiarities of the reflector.

Extending the discussion on the theory of science from historical-dialectical materialism in general, it should be noted, however, that the opposition of objective reality and its apprehension by living beings is not only to be found in humans. Thus, terms such as consciousness or subject are appropriate for humans, since they characterize essential determinations of being human. However, there are also other living beings that are capable of grasping objective reality: In them, however, subjectivity, as it is in humans, is not to be found.

Thus, the approach step to Widerspiegelung via the debate of scientific-theoretical framing in historical-dialectical materialism must be followed by a further step. What is to be established for Widerspiegelung if one considers Widerspiegelung in general, i.e. also beyond the segment of human beings? In doing so, the argument must introduce another scientific-theoretical approach in order to unfold the specificity of Widerspiegelung: This is the historical approach with the categorial analysis. The historical approach with categorial analysis continues historical-dialectical materialism and examines developments and developmental steps that can be noted in the apprehension of objective reality by living beings. The historical approach does not replace historical-dialectical materialism. The historical approach is to be understood as a further step on the way from the abstract to the concrete. The presented principles of historical-dialectical materialism, that matter exists as an objective reality, that matter is always in motion and that matter can be grasped, remain. However, it remains to be specified how this

---

[23] cf. Chap. 3 in this volume.

[24] Klaus and Buhr (1976a, vol. 1, p. 32).

grasping of objective reality by living beings takes place and what different forms of such grasping are ascertainable. From this again principles of Widerspiegelung are to deduce, which are valid for all living beings, which are able to grasp their environment by Widerspiegelung. This will be dealt with in the next chapter.

2.2 Principles of Widerspiegelung

So far, the breakdown of Widerspiegelung has been approached from the widely abstracting scientific-theoretical standpoint of historical-dialectical materialism. The connection between matter and human consciousness has been presented from such science-theoretical premises of historical-dialectical materialism. This scientific-theoretical breakdown provides cornerstones behind which further analysis must not fall back: knowledge about matter, i.e. objective reality, is generated and, in the process, processes of sensory apprehension of the world are brought into relation to one's own standpoint.

With these provisions, important basic components of Widerspiegelung have been defined. At the same time, however, the need for further concretization and specification becomes clear: It should be noted that many animals can also reflect their environment. This in turn is based on the fact that many animals have the possibility to gain impressions of the environment and to link such impressions to their needs.

That a comprehension of objective reality and thus of the world is possible follows from historical-dialectical materialism. *How* such a comprehension takes place, however, is not yet clarified. A further question is, *who is* capable of such a grasp? The third question to be asked is, what *differences* and *developments can be* discerned in the comprehension of the world? These questions cannot yet be answered on the basis of historical-dialectical materialism alone. What is necessary for this is the continuation through the historical approach and the categorial analysis.

What the historical approach can do and how it operates as a school of philosophy of science – on the basis of historical-dialectical materialism – is to be explained in relation to phylogenesis. Phylogenesis is the process of evolution and change of species. Phylogenesis conspicuously represents the principle of matter, which is always in motion and change. The phylogenetic process by which species have evolved and changed is a process by which all living things have evolved. Thus, humans, since they are indisputably living beings, are also first part of phylogenesis. The phylogenetic process takes place as the development of species and is based on the genetic variability of living beings. What of such resulting genetic

2 Widerspiegelung: An Approach

changes solidifies and prevails depends on environmental conditions and on the probability of survival in these environmental conditions. Thus, new living beings result from genetic variability. Whether these living beings become established, that is, whether they survive long enough to reproduce again, depends on environmental conditions. Phylogenesis is thus a process of biology in which species arise and it is open whether these species are capable of lasting survival.[25]

For the breakdown of Widerspiegelung it is necessary to embed the historical approach in historical-dialectical materialism: Historical approach and historical-dialectical materialism are not two separate science-theoretical position formations; historical approach continues historical-dialectical materialism. In terms of philosophy of science, the historical approach focuses historical-dialectical materialism on the analytical consideration of phylogenesis. The historical approach works out what developments matter – in this case: the origin and development of species – takes and what steps can be identified in the process. The historical approach provides the tools to be able to analytically grasp the development in phylogenesis. For this purpose, the historical approach uses the method of categorial analysis: The tracing of a category in its development through the phylogenetic process of the origin and change of species is called categorial analysis. This involves examining how a category evolves from its basic form to its final form. This enables the tracing of the becomingness of a category and its tracing in its phylogenetic development. Thus, if such a category is part of phylogenetic development, it is not the ability of a single living being, but an ability that has solidified in the course of the development of a species and whose preconditions are passed on genetically. The categorial-analytical approach is not designed as a search for chance findings; rather, the longitudinality, i.e. the temporal extension of developments, is examined. This results in steady developments, but also in qualitative leaps. This must be broken down with reference to the category under consideration. The categorial analysis therefore examines the entire development chain, not just a single point in time.

Observation in recent, that is, living, creatures can extend categorial analysis into the present. Through such observations, the expression of a category in the present can be illuminated: The analytic process of examining the development of a category from its basic form to its – tentative – final form in the most highly developed living beings is thus accomplished. Categorial analysis as a scientific-theoretical procedure does not end with phylogenesis, but involves the transition of a category to humans: In the case of humans, it is the case that a category builds on phylogenetic roots, but then undergoes a serious qualitative leap through the turn to

---

[25] For more details, see: Scheu and Autrata (2018, p. 152 ff.).

social-historical development and receives a new framing. What this means for the Widerspiegelung in humans will have to be explained later for the subjectivity emerging in humans. For a detailed description of categorial analysis as a scientific-theoretical procedure, we can only refer to earlier publications at this point.[26]

The historical approach thus continues historical-dialectical materialism and provides scientific-theoretical guidelines as to how the object to be elucidated, namely Widerspiegelung and above all social Widerspiegelung, is to be investigated. The aim, then, is to identify Widerspiegelung and social Widerspiegelung in the phylogenetic process and to single them out from this process in their categorial particularity. Special attention is paid to the change of the category in order to be able to determine the course of development from basic forms to final forms. For this purpose, the view is to be directed to the phylogeny.

In the course of phylogenesis, sensory abilities developed in living beings that allowed them to absorb information from and about the environment. The ability to absorb and process such information increases the likelihood of survival: if organisms can determine where food sources are located and where there are dangers to their own lives, a corresponding locomotion promises advantages for survival. In order to be able to determine such conditions, a corresponding sensory equipment and the potential to process such sensory impressions are essential. This can be subsumed as a category under the concept of the psychic: "Das Psychische umfasst als Kategorie die gesamte Breite der Widerspiegelung der Umwelt. Die Entwicklung bis zur Entstehung des Psychischen als Informationsverarbeitung und Tätigkeitssteuerung ist als eine Auseinandersetzung von Organismen mit den Umweltbedingungen zu verstehen".[27]

Psyche as a category thus denotes a certain relationship to the surrounding world: without psyche, a comprehension of the environment and, accordingly, a subsequent control of activities is not possible. Psyche characterizes the possibility of living beings to grasp the environment and to adapt activities to this grasp of the environment. Psyche is the Widerspiegelung of the environment and conditions via the embedding in phylogenesis that Widerspiegelung cannot be a consequence-free observation: Widerspiegelung is embedded in engagement with the environment and can increase or decrease the probability of survival. Widerspiegelung is thus of central importance for organisms that possess this quality.

The development and unfolding of the psychic through stages and qualitative leaps has been traced and presented in detail elsewhere. The psychic ranges from preliminary forms of simple sensibility, for which no special sense organs and no

---

[26] cf. e.g. Scheu and Autrata (2018, p. 147 ff.).
[27] Scheu and Autrata (2018, p. 155).

2 Widerspiegelung: An Approach

central nervous system are yet required, to animals with highly developed organs and an efficient brain. Reference can only be made to this at this point.[28]

The development of the psychic in animals is to be classified in the process of phylogenesis: A development of the psychic, which includes the Widerspiegelung of the environment, has chances to prevail, i.e. to become genetically consolidated, if it causes an increase in the probability of survival. The development of Widerspiegelung in animals is thus related to the survival probability of animals in the process of evolution via mutation and selection. In short, psyche is the quality of reflecting the environment and translating these Widerspiegelungen into adequate activities. At the interface between Widerspiegelung and activity, the result of Widerspiegelung must be transformed into activity, which in turn must be contingently related. If the activities were arbitrary, i.e. if they were not derived from the Widerspiegelung of the environment, this would entail an evident survival disadvantage: For example, the activity of seeking food is promising if it is based on a Widerspiegelung of food sources. Similarly, flight is a reasonable response if the predator could be previously reflected. Between Widerspiegelung and activity, however, there must be processing that leads to a determination of direction for the activity.

Components of the mental process, one can deduce, are cognition and emotion: Cognition is the part of the mental process that is responsible for the reception of information. For this, sensory organs are necessary that can take in information from the environment; this can take place through forms of seeing, hearing or smelling, among others. Cognition, as the second part of the mental process, includes emotion, which is responsible for evaluating information. From the wealth of information received via cognition, what, for example, is relevant to foraging for food or avoiding danger? What activity is appropriate as a consequence?

Especially the second part of the psyche, namely emotion, is in danger of being misinterpreted as blind feeling in everyday language. If, on the other hand, emotion is derived, it becomes clear that emotion includes feelings: When animals identify an approaching other animal as a predator, this is followed – soberly put – by the evaluation that the appropriate activity might be flight. The process of evaluation, however, also involves feelings that mobilize energy reserves. On the other hand, feelings such as joy or pleasure accompany the discovery of the food that is eaten most readily. Such emotions already exist in animals, but they are not blind feelings, but are part of the mental process.

It should be noted that forms of Widerspiegelung have already developed in – more highly developed – animals with the development of the psychic. Via

---

[28] For more details see: Scheu and Autrata (2011, p. 141 ff.).

Widerspiegelung, which in turn presupposes the possibility of mental processes, information about the environment is obtained that is relevant for the life and survival of the respective animals. This means two things: firstly, animals must be able to obtain such information about their environment via sensory organs – such as eyes, ears, nose or organs of touch. Second, animals must be able to sort out from the wealth of available information those that are meaningful to the animals' lives. For this second part, this means there must also be an organ – a central nervous system or brain – that can process sensory information: Sensory received information must be able to be linked to needs via processing. Sensory information must be evaluated in terms of its relevance for the life and survival of the animals.

As for the mutual demarcation, it must be said that Widerspiegelung is a part of the psychic. Widerspiegelung of the world belongs to the psychic, but the psychic also includes the organic prerequisites necessary for the apprehension of the world, such as sense organs and central nervous system or brain. The development of the psychic would be phylogenetically meaningless if the unfolding of the possibility of reflecting the environment did not result in corresponding activities. The psychic encompasses the totality of engagement with the world. Widerspiegelung is that part of the psychic with which the apprehension of the world is accomplished.

The basic considerations that were made on the basis of the categorial analysis for the psychic are to be focused on the recording of the principles of Widerspiegelung: Widerspiegelung as a subarea of the psyche exists on different levels and in many different animals. However, as soon as Widerspiegelung of the environment is possible, principles can be determined which are always given. The comprehension of the world, i.e. its Widerspiegelung, always begins with sensory processes. If sensory processes are not possible in living beings, there is no perception of the environment. Widerspiegelung begins with the sensory perception of the environment through the sense organs: The perception of the world "(…) ist gebunden an die physisch-stoffliche Wechselwirkung zwischen den Dingen und *'sensiblen' Bereichen des Organismus*, den *Sinnesorganen*. Ist diese physische Wechselwirkung unterbrochen (…)",[29] a grasp of the world does not take place. To differentiate, it must be clarified: Widerspiegelung exists only in animals and humans,[30] but not in all animals. For example, some unicellular living beings belong biologically to the animals, but have no sense organs and are therefore not capable of Widerspiegelung. Other living beings than animals generally do not

---

[29] Holzkamp (1978, p. 22); Herv. i. Orig.

[30] Biologically, humans belong to the animals. The statement that there is Widerspiegelung in animals and humans is therefore redundant: humans are already included with animals. In order to prevent misunderstandings, humans are mentioned specifically.

2 Widerspiegelung: An Approach

have sense organs, so that in principle no Widerspiegelung can be found in them. Thus, it makes sense to conceptually associate Widerspiegelung exclusively with animals.

This first principle of Widerspiegelung results from the already presented specificity of matter[31]: All animals live in relation to the objective reality, which in turn interacts with the living beings. For example, the waves of the sea rush or the hooves of large grazing animals stamp. This in turn enters into interaction with sense organs of animals, which grasp the peculiarities and structurings of the world via these sense organs.

The second principle of Widerspiegelung is that Widerspiegelung is an active process. This is already expressed in the concept of Widerspiegelung: Widerspiegelung is not a mirroring, but expresses the active relation of living beings to the environment they grasp. The concept of Widerspiegelung allows us to adequately grasp the active side of the processes involved in the reception of information and impressions from the environment. Relevant for Widerspiegelung is the dimension of one's own activity and locomotion: A mirror hangs – normally – unchanged and always in the same position on the wall. The fact that an image can be seen in the mirror or in the water is a process on which the mirror or the water has no influence. That would be a simple Widerspiegelung.

It is different for reflecting animals. You might not be able to see an object because of trees or rocks in the way. The eyes would be open and not closed, but visual reception is precluded by the location. One cannot hear sounds or tones because their source is too far away and thus beyond the sensory capacity of the ears. In such cases, a Widerspiegelung of the environment is not possible, or only possible to a limited extent, if one maintains the assumed point of view. Most animals, however, can change their point of view[32]: they can move in such a way that they have a different perspective for a visual Widerspiegelung; they can also move in such a way that they improve their hearing by moving closer.

However, the fact always remains that Widerspiegelung is based on the reception of impressions from the environment. Sensory perception is the starting point of Widerspiegelung. However, sensory perception by animals can also be influenced by animals: They can approach or move away from factual objects, for example, to gain a better overview. Highly developed animals can, if the objects allow

---

[31] cf. par. 2.1 in this volume.

[32] An exception are for example the sponges (Porifera). Although sponges belong to the multicellular animals (Metazoa), they live sessile, i.e. immobile. However, sponges have no organs and especially no sensory organs: Widerspiegelung is therefore only possible to a very limited extent, and locomotion would not help either.

it, pick up such objects and hold them in such a way that a section or part can be seen better. Widerspiegelung can be made more precise by combining sensory impressions: If something cannot be seen precisely, it may be possible to obtain further impressions by touching it.

Leontyev says that Widerspiegelung "(…) zum Unterschied von der Spiegelung und anderen Formen der passiven Widerspiegelung (…) nicht passiv, sondern aktiv ist (…)".[33] The concept of Widerspiegelung emphasizes that, on the one hand, it is the reception of objective reality: Information and impressions about this objective reality are received via the sensory potentials. The objective reality is thus mirrored sensory. No groundless fantasies are made about the objective reality, rather the objective reality is found in its Widerspiegelung.

On the other hand, Widerspiegelung is more complex than the image that appears in a mirror. Widerspiegelung is an active process. Many animals can influence the Widerspiegelung simply by choosing their location: Objective reality remains the same in itself, what is reflected from it, or what section of it, results from activities of animals. What is hidden from view cannot be reflected. But how the field of vision is laid out can be controlled by locomotions.

The result of Widerspiegelung thus remains connected to the object of Widerspiegelung, namely parts of objective reality. But the result of Widerspiegelung is also not simply a mirror image. Rather, the result of Widerspiegelung is the *active* transformation of sensory information into an image.

The first two principles of Widerspiegelung, namely that Widerspiegelung is based on sensory perception and is an active process, are still immediately plausible: one can observe that animals take a close look at something, touch it or put up their ears; one can also observe that animals change their location in order to get closer to something. The third principle of Widerspiegelung, that in the process a Widerspiegelung of objective reality is created, cannot be observed directly. Inferences and analytical considerations are necessary to prove that a Widerspiegelung must result in an image.

The starting point is the fact that Widerspiegelung must filter out relevant information from an abundance of information. Even if animals perceive the environment via sensitive sensory organs and still exert influence through active control, important and unimportant information remains in a disorderly mixture. For the life and survival of animals, however, it is important to grasp relevant information appropriately and, ideally, to do so quickly. This is possible through the dimension of meanings. The wealth of information gained by reflecting the environment is condensed into meanings. The extent to which animals can grasp meanings varies.

---

[33] Leontyev (1982, p. 57).

2 Widerspiegelung: An Approach

Meanings can also be passed on differently: There are meanings that are genetically fixed and passed on accordingly through heredity. Other meanings are not genetically transmitted and must first be acquired. It should be noted, however, that it is the mediatedness of meaning that enables animals to generate an image within the framework of Widerspiegelung.

This can be illustrated by an example of the meaning-mediatedness of information: When chickens spot a bird of prey, i.e. a predator, they react by fleeing; however, the flight is already triggered by a black triangle above the chickens.[34] This makes two things clear: first, a black triangle already has the meaning structure of the predator; the Widerspiegelung of the environment in this case condenses to the identification of a black triangle. This meaning structure can be identified in the Widerspiegelung: Thus, an image is created. The image thus captures the structure of meaning, but again is not immune to deception: even with a black triangle showing above chickens, the same image is obviously formed as with birds of prey. Second, in chickens, the behavior exhibited immediately after the appearance of the black triangle, that is, the meaning-mediated predator, is flight. Widerspiegelung and resulting activity occur almost simultaneously. This results from the fact that flight upon recognition of the predator is a biologically fixed program that cannot be modified by animals equipped with this program. The survival advantage is obvious: If chickens could not immediately create an image when the predator approaches and would hesitate, they would be eaten. The fact that researchers are now incorporating black triangles into an experimental set-up is not foreseen in the biological make-up of chickens.

The result of Widerspiegelung is an image of objective reality. A Widerspiegelung is not a simple mirror image; elements of sensory perception, activity and mediated meaning are involved in the formation of the Widerspiegelung. However, it should first be noted that Widerspiegelung does not aim at obtaining a mirror image of objective reality, but an image. According to Leontyev, when "(…) Forscher an die Untersuchung der Perzeptionstätigkeit herangehen, vereint sie die Anerkennung ihrer Notwendigkeit, die Überzeugung, daß gerade in ihr der Prozeß der 'Übersetzung' der auf die Sinnesorgane einwirkenden äußeren Objekte in das psychische Abbild erfolgt."[35] Between sensory perception and the image, which is ultimately the result of Widerspiegelung, we must therefore assume a process that Leontyev has called "Übersetzung".[36]

---

[34] cf. Scheu and Autrata (2011, p. 147 ff.).

[35] Leontyev (1982, p. 61).

[36] Leontyev (1982, p. 61).

For the understanding of Widerspiegelung, two poles can be identified: On the one hand, this is the objective reality, on the other hand, this is the Widerspiegelung of this objective reality. This Widerspiegelung is not a mirror image of the objective reality. Thus ex negativo determinations are made as to what the image as the result of Widerspiegelung is not. But this is not enough to adequately grasp the result of Widerspiegelung. In order to be able to illuminate both the result and the process of Widerspiegelung in its entirety, it is necessary to clarify what occurs between the reception of information about objective reality – which takes place via sensory perception – and its condensed output as an image.

One can first postulate that as a fourth principle of Widerspiegelung something like a processing of the incoming information and its transformation must be possible: If animals can make out differences in brightness via sensory perception, this does not yet provide a Widerspiegelung of objective reality. If animals can localize sounds or tones and perhaps even detect differences in loudness, this too is not yet suitable for generating an image of objective reality. Sensory perception is indispensable: how else is information about the objective reality of the environment to be obtained? In themselves, however, such sensory impulses are meaningless, or at least cannot be divided into the relevant and the irrelevant. Only the possibility of their processing and classification opens up the potential for capturing objective reality and generating an image of it. This is to be noted from the point of view of the mediatedness of meaning of objective reality: In objective reality, animals have, for example, predators, food sources, storage sites and sexual partners. It must be possible to assign this to the respective meaning via a processing process.

For the processing and evaluation of the impressions that arrive via sensory perception, a processing process is necessary. For example, irrelevant information must be distinguished from relevant information: Not everything that is sensory received from and to the environment is important. But what is presumably important must be sensory reviewed with more attention and perhaps repeated effort: This is again to be placed in the dimension of activity that distinguishes Widerspiegelung. Animals do not just passively wait to see if and what information about the environment reaches them; rather, Widerspiegelung is an active process that can be intensified or reduced. In order for activity in turn to do justice to the environment, control processes are necessary that set priorities. This, too, is a thought-processing process: what is or can potentially become important is 'looked at' more closely.

Such classifications of whether something is important or not require the formation of appropriate criteria: The process of evaluating and classifying what is established via sensory perception must be able to make connections with other information. The weighting and importance of sensory perceptions only results from the

2 Widerspiegelung: An Approach

fact that comparisons are possible. It should be emphasized that – according to the level of mental development – differences between animals in the processing of information can be observed. Animals have very different stocks of meanings to deal with. Accordingly, processing as the fourth principle of Widerspiegelung can be more extensive or narrower.

The processing results in ideas about the perceived and found objects or facts. Such conceptions in turn enter into the result of Widerspiegelung, namely what has been called a likeness. An image in the context of Widerspiegelung is rather to be seen as the result of the processing in which perceptions were compared with known meanings.

The processing that takes place in the context of Widerspiegelung has thus been outlined on the one hand as a process of comparison with what is known. On the other hand, the processing process in the context of Widerspiegelung is also a process of comparison with one's own needs and wants. For example, the Widerspiegelung that something is a source of food is brought into relation with the needs and wants. Possibly the result of the processing is that the food source corresponds to the basic need for food, but at the moment there is no need for food intake: The reflecting animal is full. Leontjew finds the following formulation for this connection: "Der Zusammenhang zwischen Abbild und Widerspiegelung ist nicht der Zusammenhang zweier Objekte (Systeme, Mengen), die in gegenseitig-gleichartiger Beziehung zueinanderstehen – ihre Beziehung reproduziert die Polarisiertheit eines jeden Lebensprozesses (...)."[37] An object is confronted with an active animal, which carries out the Widerspiegelung of the object under the sign of wanting to gain advantages for its life with it.

The last formulation, that Widerspiegelung serves animals to achieve advantages for their own life, leads to the fifth and last principle to be named: It must therefore be possible, it is to be concluded, for such animals to grasp what is to their advantage. To keep in evidence is, that these considerations are on the level of animals, so anthropomorphizations are to avoid. Nevertheless it is necessary to assume an internal controlling instance for animals, which are able to reflect: Widerspiegelung, together with its four principles introduced so far, would be meaningless if it could not be intentionally linked to activities – on the basis of the detection of one's own needs and wants. The fifth principle of Widerspiegelung is thus its inherent intentionality.

The introduced principles of sensory perception, activity, the formation of an image and the necessary processing only gain meaning through the fact that they are connected to needs and wants via intentionality. The advantage of

---

[37] Leontyev (1982, p. 58).

Widerspiegelung for animals lies in the increase in the probability of survival in the process of phylogenesis: if successful Widerspiegelung of the environment succeeds in ensuring one's own survival or at least the survival of one's own species, forms of Widerspiegelung can be passed on genetically.

Thus, Widerspiegelung is primarily not an unintentional observation of the environment, but an intentional, built-in grasp of the environment that is directed towards increasing the probability of survival. However, it cannot be assumed that animals 'know' that they increase their probability of survival in the phylogenetic process through successful Widerspiegelung. Intentionality must necessarily be present to explain the emergence and further evolution of Widerspiegelung in the phylogenetic process: If Widerspiegelung were disconnected from the needs and wants of animals, it could do nothing to increase the probability of survival. There must be an intentional control that regulates whether, when reflecting, it is advisable to approach or move away from the object just reflected. If there were no such thing, animals would approach predators and move away from food sources. Both can happen, but these should remain exceptional cases in order to maintain the probability of survival. The guiding authority here is intentionality.

Intentionality is to be characterized as intentionality: the Widerspiegelung itself, as well as the activities based on it, are therefore not accidental, but intentional. It should be noted that intentionality belongs to Widerspiegelung as a principle that is realized in Widerspiegelung. But there are considerable ranges of what intentionality includes. Intentionality exists in simple animals like earthworms: They have a nervous system as well as mental processes made possible by it. Earthworms can find other earthworms for reproduction by Widerspiegelung and mate with them. The sequence of Widerspiegelung and subsequent mating cannot be imagined without intentionality: this is not a random sequence of processes, but is a sequence of processes behind which there is intentionality. Yet intentionality is straightforward and not very complex.

On the other side of the spectrum that intentionality can occupy are the highly evolved chimpanzees. De Waal reports, "(…) in freier Wildbahn würden hochrangige Schimpansen andere Tiere bestechen, indem sie Fleisch selektiv mit potentiellen Verbündeten teilen und es Rivalen vorenthalten."[38] The male and high-ranking chimpanzees occasionally capture rare and prized food, namely meat. They share this food selectively, with allies getting consideration and rivals getting nothing. The intentionality of this is clear: allies are supposed to be favored by the givers because of the food gifts, rivals are supposed to feel the deference and – perhaps – become allies in the long run. A complex internal view is necessary for distinguish-

---

[38] Waal, de (2009, p. 232); see also Scheu and Autrata (2013).

2 Widerspiegelung: An Approach

ing whether other animals are something like allies or rivals: The animal that can make such distinctions and translate them into activities must have the mental capacity to mirror itself. Whether another animal is potentially a rival or an ally can only be known in relation to its own position and, more importantly, on the basis of Widerspiegelung from itself. Intentionality thereby becomes complex, involving anticipation and tactical detours.

To summarize, there are five principles of Widerspiegelung that are found in all animals that have Widerspiegelung as a means of the psychic. We must begin with the basic fact: Widerspiegelung always refers to objective reality, that is, to matter. The first principle of Widerspiegelung is that it makes use of the forms of sensory perception of matter, such as seeing, hearing or smelling. Second principle of Widerspiegelung is activity: all animals that have Widerspiegelung as a possibility can intervene in their sensory perception by their own activity. The third principle of Widerspiegelung is that the result of Widerspiegelung is an image: this image weights and evaluates the incoming information. The basis of the formation of the image is the fourth principle of Widerspiegelung, namely processing: in evaluating sensory perceptions, animals rely on inherited or acquired interpretations that result from the mediatedness of meaning of objective reality. The fifth principle of Widerspiegelung is its inherent intentionality: Widerspiegelung is performed intentionally and establishes the relation to one's own needs and wants.

The above principles of Widerspiegelung are given in all animals that can reflect objective reality. This corresponds to the introduced procedure of categorial analysis: a category develops from the basic form to the final form, but always retains the specificity of the category. Thus, Widerspiegelung corresponds to the same categorial determinations in all animals that have it, as in humans. In humans, where the final form of the category is to be found, extensions occur. Thus, the specifics of Widerspiegelung in humans, which occur as extensions to the determinations of the category, are still to be elaborated. The specifics of Widerspiegelung in human beings, it can be said in advance, are based on the specifics of being human. What constitutes being human for Widerspiegelung is to be explicated under the guiding concept of subjectivity. Subjectivity in Widerspiegelung does not mean that Widerspiegelung detaches itself from the intention to recognize objective reality. Rather, subjectivity in Widerspiegelung means that Widerspiegelung is formed anew in human beings through the specificity of being human and experiences an orienting standpoint through subjectivity. In explaining Widerspiegelung in humans, the next step is to introduce the specificity of being human: This will be explained in the next subchapter, before the specificity of human Widerspiegelung can be presented in the subchapter after next.

2.3 Hominization

Before the specificity of the Widerspiegelung of human beings can be explained, hominisation, i.e. the origin of human beings, must be outlined in brief.[39] That humans are humans is known; what needs to be clarified is what *constitutes the* specificity of humans. This, in turn, is only possible in connection with the specific form of life and organisation of human beings: society. It seems that the concept of 'society' is banal. When asked what is meant by society, it is not uncommon to receive the following answers: society is a synonym for culture, environmental (conditions), the political system, institutions and much more. However, these answers are not comprehensively helpful in grasping the concept. In order to grasp the concept of 'society', reference to theories of society is necessary. For example, it is necessary to clarify how living conditions arise and how they are formed. In order to clarify this, theories – i.e. social theories – are necessary. Now there is a multitude of social theories. The authorship of the present publication refers to a social theory that is able to analyse the present social situation of capitalism and thus to explain and understand it. Thus, a view of society is represented here that assumes that living conditions were created by humans and are thus also changeable. However, society does not only 'consist' of 'things' or objects, but knowledge is also found in society, for example, about how objects, institutions and environments came into being and what social significance they have for humans.

If one deals with the topic of 'societal knowledge', then this presupposes that man is regarded as a social being who lives in social conditions, but is by no means determined by them. Rather, man relates to his respective specific social relations. This relation is to be regarded as a relation of possibility.

Societal knowledge thus means that humans who establish a relationship to their respective specific conditions of life have a knowledge of these conditions of life that is mediated through society, that they know about the socially mediated meanings of, for example, the conditions of life, that they know what knowledge is inherent in the objects. The specificity of being human is only possible in the connection of the individual human being to his form of life in society. For human beings – in contrast to animals and other living beings – the specificity arises that the phylogenetic process of development is superimposed and partially replaced by the social-historical process. Human life and its development are therefore no longer based solely on the biological process of the emergence and change of species.

---

[39] In detail: cf. Autrata and Scheu (2011, esp. p. 141 ff.).

2 Widerspiegelung: An Approach   33

The existence of human beings is embedded in the social process: The life and survival of human beings is essentially based on social circumstances.

Human life is also life in and with nature: humans are born, they age and die; furthermore, humans are dependent on the intake of food and the presence of air to breathe. However, human life is also a form of life that is allowed to intervene in nature in a formative and formative way. The possibility of intervening in nature does not only mean the acquisition of food: for example, herbivorous animals can only eat the plants they find at the moment; at most, individual animals have the possibility of storing plant food in hiding places for later consumption. In contrast, humans who want to eat plant food can grow, harvest and process food plants. In this way, nature is intervened in a targeted and precautionary manner in order to detach the acquisition of food by humans from the vicissitudes of nature and thus to adapt it to the needs of humans. What remains, however, is the physical endowment of the human being: Humans have a body that has evolved in the phylogenetic process, and part of its physicality is that it is dependent on certain food. The food supply of present-day humans, however, is not regulated by humans going in search of appropriate food in nature. Rather, food is produced in a social process that is made available to humans, again regulated by social processes of distribution. The relationship to securing food has thus become social for humans. Stepping out of the immediate relationship to nature is not partial, but a fundamental development in and for human beings.

The step out of the immediate relationship to nature is therefore the decisive step that made the specificity of human life possible. How is it conceivable, however, that this step could be taken in hominization? The decisive movens was the use of tools. Tools expand the possibilities for securing life.[40] The step towards hominisation becomes clear if we contrast the use of tools that is possible for humans with that of the most highly developed animals: chimpanzees, for example, are able to use small twigs as tools for capturing termites in their burrows. The use of tools extends the physical possibilities of chimpanzees: they are not able to break open termite burrows and cannot penetrate the termite burrow with any part of their body deep enough to reach the termites. The described use of tools therefore creates a survival advantage for the chimpanzees: they can capture and eat termites with the tools used.

The abilities of the chimpanzees, however, only allow them to *use* such tools as twigs. The twigs grow on trees, are searched for by chimpanzees and broken off; at most, leaves are stripped from the twigs in order to be able to operate better with

---

[40] In the case of tool use, only animals are to be considered. Other living beings already lack the physical and psychological prerequisites for tool use.

them. After use, the twigs have no more meaning for the chimpanzees, they throw them away. In the next attempt to capture termites, such a branch could be useful again: However, this apparently does not translate into chimpanzees storing used twigs for later use. Analytically generalizing to this, we can state that tool use is possible for chimpanzees – and other animals. However, the tool used has only situational meaning for them. A meaning of the tool that goes beyond the situation is not reflected in activities, i.e. it is not represented psychologically.

Tool use, which occurs in some animals, expands in hominization to include the qualitative leap to *tool making*: "Nach allgemeiner Auffassung beginnt die menschliche Technik mit der Herstellung von Werkzeugen."[41] Tool making is the qualitative leap that makes hominization possible. Yet tool-making in the context of hominization is to be imagined as a staged process: Early humans did not start making an entire toolkit all at once. Rather, toolmaking unfolded from – from a manufacturing perspective – simple techniques. At the beginning of toolmaking was the processing of stones into cutting or percussive tools: "Zufällig entstehende scharfkantige Abschläge wurden als Schneidewerkzeuge eingesetzt – eine Revolution in der Fleischbearbeitung und der Zerlegung von Kadavern."[42] Even such simple tools expanded the possibilities enormously and thus brought far-reaching survival advantages. The emergence of tool making can be imagined as a sequence of steps: the sharp-edged stones or stone parts mentioned by Schrenk were found by early humans and then used to divide captured animals. This can only be classified as tool use. Obviously, however, such stones or stone parts were kept by early man and used several times. This was followed by simple forms of working: Pieces were cut off suitable stones in order to create sharp edges. This is already the stage of tool making. Even later, stones were deliberately worked in such a way that stone wedges were created. By connecting a stone wedge with a handle made of wood, the efficiency of the tool can be greatly increased: Thus tool-making has already reached the possibility of making stone axes or stone hammers.

However, the sequence of steps in the tool-making process that emerges in humans can only be explained by the fact that the meaning of tools changes. Whereas tools in chimpanzees still had a purely situational meaning and were thrown away again after use, tools for early humans have a generalized meaning: they are kept because they can also be used in other situations and thus regularly. Further, tools are purposefully made so that they conform to the generalized meaning. The generalized meaning of cutting is already incorporated into the stone wedges. The meaning of cutting is exploitable in the cutting of a killed animal, but it is also

---

[41] Henke and Rothe (2003, p. 69); see also: Scheu and Autrata (2013, p. 200 ff.).

[42] Schrenk in: Bohlken et al. (2009, p. 204).

2 Widerspiegelung: An Approach

retained by the tool beyond the day and for other animals. The generalized meaning is thus inherent in the tool; it was purposefully achieved through manufacture.

Tool production as well as the generalized meanings inherent in tools are in turn to be reflected back to the life of early humans: If tools with generalized meanings had been made and used by the maker, but subsequently the tool-making had been forgotten again, hominization could not have taken place. Only the transmission of the knowledge of tool-making, like the generalized meanings included in it, generated the specificity of the human, namely the social life of humans. The developmental core of human life is the transmission of knowledge as societal knowledge: If only one person knows how to make a stone wedge and what to do with it, it is left to chance whether this knowledge is passed on and thus preserved. If the person dies before the knowledge has been passed on, the knowledge would be lost.

Only the storage of knowledge in the social stock of knowledge ensures its transmission. It thus becomes independent of the vicissitudes of life and personal contacts: Knowledge about tools and their generalized meanings becomes societal knowledge available to humans. Even if a person who is the bearer of this knowledge dies, the knowledge remains. Knowledge enters into social forms of storage and preservation, such as written language and books, and is there accessible to humans.

The aspect of knowledge makes it clear what changes hominization has brought with it. Hominisation is, on the one hand, something that affects individual human beings; on the other hand, hominisation requires embedding in an institution that frames and outlasts the lives of individual human beings: this is society. Society thus becomes an organizational form of human beings that ensures their life and survival. Society is – as illustrated – the place and form in which knowledge is permanently stored. But society is fundamentally the form of organization that ensures human life and survival. Society includes the production and distribution of goods, but also traditions or culture and many other characteristics. Society is to be understood as a characteristic term for an object, which can be very different in its development and differentiation. The 'society' of hunter-gatherers well before the turn of time has little in common with modern capitalist or socialist societies in its phenotype, but was nevertheless also a society. Society is the term for all these forms of organization of human life and characterizes their essence: They frame and shape the lives of individuals.

If one looks back once again to the beginnings of hominization and thus also of the formation of society, this begins with the production of tools. However, not only one tool with a generalized meaning is produced, but several and later many: In addition to tools for cutting such as stone wedges, those for striking such as a stone axe were also developed. Thus the stock of generalized meanings also expanded and differentiated. If one tool was well suited for one purpose, it was not for another. Parallel to this, this knowledge of purposes was passed on and stored in the social stock of knowledge.

Before hominization there was no society, nor could there be, since society is the specific form of life and organization of humans. All living beings other than humans have only nature as their environment at their disposal: In the course of hominization, society visibly unfolded as the environment of human life and replaced dependence on nature. The production of the first tools – such as the stone wedges shown here – provided survival advantages for the humans who had them. This continued until sociality became dominant in human life. The production of tools expanded to the production of – in general – objects with a generalized purpose, i.e. an inherent object meaning. Human life thus changes from being dependent on what is created in nature to being able to purposefully produce something that is needed by humans. Through society, provision for the future in particular can be realised: provision can be made for future needs – above and beyond the assets of an individual person.

The fact that society developed as a form of organization parallel to hominization is indispensable as a framing of human life: human life is not possible without the framing in a society. This indispensable framing of human life in a society is sociality. As a definition said: sociability denotes the fact that human life is framed and shaped by society. But sociability, like society, also denotes a state of affairs that can vary widely: Sociality is indispensable, but whether it offers in all areas what humans desire is not certain.

The sociality that embeds human life holds things and facts that humans know about and can adopt and use. This has become dominant for human life in the course of hominization, reducing dependence on nature and creating new possibilities. Humans entered a new developmental context via this shift in dominance: Phylogenesis was replaced by social-historical development for humans. The further development of humans after hominization is no longer guided by phylogenesis with processes such as mutation and selection, but by the specifics of social-historical development.

Humans have thus left the immediacy of the relationship to nature, which can be conceptually understood as a transgression of immediacy.[43] Transgression of immediacy does not mean that humans live completely independently of nature: Humans are living beings and thus dependent on nature in many ways. However, transcending immediacy entails that humans *can* transcend immediacy to nature. The fact that humans have succeeded in transcending immediacy is to be understood

---

[43] cf. Scheu and Autrata (2011, p. 162 ff.). and Holzkamp (1985).

2 Widerspiegelung: An Approach 37

as a qualitative statement: Humans have made the decisive developmental leap that allows them to step out of immediacy to nature. This is to be distinguished from what is true for all other living beings: they remain completely and always arrested in immediacy to nature. In humans, on the other hand, the transgression of immediacy has begun through the production of tools with generalized meaning. Holzkamp states that "(…) die Menschen in einem bisher nicht gekannten Ausmaß *aus der Natur heraus und ihr durch ihre geplante Veränderung gegenüber (…)*" stand.[44] The transgression of immediacy is thus the beginning of an entirely different relationship to nature, which in turn entails a way of life for humans that is essentially different from that of other living beings.

The result of transcending immediacy is that humans have possibilities at their disposal and can make decisions. The step of being able to step out of the immediate relationship to nature allows for a formative influence on nature. This can be exemplified in this way: Tools and their generalized meaning are stored in society's stock of objects and knowledge. Humans can access this stock. However, it is not just one tool that is available to humans, but several. This allows for the selection and decision of which tool is best suited for a task at hand. The tool that is appropriate for completing the task at hand can be selected and used. This makes the engagement with the world different in structure for humans than it is for all other living things: Humans can draw on the social supply of knowledge and goods and use that for their purposes. In the same way, however, humans can also shape what society offers: They can, for example, change tools or adapt them situationally. Thus, on the one hand, humans's engagement with the world becomes a selection from this offer, i.e. a selection among possibilities; on the other hand, however, humans can also shape these possibilities.

For humans, this changes their access to the world: humans have options between which they can choose. This is the central principle of the relationship of humans to the world. Humans are able to choose from possibilities and thus to influence the world. This is a new dimension that is not found in other living beings or in highly developed animals. Only the organizational form of sociality has created this reservoir from which the possibility structure of the relation to the world has grown for humans.

This should be explained again in its basic features: it was humans who developed the ability to make tools. Society was not able to do this. Society, in turn, enters as a form of organization and creates the potential to absorb and store the results of human activity. Society is necessary to accumulate, but also to multiply, the potentials of the human. The result of a human being's activity could be lost or

---

[44] Holzkamp (1985, p. 182), Herv. i. Orig.

forgotten; society, on the other hand, can secure such results across generations. In a next step, such socially stored results are in turn available to humans who can access them. Access to social goods and knowledge can be shaped and controlled by humans: They have options at their disposal from which they can choose.

Mediated through society, the relationship of humans to the world is thus a relationship of possibility. It is decisive for the specificity of being human that humans have possibilities at their disposal. Humans can make a choice between these possibilities. Since it is possibilities that constitute the relationship of human beings to the world, it is thus also understood that human beings always have to make a choice between possibilities. The possibility structure of humans's relation to the world is always preserved; this is the result of deriving being human from transcending immediacy. Humans are not determined, so they do not lose their scope for decision: the decision between possibilities is always preserved.

However, the determination that the relationship of humans to the world has a structure of possibilities does not include that the possibilities available are the best imaginable and completely satisfying. The possibilities available to humans arise from the social process. The social process has a relevant historical component: it may be that at a certain historical point in time possibilities are not – yet – available, because they have not yet been invented. Other possibilities are not available because the social process has inequalities, specifically inequalities in the distribution of possibilities. The analytical statement that the possibility structure to the world is always preserved for human beings and can never sink to the level of determinacy does not imply that the given possibilities are suitable to fulfil all desires.

2.4   Widerspiegelung in Humans

Once again, we should refer to the problematic situations that arise when looking at and breaking down Widerspiegelung. This can be illustrated by our protagonists from Greek antiquity: when Eurykleia says to Odysseus that she has recognized him, one might be inclined to assume that one knows what led to this activity. The basis of the activity, in this case the verbal utterance, must surely have been a corresponding Widerspiegelung. This is consistent in itself, but it unifies the complexity of the Widerspiegelung under the leitmotif of the subsequent activity. Eurykleia did not, after all, enter the room in which Odysseus was in order to recognize him: Rather, she had the task of washing the feet of the for the time being unknown man as a form of polite hospitality. So Eurykleia, on entering the room, had to consider, for example, where to put the vessel she had brought with her containing the water, where to place the cloth to dry it, and whether perhaps any part of the room was

2 Widerspiegelung: An Approach

exposed to the sun's rays. This is not described in detail in the Odyssey, as it is of secondary importance to the progress of events. In fact, however, the preoccupation with the world requires that the world be apprehended as accurately and as correctly as possible. Had Eurykleia placed her water vessel on a wobbly stool, it might have tipped over and the subsequent washing of her feet would have become questionable. Eurykleia therefore had to grasp what was given in the room as a whole and direct her activities towards grasping the situation. The recognition of Odysseus in the context of the Widerspiegelung event in the said room of the court in Ithaca is a product of chance and by no means the original goal of Eurykleia's Widerspiegelungen of the given.

Further, the part of the Widerspiegelung of the given by Eurykleia, which then leads to the recognition of Odysseus, is to be seen as a process. The result of the process is recognition. Before that, however, Eurykleia first had to reflect where and how the stranger was situated in the room: was he already seated so that his feet could be easily reached for washing, or did he first have to be asked to sit down? The washing of another must accurately reflect how the activity can be done given the situation. If then something like beginnings of recognition arise from the Widerspiegelung, it is to be presumed that recognition has to deal with doubts: Can this really be Ulysses? It can be assumed that Eurykleia tries to check whether what she thinks she recognizes can be true: does the shape correspond to her memory, is the eye color that of Odysseus? But these are again processes which Leontyev names as one of the most difficult problems facing psychological research, namely "(...) das Problem des Zusammenhangs der psychischen Prozesse und der Gehirnprozesse, der physiologischen Prozesse".[45] Both, the psychological as well as the physiological processes, must work together for Widerspiegelung. In the process, inconsistencies and sometimes even − supposed − contradictions have to be eliminated: Isn't Odysseus already dead? The process that ultimately leads to a result of Widerspiegelung does not always have to move linearly towards a goal. Widerspiegelung has to deal with information and process it. However, detours or several attempts are quite conceivable.

Widerspiegelung is thus influenced by the fact that it is exercised by humans and 'passes through them'. Widerspiegelung refers to objective reality as an object: this has already been explained in detail.[46] Now, considering Widerspiegelung for humans, it is to be postulated: The process of Widerspiegelung itself is inherent in human beings and to that extent takes on the specificity of human beings. It has already been explained that there is a Widerspiegelung of the world not only in

---

[45] Leontyev (1982, p. 12 f.).

[46] cf. Sect. 2.1 in this volume.

humans, but also already in animals.[47] The general prerequisite for Widerspiegelung is that there is an interaction of physiological and psychological processes that is suitable for determining the conditions of the world. This is now continued in the specification of Widerspiegelung, as it is only possible for humans. For the time being, the Widerspiegelung of other humans by humans, the social Widerspiegelung, remains excluded. This will be discussed in the next chapter.[48]

The five principles of Widerspiegelung introduced – sensory perception, active control, processing, intentionality as well as the creation of an image – are also preserved for humans in the sense of the categorial analysis, i.e. they can also be found in human Widerspiegelung. In humans, however, there are specifications of Widerspiegelung that can be derived from the specificity of humans. Widerspiegelung in and by humans is to be distinguished from the introduced five principles, which apply to all living beings, at two points: The principle of processing results obtained via sensory perception becomes a process of gnostic processing. The principle of intentionality expands to subjectivity, which is unique to humans. This will be further elaborated below.

The explanations of hominization in the previous subchapter close a gap which now makes possible the presentation of the change and extension of the principles of Widerspiegelung to human Widerspiegelung. The principle to be considered in this connection is that of processing, which in man becomes a gnostic process of processing. What is meant by this? A core area of human Widerspiegelung is recourse to societal knowledge and comparison with societal knowledge. In this regard, the question arises as to where humans get such knowledge? The answer arises from hominization. The process of hominization is constituted by the acquisition and incorporation of generalized knowledge into the stock of societal knowledge that humans can access. Humans thus hold such knowledge and can update it in the context of Widerspiegelung. Thus, humans do not have to continuously 're-invent the wheel', but can recognize, on the basis of the knowledge available to them, whether the object they are currently sensory perceiving is a wheel with its inherent object meaning or not. In order to arrive at an adequate image of the object found, it is therefore not necessary to reproduce the wheel in a model or to produce a painting of it; it is sufficient if one can apply the associated linguistic concept.

In humans's Widerspiegelung, sensory perceptions of objective reality are compared with existing knowledge about objects and their generalized scopes. Putting this in the context of humans's social lives, it would be fatal if humans regularly

---

[47] cf. Sect. 2.2 in this volume.
[48] cf. Chap. 3 in this volume.

2 Widerspiegelung: An Approach 41

came to the wrong conclusions about Widerspiegelung: Someone who does not recognize a wheel as a wheel might use the wheel as a doorstop. But this does not do justice to the wheel in its object meaning. As a result, humans with such Widerspiegelung problems are likely to find it difficult to participate in social life. Under certain circumstances, survival may even be impaired or endangered.

These are not far-fetched speculations that have nothing to do with reality: If one thinks of the clinical picture of dementia, a typical example of the problematic situations of those affected is that one no longer knows, "(…) dass das Zerkleinern von Fleisch mit dem Messer besser geht und benützt zum Fleisch-Schneiden den Löffel. Nochmals auf das (…) 'Löffel-Beispiel' zurückzukommend, zeigt sich, dass nicht einfach 'vergessen' wird, welches Werkzeug zum Zerkleinern von Fleisch geeignet ist, sondern dass die Bedeutung des Gegenstandes (hier: das Messer) 'vergessen' wird. Man 'vergisst', welche Bedeutung ein alltäglicher Gegenstand hat, dass man mit dem Messer zerkleinert oder schneidet und mit dem Löffel schöpft."[49] Thus, the gnostic process in the context of Widerspiegelung can no longer access knowledge about object meanings: This knowledge is no longer available, an adequate image of the perceived object cannot be formed.

In humans suffering from dementia, the necessary knowledge is *no longer* available for comparison in the gnostic process. On the other hand, it is also possible to identify the fact that such knowledge is *not yet* available: "Vor allem im frühkindlichen Alter findet im Kontext der Ontogenese Bedeutungsaneignung statt. Illustriert wird das durch das Beispiel eines zweijährigen Kindes, das vergeblich versucht, mit der Gabel die Suppe zu löffeln, weil es sich die Bedeutung des Gegenstandes Löffel/Gabel noch nicht angeeignet hat. Anders ausgedrückt: Das Kind verfügt noch nicht über das gesellschaftliche Wissen über den verwendeten Gegenstand".[50] In the case of the child who tries to spoon soup with a fork, the adequate Widerspiegelung has also failed because the societal knowledge about object meanings is not available: sensory perceptions cannot be processed to the end point of an image that takes into account the generalized meaning of an object.

The examples presented of humans with dementia and children make it clear that the process of Widerspiegelung from sensory perception via gnostic processing to the image does not always have to lead to a uniform result. These differences result from influences on the process of Widerspiegelung, which can arise, among other things, with regard to the societal knowledge necessary for this. Also conceivable would be impairments of sensory perception such as visual or auditory

---

[49] Scheu in: Sozial Extra (4/2014, p. 25).
[50] Scheu in: Sozial Extra (4/2014, p. 25).

disorders, which can also have an impact on the possibilities of Widerspiegelung. The important ontogenesis for children, within which societal knowledge is acquired as the basis of Widerspiegelung, is a necessary and indispensable development in contrast to disorders or impairments.

Another principle to be modified for the analysis of human Widerspiegelung is intentionality, which unfolds into subjectivity. Leontiev finds the following formulation for this: "Die These, die psychische Widerspiegelung der Realität ist ihr subjektives Abbild, bedeutet Zugehörigkeit des Abbilds zum realen Lebenssubjekt. Aber der Begriff Subjektivität des Abbilds im Sinne seiner Zugehörigkeit zum Lebenssubjekt schließt dessen Aktivität ein. (…) Mit anderen Worten, Subjektivität auf der Ebene der sinnlichen Widerspiegelung darf man nicht als deren Subjektivismus verstehen, sondern vielmehr als deren Subjektivität im Sinne ihrer Zugehörigkeit zum tätigen Subjekt."[51] Although this assessment thematizes the connection between Widerspiegelung and subjectivity, it cannot yet adequately explain the share of subjectivity and subjects in Widerspiegelung. A wheel is a wheel in any case, one might object: If one relates sensory perceptions in the gnostic process to existing knowledge, the resulting conclusions would have to be the same. Still conceivable would be inadequate perceptions or incomplete knowledge of objects and their generalized meaning, which could lead to differing results of the gnostic process of cognition. Such errors or weaknesses occur in Widerspiegelung, but this is not what Leontiev means by the *subjectivity of Widerspiegelung*.[52] The determination that Widerspiegelung is subjective is not meant to discredit Widerspiegelung: Widerspiegelung is not imagination.

It becomes clear that Leontjev recognizes the subject-bound nature of Widerspiegelung. How exactly the connection between subjectivity and Widerspiegelung is to be understood, however, is not yet clear. What is the basis of the aforementioned subjective shaping of Widerspiegelung? This is basically to be unravelled by introducing the determinacy of subjectivity, which is not to be found in Leontjew.

It has been argued that after transcending immediacy, human beings stand in a relation of possibility to the world: Humans have left immediacy to nature on a large scale. They have a changed relationship to the world on the basis of the production of tools with generalized meanings and the social transmission of these generalized meanings. This is the aforementioned relation of possibility to the world, which allows one to choose between possibilities.

---

[51] Leontyev (1982, p. 58).

[52] cf. Sect. 2.2 in this volume.

2.5 Subjective Quality of Life

But the fact that there is a choice among possibilities for humans only makes sense if there is an internal standard that guides this choice. If the choice between possibilities were given, but were made only at random, it would be meaningless and would not bring humans any advantage in their way of life. Only when the relation of possibilities can be used purposefully does it benefit the quality of life of the respective humans.

This names the criterion for choosing between the options: It is humans's own quality of life. Humans therefore choose between options in such a way that their own quality of life is at least maintained, but rather improved. However, quality of life is not an objective criterion that is the same for all humans: quality of life is subjective. The relationship of possibility to the world as well as the subjective quality of life belong as two sides of the same coin to the specificity of being human: If there were no structure of possibility, no *subjective* quality of life could develop. The formation of a subjective quality of life would be meaningless, since no decisions could be made between possibilities. If there were only the possibility structure, but no subjective quality of life, that would also be meaningless: What would possibilities be useful for if they were not matched by subjectively meaningful choices? Possibility structure and subjective quality of life are two complementary features that stem from the transgression of immediacy.

Subjective quality of life is a central concept in determining the specificity of being human and, derived from this, the specificity of human Widerspiegelung. Since quality of life is subjective, there can be no objectifiable determination of quality of life that is valid for all human beings. Nevertheless, the question remains as to what can be said about the content of quality of life. Thus, further statements in this regard shall be consulted: The International Association of Schools of Social Work (IASSW), in its definition of professional and disciplinary social work, refers, among many other things, to the improvement of humans's well-being. It states, "Soziale Arbeit ist ein praktischer Beruf und eine akademische Disziplin, die den sozialen Wandel und die soziale Entwicklung, den sozialen Zusammenhalt sowie die Stärkung und Befreiung der Menschen fördert. Grundsätze der sozialen Gerechtigkeit, der Menschenrechte, der kollektiven Verantwortung und der Achtung der Vielfalt sind für die Sozialarbeit von zentraler Bedeutung. Unterstützt durch Theorien der Sozialen Arbeit, der Sozialwissenschaften, der Geisteswissen schaften und der indigenen Kenntnisse, der Sozialen Arbeit engagiert Menschen und Strukturen [sic], um die Herausforderungen des Lebens anzugehen und das

44   2 Widerspiegelung: An Approach

Wohlbefinden zu steigern".[53] From the IASSW's determination, the mission of social work can be seen as being challenged to address challenges of humans's lives
as well as increase humans's well-being. However, a more precise clarification of
what exactly could be meant by this task does not result from this.

The definition of the International Federation of Social Workers (IFSW) and the
German Professional Association (DBSH) argue similarly. There, however, it is
stated that *well-being* is to be improved: "Soziale Arbeit fördert als praxisorienti-
erte Profession und wissenschaftliche Disziplin gesellschaftliche Veränderungen,
soziale Entwicklungen und den sozialen Zusammenhalt sowie die Stärkung der
Autonomie und Selbstbestimmung von Menschen. Die Prinzipien sozialer
Gerechtigkeit, die Menschenrechte, die gemeinsame Verantwortung und die
Achtung der Vielfalt bilden die Grundlage der Sozialen Arbeit. Dabei stützt sie sich
auf Theorien der Sozialen Arbeit, der Human- und Sozialwissenschaften und auf
indigenes Wissen. Soziale Arbeit befähigt und ermutigt Menschen so, dass sie die
Herausforderungen des Lebens bewältigen und das Wohlergehen verbessern, dabei
bindet sie Strukturen ein."[54] DBSH also talks about the challenges of life and the
well-being of humans to be improved.

The task of social work is therefore, among other tasks, to both increase and
support the well-being and welfare of humans who are accompanied and supported
by professional social work. However, the official definition of social work does
not say what constitutes the well-being and welfare that is to be increased and improved. There are, however, ideas on the part of some university lecturers as to
what might be included. For example, Leupold suggests using the capability approach to clarify the question. He summarizes it as follows: "Dieser [capability
approach, author's note] justiert, vereinfacht ausgedrückt, Wohlergehen als ein
Verfügen über bestimmte Fähigkeiten, die als unverzichtbar für ein gutes menschli-
ches Leben bewertet werden".[55] Well-being is thus achieved when humans have the
capabilities to lead a good life. Nussbaum formulates what these capabilities might
be in her Capabilities Approach.

What is questionable is whether or not the Capability or Capabilities Approach
is a theory. Nussbaum herself admits that the Capabilities Approach she formulates
is a vague theory.[56] This has been taken up critically by the authorship of the present

---

[53] International Association of Schools of Social Work 2020.

[54] German Professional Association for Social Work 2020.

[55] Leupold in: Begemann et al. (2016, p. 58). In addition to the *capability* approach, there is
also talk of the *capabilities* approach.

[56] Nussbaum in: Douglass et al. (1990, p. 218).

2 Widerspiegelung: An Approach

45

paper: According to the authorship, there is no such thing as a vague theory; at least, an utterance that remains vague should not be called a theory.[57]

Returning to what the Capabilities Approach says, it can be stated: In the Capabilities Approach, Nussbaum assumes that humans must possess basic abilities in order to be able to lead a good life. To this end, she formulates ten basic abilities to which humans must be enabled in order to lead a good life. Following Galamaga, who in turn summarizes Nussbaum, these will be briefly listed below: Humans must be able or be enabled "(…) das Leben bis zum natürlichen Tod zu leben, (…) sich angemessen zu ernähren, sich guter Gesundheit zu erfreuen und eine Unterkunft zu haben, (…) sich gegen Gewalt zu schützen, nach lustvollen Erlebnissen zu suchen und schmerzvolle Erlebnisse zu meiden."[58] Furthermore, humans should be able to "(…) sich des eigenen Verstandes zu bedienen, angemessenen Zugang zur Bildung zu haben, am kulturellen Leben teilzunehmen und von Meinungsfreiheit Gebrauch zu machen, (…) Gefühle frei auszudrücken und sich emotional ohne Angst und Einschüchterung zu entwickeln, (…) eine eigene Konzeption des Guten zu verfolgen und über die Planung des eigenen Lebens kritisch zu reflektieren, (…) in soziale Interaktionen zu treten, sich in die Lage des Anderen hineinzuversetzen und respektvoll mit Anderen umzugehen, (…) in Respekt für die Tier- und Pflanzenwelt zu leben, (…) zu lachen, zu spielen und Freizeitbeschäftigungen nachzugehen, [and, author's note] (…) ein eigenes Leben zu führen, an politischen Prozessen zu partizipieren, Eigentum zu besitzen, nach Arbeit zu suchen etc. [sic]".[59] It is thus a motley mix of ideas that can be detected in Galamaga, who in turn references Nussbaum.

Leupold in turn states, "(…) dass Wohlbefinden mindestens ein grundlegendes Bestimmungsstück gelingenden Lebens ist".[60] It should be noted here that although Leupold refers to the Capabilities Approach, he changes the terminology used there. Thus the Capabilities Approach speaks of well-being, whereas Leupold speaks of well-being. Furthermore, the Capabilities Approach speaks of a good life, whereas Leupold speaks of a successful life. That is, Leupold equates well-being with well-being and good with successful. This imprecise use of terms will not be pursued further here. It should be emphasised, however, that in the context of the capabilities approach, well-being is achieved when humans have capabilities that make this well-being possible. It is not clear whether the capabilities to be

---

[57] cf. Autrata and Scheu (2015, p. 183 ff.).

[58] Galamaga (2014, p. 60).

[59] Galamaga (2014, p. 61).

[60] Leupold in: Begemann et al. (2016, p. 58).

achieved are conclusively and comprehensively outlined by Galamaga's or Nussbaum's catalogue of capabilities.

Leupold emphasises that the subject of 'well-being' also plays an important role in the philosophical context. He refers to the two hedonistic approaches of Aristipp and Epicurus. Both ancient philosophers are concerned with 'well-being'. Aristipp determines well-being as "(…) ein grundlegendes Bestimmungsstück gelingenden Lebens."[61] Following this understanding, it means that well-being occurs when a person has positive emotions. Epicurus – as Leupold notes – on the other hand considers "(…) Wohlbefinden als Abwesenheit von Unlust bzw. Von negativen Emotionen".[62] Sceptical of both the representatives of the capabilities approach (Galamaga, Nuss baum) in the narrower sense and Leupold, it must be objected that both positions have recognizable weaknesses: Where does the idiosyncratic catalogue of requirements that Galamaga lists with reference to Nussbaum come from? Are these requirements valid for all human beings or only a provisional list? Leupold's Widerspiegelungen on humans's well-being or positive emotions are similar: do humans themselves determine whether well-being or positive emotions have arisen in them? Do such non-derived and not further determined terms like well-being or positive emotions provide analytical clarity? Thus, the question of whether well-being and well-being in the sense presented here are synonymous with quality of life cannot be answered with certainty.

Norbert Rückert deals specifically with quality of life. He also equates quality of life with a successful life.[63] To define the term, he also draws on the definition of the World Health Organization (WHO), among others. Here quality of life is defined as follows: "'Lebensqualität'ist die individuelle Wahrnehmung der eigenen Lebenssituation im Kontext der jeweiligen Kultur und des jeweiligen Wertesystems und in Bezug auf die eigenen Ziele, Erwartungen, Beurteilungsmaßstäbe und Interessen".[64] Rückert also refers to the 2011 report of the Organisation for Economic Development and Cooperation (OECD), the Stiglitz-Sen-Fitoussi Commission. There, quality of life is explained on the basis of 15 indicators. These indicators are "(…) Gesundheit (…), Beruf und Privatleben (…), Bildung und Qualifikation (…), Soziale Beziehungen (…), Ziviles Engagement und

---

[61] Leupold in: Begemann et al. (2016, p. 59).
[62] Leupold in: Begemann et al. (2016, p. 59).
[63] cf. Rückert in: Begemann et al. (2016, p. 90).
[64] WHO QOL Group (1997); quoted from Rückert in: Begemann et al. (2016, p. 92).

2 Widerspiegelung: An Approach 47

Politikmitgestaltung (...), Umweltqualität (...), Persönliche Sicherheit (...), Subjektives Wohlbefinden".[65]

According to Rückert, a good life can also be achieved if a person has "(...) psychische Ressourcen (...) wie Motivation, Selbstwertgefühl, internale Kontrollüberzeugungen, Selbstwirksamkeitserwartungen, Kohärenzgefühl und identitätsrelevante Ressourcen bzw. Innere Ressourcen ...)".[66] According to this, humans are able to lead a good life or have a good quality of life if they have psychological, i.e. inner, resources at their disposal.[67]

In the previous explanations, 'inner' and 'outer' aspects – which can also be reciprocal and/or related to each other – have been mentioned, which can lead to a good life or make up the quality of life. However, the human being is completely disregarded. Rückert formulates this as follows: "Die Person selbst ist als Organismus oder System (nur) der Schauplatz des Geschehens, aber nicht 'Mitspielerin'".[68] Here Rückert is not to be agreed with. Ideas about quality of life that leave the person, or better: the subject, out of the equation do not seem very meaningful. How could one imagine a subject-independent quality of life? Would it be helpful to draw up a catalogue of criteria on the one hand and to refer to psychological resources on the other, in order to come to the conclusion that the quality of life is outside the sphere of influence of humans? With Rückert, one would have to come to the paradoxical assessment that the quality of life of humans has little to do with humans.

After these critical remarks, we need to take another look at the debate on quality of life: Here, it is primarily a matter of determining how the individual subject conceives of his or her specific quality of life. For this purpose, reference should be made to the findings of subject science. There, quality of life is described in general terms as the disposal of living conditions. Holzkamp summarizes this as follows: "*Die Qualität der individuellen Lebenserfüllung* akzentuiert sich mithin hier aus der Kraftentfaltung, dem Beziehungsreichtum etc. bei der *Rückgewinnung* der Handlungsfähigkeit, was selbst schon – indem auf Verfügungserweiterung gerichtet – einen *je gegenwärtigen Zuwachs an erfahrener Bedingungsverfügung, damit menschlicher Lebensqualität*, einschließt."[69]

---

[65] German Bundestag (2013; p. 324 ff.) o. O.; quoted from Rückert in: Begemann et al. (2016, p. 94).

[66] Rückert in: Begemann et al. (2016, p. 96).

[67] Humanistic psychology argues in a similar way: cf. e.g. Seligman 2005.

[68] Rückert in: Begemann et al. (2016, p. 97).

[69] Holzkamp (1985, p. 246); Herv. i. Orig.

However, Holzkamp's argument needs to be made more precise: Quality of life has to do with the disposition over conditions. The simple equation – quality of life is the increase in the availability of conditions – is not true. There are conditions that are important for one's own quality of life. A disposal of these conditions is in one's own interest, promotes one's own quality of life. Other conditions are not important for one's quality of life: having them at one's disposal does not enhance one's quality of life. Only if one adds that the extended disposal is only purposeful in the case of those conditions that serve to improve one's subjective quality of life, does the connection become clear.[70] Explained by means of an example: If someone first has a few books at his disposal, and then later has many, this represents an increase in conditional disposition; however, this person may not like to read in general or may not be able to read at all. In this case, there is an increase in conditional disposition, but there is probably no increase in quality of life.

That is, humans achieve subjective quality of life when they can dispose of their own living conditions in such a way that this contributes to maintaining or increasing their quality of life. This can be explained with another example: When humans suffer from hunger, they suffer from hunger because of a lack of food, but they also suffer from the fact that they have no access to those living conditions that would make hunger obsolete, and this also affects their quality of life. Quality of life would therefore exist if there were enough food available and if the starving person had those living conditions at his disposal which would make hunger unnecessary. As far as possible, the food available should correspond to what the hungry person can and wants to eat: for very small children or vegan humans, a steak is probably not the most suitable food. Subjective quality of life is realized through the availability of conditions. In which areas, however, the realization of subjective quality of life is pursued depends on the interests and needs of the person who does so.

It can therefore be stated that quality of life cannot be meaningfully determined without linking it back to subjectivity. All the versions of quality of life presented in catalogues, such as those formulated by the capabilities approach, suffer from the fact that they provide lists of desirable things: Who exactly desires this, however, and whether there are not also other conceptions of quality of life, cannot be elucidated with this. Quality of life, as subjective quality of life, remains referred to the fact that it is pursued by subjects. What subjects in turn seek to realize as quality of life is left to the decision of the subjects. This means that the discourse on quality of life as a concept, which is relevant in various contexts, must be left behind again: It is now again a matter of placing quality of life as a specifically human quality in the context of Widerspiegelung.

---

[70] cf. Scheu and Autrata (2013, p. 257 ff.).

2 Widerspiegelung: An Approach

It is only human beings who have the possibility structure to the world as well as subjectively determined quality of life. This is based on human existence in society, which allows humans to make a choice among social possibilities, but which also confronts humans with the task of making this choice according to subjective standards. This is the root of human subjectivity. Subjectivity is – in the Latin sense of the word – what underlies humans's choices: subjectivity derives from the Latin *subiectum esse*, which can be translated as *to underlie*.[71]

Subjectivity of humans is the answer to the question of why: Why do humans do exactly what they do? Subjectivity is what underlies humans's actions. Humans have to fathom out for themselves what is and what is not the quality of life to which they aspire. Quality of life can only be determined subjectively, i.e. according to a gnostic process in which humans grasp themselves.

Subjectivity thus captures the inner constitution of a person, his preferences and interests. Subjectivity guides the relationship of humans to the world: decisions are made and actions triggered from the perspective of subjectivity. Subjectivity subsequently shapes itself into goals and strategies: That which is pursued vis-à-vis the realities of the world has its starting point in one's own subjectivity.

Subjectivity is not recognizable from the outside: at most, one can draw conclusions about the subjectivity behind it from decisions that have been made or actions that have been performed. But this remains – necessarily – attached to the surface: actions can be seen or their consequences felt, the subjectivity that led to actions cannot be seen or felt. For example, from the outside it cannot be seen or felt with certainty what the relation is between an action and a person's subjectivity. The action carried out must be based on a decision attributable to subjectivity, but may perhaps have been influenced by considerations or have incorporated tactical detours: But even such considerations or tactical detours are based on subjectivity. So whether judgments about other humans's subjectivity are valid or subject to fallacies remains uncertain.

Subjectivity as well as subjective quality of life are thus fundamentally introduced and explicated. In summary, it can be stated: Subjectivity has its origin in the relationship of humans to the world. In this context, an internal yardstick is employed, namely the subjective quality of life. It is this yardstick that guides the choice between possibilities.

This is to be continued for the presentation of the connection between Widerspiegelung and subjectivity. Widerspiegelung of objective reality is a part of human life. Thus, when analyzing Widerspiegelung by humans, the specificity of being human must be taken into account. Less influenced by the specificity of be-

---

[71] own translation, d. Verf.

ing human is sensory perception: sensory perceptions are bound to biological processes that take place via organs of perception. Seeing, hearing, smelling or touching are such processes of sensory perception. Thus, for example, touch is sensory very powerful in humans due to the development of the free use of the hand, which in turn was made possible by the upright gait.

However, there is also evidence of performance differences in sensory perception, which in turn are attributed to activities in certain occupational groups. Rubinstein reports, for example, "(...) daß Weber, die an schwarzen Geweben arbeiten, Dutzende von Schwarztönen unterscheiden, während andere Menschen nicht mehr als drei bis vier unterscheiden können".[72] Rubinstein thus found weavers to have a high ability to differentiate between shades of black, which apparently corresponds to the occupational necessity of having to detect color differences between fabrics, all of which are to be classified as black. The sensory perception that contrasts with this is vision. There are similar findings for other professions and other parts of sensory perception: For piano tuners or musicians it is found that they can distinguish the pitch of tones better than other humans. The sensory perception through hearing is in question here. Cooks or wine growers often have a high ability to differentiate between tastes, which in turn is based on corresponding sensory perception. On the one hand, it seems plausible that sensory perception is refined and made more precise in a specific professional context.

On the other hand, sensory perception is only a part of Widerspiegelung: impressions from sensory perception are compared with societal knowledge in the gnostic process. Humans with appropriate occupations then know that a darker black is the result of a more intense coloring process. Higher or lower tones on the piano are based on mood and can be changed by appropriate intervention. Flavors of food or wine are created in the making and can be corrected by adding or omitting ingredients. Thus, there are areas of social life in which humans deal with facts that require a combination of sensory perception and societal knowledge about the object that is appropriate to the object. Thus the exemplarily mentioned differentiation of many shades of black by weavers is the result of a sensory perception refined by repetition, which in turn, however, requires processing in a gnostic process that is also trained in this respect.

Sensory perception, as the references to special deepenings have already shown, is not merely a passive reception of information from the environment; sensory perception is a process that is actively controlled. This is to be pursued further under the leitmotif of subjectivity. Sensory perception is subject to being tied back to the subjectivity of humans through active control.

---

[72] Rubinstein (1972, p. 92); quoted in Holzkamp (1978, p. 273).

2 Widerspiegelung: An Approach

The fact that and how subjectivity finds its way into sensory perception in humans via active control,[73] should be underlined by an example: An object as a part of objective reality receives attention because it could potentially be important for the subjective quality of life. Other objects, on the other hand, are quickly eliminated from further sensory perception because they are obviously not significant for one's quality of life. The objects that are perceptually reflected are, for example, food. In contrast to non-vegetarians, vegetarians or vegans make different preselections: Non-vegetarians will perhaps examine pieces of meat more closely in a supermarket to see whether they are fresh and of high quality, humans who do not eat meat will quickly – presumably with emerging reluctance – end the sensory perception of pieces of meat. In each case, what meets subjective quality of life hits sensory perception: One takes in something more closely because it lies in the corridor of one's own subjective quality of life, or one quickly directs one's attention to other things because one's own quality of life suggests it.

The segment of Widerspiegelung in which subjectivity finds its expression is the gnostic process. The gnostic process has to connect two reference points with the aim of generating an image as a result of the Widerspiegelung. These two reference points are objective reality and the subjectivity of the reflecting person. Since there can only be one image as the result of the Widerspiegelung, the two points of reference must be transferred to a coincident result via and in the gnostic process.

Thus it is the task of the gnostic process to overcome an apparent paradox: The objective reality of what is *reflected* as well as the reality of the subjective of the *reflected are* to be compressed into a common result, the image, via the gnostic apprehension and processing. The question of whether and how this might be possible is already raised by Engels and taken up again by Holz: "How do our thoughts about the world surrounding us relate to this world itself? Is our thinking capable of recognizing the real world, are we able to "(...) daß Weber, die an schwarzen Geweben arbeiten, Dutzende von Schwarztönen unterscheiden, während andere Menschen nicht mehr als drei bis vier unterscheiden können?"[74] Apparently, then, objectivity and subjectivity are incompatible. In fact, however, this is a contradiction, but one that can be resolved.

Mentally, the principle of dialectics is to be recalled: Thesis and antithesis are in contradiction. A simple unification as an average value is not possible. A synthesis must be sought and found that can reach a higher level of understanding via a qualitative leap.[75]

---

[73] cf. Autrata and Scheu (2011, esp. p. 130 ff.).

[74] Marx and Engels (1962b, MEW 21, p. 275); quoted in Holz (2003, p. 48).

[75] cf. Autrata and Scheu (2011, esp. p. 130 ff.).

This can be clarified by looking at the prerequisites of Widerspiegelung: On the one hand, Widerspiegelung must fulfil the prerequisite that it provides knowledge about objective reality. If Widerspiegelung did not achieve this, the effort to reflect would be pointless, would be an unnecessary consumption of resources. If Widerspiegelung did not provide results that were relevant to one's own subjective quality of life, it would again be pointless, since it would not contribute to maintaining or increasing this subjective quality of life. Widerspiegelung must satisfy both conditions, otherwise it would be pointless and would probably not take place.

In the gnostic process, Widerspiegelung must therefore do justice to the reference point of objective reality: Widerspiegelung cannot slide into fantasizing, but must break down, in a discerning process and with the aid of societal knowledge, which object or state of affairs is being reflected. In the same way, Widerspiegelung must do justice to the reference point of the reality of the subjective: In this relation, the cognitive process aims at the fact whether and to what extent the reflected fact or object can contribute to one's own subjective quality of life.

Widerspiegelung must therefore focus these two points of reference, objective reality and subjectivity, in such a way that they coincide in one image. How this can be done will again be explained by means of an example: One finds a large object at a household clearance, perhaps initially difficult to discern in its nature. The object is covered by boxes and other material. After clearing it away – and initial cleaning – it becomes apparent that the mysterious object is a piano. Through more accurate sensory perceptions such as palpating the surfaces, carefully striking the keys, and listening closely for the sounds that emerge, further information important to accurate Widerspiegelung is absorbed. The gnostic recognition including the comparison with the object meaning comes to the conclusion that the piano is still in good condition. Parallel to the recognition of the objective reality runs the comparison with subjectivity: could the use of the piano in accordance with its object meaning, i.e. through playing the piano, contribute to one's own subjective quality of life? Possibly the gnostic process in this regard comes up against the memory of piano lessons one had as a child: Only for a long time one did not have a piano to play on. So it could be that the found object fits exactly into this gap: It is, in its objective meaning, a piano. If it were not a piano but a chest of drawers, the idea that one would like to play the piano again could not be updated in the sense of the realization of subjective quality of life: One might want to play the piano, but if one does not have the instrument to do so, the wish remains unfulfilled. If, on the other hand, it is irrelevant for one's own subjective quality of life whether one owns a piano or not, one will hardly pay attention to a piano one has found. In the exemplary case shown, however, the following result of the

2 Widerspiegelung: An Approach

Widerspiegelung in objective and subjective terms is obtained: Now I have finally found the piano I have been looking for for a long time!

The fact that Widerspiegelung is almost dramatic, however, should be the exception rather than the rule: such a chance find, as described in the example above, may occasionally occur. If one looks at the everyday life of humans, Widerspiegelung runs along quieter paths. But there, too, the interlocking between the determination of objective reality and the consideration of one's own subjectivity can be observed.

Thus, there are likely to be few humans who consistently and accurately record – as in an inventory list – everything that is in their house or apartment. That would follow the model of establishing objective reality. This would probably only be done – if at all – in a special case, perhaps when the house or apartment is sold: But then subjective quality of life would be involved again. One would have to decide whether to take the household effects with one, dispose of them, or try to incorporate them into the purchase. A customary Widerspiegelung, on the other hand, would be guided by the idea of checking what is missing or running out. What is clear here is the interlocking of objective reality and subjectivity in Widerspiegelung. On the one hand, one must determine and recognize what one has and what of it is still usable, should it be perishable food, for example. Thus, through the means of sensory perception such as sight, touch, and smell, one must attempt to gain meaningful impressions about the stock and the goodness of the stock. In addition, one must activate knowledge about the nature and shelf life of such goods in order to arrive at an identification and assessment: What could be the contents of the ominous package in the freezer and is that likely to still be edible?

Actually, subjectivity and the gnostic view of one's own subjective quality of life was already involved in the above-mentioned sifting, whether one realized it or not. Once one has sifted through the stock of food, the subjective issue is whether one still has enough stock for the next meals and what those things are that are in the stock. Subjectively speaking, one wants to eat. This general goal is in turn influenced by the fact that one wants to eat what tastes good or seems digestible. Vegetarians will disapprovingly take note of large meat packages in the refrigerator and will not assume that they will be able to realize their ideas of good food for the near future. Their subjective quality of life in this respect is endangered due to the reflected actual state.

The interlocking of the objective and the subjective and the coincidence of both in the Widerspiegelung becomes clear: On the one hand, it must be a matter of reflecting the objective reality as well and appropriately as possible. If mistakes are made, for example if something is overlooked, the Widerspiegelung is impaired. However, the Widerspiegelung of objective reality cannot be about creating an inventory of the trivial. Widerspiegelung must therefore also concentrate on the other side, that of the subjective: What of what is found is significant to one's quality of life? But it would also make little sense, starting from the side of the subjective, to fill out a wish list of desiderata: What would I like to have in order to fully satisfy my ideas of quality of life? This too is subject to the danger of slipping into the trivial. Rather, it is the task of Widerspiegelung to grasp reality both as objectively given and in its relationship to one's own subjectivity.

The Widerspiegelung must therefore be detached from neither its objective nor its subjective context. For example, when looking at the contents of the refrigerator, one must consider both that one correctly recognizes all products and whether the recognized products correspond to one's own taste.

Widerspiegelung thus stands in a double gnostic relation. First, the gnostic process of cognition is directed towards objective reality. Secondly, the gnostic process is also directed towards one's own subjectivity, towards the elucidation of the question of what does justice to one's own subjective quality of life.

This double gnostic relationship is easily manageable for the sighting of the refrigerator: if one finds milk or not, for example, it is probably easy to decide whether milk is beneficial for one's subjective quality of life or not. Similarly, identifying milk in a printed bottle should not be difficult. However, if one considers more complex circumstances that need to be reflected, it becomes clear that Widerspiegelung is by no means always so easy.

The challenge of adequately performing Widerspiegelung concerns both sides of the gnostic process: the gnostic apprehension of the objective can be difficult, just as the gnostic apprehension of one's own subjectivity, that is, the gnostic relationship to oneself, can also be difficult. The exemplary Widerspiegelung of milk will not be particularly problematic, either objectively or subjectively: One can already recognize the milk in the bottle by the imprint; likewise, the inward question of whether one appreciates milk or not is not likely to trigger a very complex gnostic process to oneself.

However, if one recalls the example in which a piano was found in a household clearance, multi-layered relationships are hinted at: Is it so easy to elucidate whether or not resuming piano playing after years contributes to an increase in subjective quality of life? One may have to allow for a longer period of practice before actually being able to play the piano again. Perhaps it is to be feared that one will not be able to connect to earlier skills. In such a case, it could be that the joy of playing the piano is not restored, but the disappointment that one no longer masters the piano to the same extent as before predominates. The gnostic process to oneself may also need to consider the past: Did one actually play the piano well

2 Widerspiegelung: An Approach

at a young age, or did one allow the biased praise of relatives to influence one as a child? In any case, in the gnostic process towards oneself, it is not easy to clarify beyond doubt how the subjective quality of life is to be evaluated. Subjective quality of life does not appear – always – as a simple proposition. Subjective quality of life often exists in the form of statements that oscillate between 'indeed' and 'however': There are ideas about one's own subjective quality of life, but there are also doubts and reservations. In this respect the gnostic process, which wants to recognize the side of the subjective within the framework of a Widerspiegelung, is sometimes laborious and in itself not free of contradictions.

The complications and detours demanded by the gnostic process of recognizing the subject side in Widerspiegelung are also to be found on the side of recognizing the objective. One will not have to go to great lengths to recognize a piano. In such a case, Widerspiegelung of objective reality should quickly come to an unambiguous result. However, if one imagines that one is inspecting a used car that one might want to buy, the requirements for Widerspiegelung become greater. Whether it is a car that one is viewing should be quickly clarified. If you do not have any knowledge about cars and their condition, the question arises where and how to start the Widerspiegelung. Can you tell from the engine's running noise what condition it is in? Where and how do you have to feel in order to detect previous damage? Which characteristics are decisive for determining the value and ultimately the purchase price? Even in such a context, doubts and contradictions can enter into the process of Widerspiegelung; the formulation of a gnostic result, on the other hand, is difficult.

Finally, it should be noted that the gnostic process is analytically divided into a part directed towards objective reality and a part directed towards subjectivity. In fact, however, Widerspiegelung, including the gnostic process, is a process that leads to a result or image. Widerspiegelung of a used car leads to a result in which the capture of the objective as well as the subjective can be found. In the same way, the Widerspiegelung of a piano found by chance leads to a Widerspiegelung: this is an instrument that is still quite usable, on which I can fulfil my long-cherished wish of playing the piano again. If the instrument were indeed a piano, but as a result of the objective Widerspiegelung in such a desolate condition that one could no longer play it, the subjective desire to want to play the piano again would necessarily not be able to come to fruition. If the piano were still playable, but one's doubts about one's own playing qualities or one's own willingness to make an effort were so predominant that one did not trust oneself to make a new start, the objective qualities of the found piano would be of secondary importance.

It can also be that Widerspiegelung is not a snapshot that comes to a decision and an image of what is found in a short moment. There are such quick results of Widerspiegelung: if one discovers a cold drink in the refrigerator on a hot day that suits one's taste, the emergence of an image will probably proceed quickly and be transformed into activity: One drinks it up. Other Widerspiegelungen take on a process character, perhaps being repeated and intensified.

Summarizing the results achieved so far, it can be stated that Widerspiegelung is a complex process of taking in and dealing with reality. Essential for the conception of Widerspiegelung is the emphasis on activity: Widerspiegelung is to be understood in all aspects as an active process, is not a passive perception.

Reality that is reflected is given once as objective reality. The objective reality is received via sensory perceptions: One source of information about objective reality lies in these sensory perceptions. The essential other source lies in the comparison with existing societal knowledge about objects and facts. In the gnostic process of cognition, the two aforementioned sources are brought together.

The second reality that enters into the Widerspiegelung is that of subjectivity. In the gnostic process, evaluations are made, the relation to the subjective quality of life is established. The gnostic process to oneself examines what meaning the reflected has for one's own subjectivity. Thus the gnostic process is always subjective.

In conclusion, the following definition can be given: Widerspiegelung is the representation of objective reality from the subject standpoint.

Social Widerspiegelung in Humans: Fundamentals

3

In the second chapter, Widerspiegelung was discussed in general terms as the Widerspiegelung of objective reality. However, Widerspiegelung also includes the Widerspiegelung of other humans. In the first chapter, this was exemplified by the legendary Odysseus. To him, returning home to humans who could recognize him was important. This can be illustrated in this way: On the one hand, humans are to be seen for themselves. For example, what someone thinks is known only to that individual. The plans Odysseus made before he returned to Ithaca are accessible only to him. However, the classification that a person's thoughts are his alone changes in relation to other humans: Of course, Odysseus' mental reaction to being recognized by his nurse is something that takes place within him. He may have been pleased or startled because he did not expect it. However, there is also the interplay between the nurse and Odysseus to consider: Odysseus may be pleased or frightened only after the Nurse recognizes him. Parallel to Odysseus' thoughts and reactions, thoughts, feelings and plans also form in the Nurse Eurykleia: she may no longer have expected Odysseus to return and is pleased that he has come after all; but she may also be surprised at how much he has aged. All these thoughts that form in the minds of Eurykleia and Odysseus are based on the interplay of recognizing and being recognized. Humans, then, are on the one hand humans in their own right, but on the other hand they are also socially interwoven with other humans.

Since Eurykleia is a human being, she is distinguished by her being a subject. She can therefore decide whether or not to let Odysseus know that she has recognized him and whether or not to tell others about the scar she has discovered.

© The Author(s), under exclusive license to Springer Fachmedien
Wiesbaden GmbH, part of Springer Nature 2023
O. Autrata, B. Scheu, *Subjective quality of life and social work*,
https://doi.org/10.1007/978-3-658-40400-0_3

58 3 Social Widerspiegelung in Humans: Fundamentals

Her decision is guided by her own specific interests and needs, but not determined by them. The view of the legendary Odysseus, however, can only be used as an image that makes clear the individual components that make up the Widerspiegelung of other humans. In the following, it is now necessary to take a closer look at the Widerspiegelung of other humans, which means to open it up scientifically.

For human beings, being recognized and being recognized again is of great importance. This can be provisionally stated with regard to the incident described for Odysseus. However, following the purpose of the present publication, this assessment is to be pursued analytically and underpinned with appropriate terms. The first chapter introduced the concept of anagnorisis, which was already known in the fourth century before the turn of time.[1] However, anagnorisis has remained limited in its application to the realm of theatre and drama. Furthermore, the concept of anagnorisis lacks the analytical depth that would allow it to grasp the complexity of reflecting other humans, which is, after all, what this publication is about.

So what is it, from a scientific point of view, that plays such an important role in the life of Odysseus and – to put it in general terms – in the life of human beings? It is the social, one can say. With this definition, we have gained a concept that is suitable for grasping what can be found as a phenomenon in the example presented as well as in the lives of humans in general. Starting from this concept, the connection to the analyses of Chap. 2 can also be made: There is Widerspiegelung, which was explained in more detail and ultimately defined. Widerspiegelung, in turn, includes the Widerspiegelung of other humans, that is, social Widerspiegelung. The specifics of Widerspiegelung in the social are to be outlined more precisely in this chapter. In order for this to happen, the concept of the social must be dealt with in more detail.

However, before introducing and explaining the authors' own Widerspiegelungen on Widerspiegelung in the context of the social, it is necessary to look at existing research findings: It should be noted that there is research that also deals with how humans perceive other humans, but does not conceptually start from Widerspiegelung and the social. Methodologically, too, the approach is different from that of authorship. In a first subchapter – for contrast – it is unfolded how the authors to be introduced there approach the elucidation of perception between humans and to which results they come.

---

[1] cf. Chap. 1 in this volume.

3 Social Widerspiegelung in Humans: Fundamentals   59

3.1 Contrast: Existing Research Findings

The theorization of the present publication pursues the path of analytically eluci-
dating how humans see each other and how they process what they see. It is thus
concerned with phenomena as they emerge in the process of recognizing and being
recognized between Odysseus and Eurykleia. The present publication is guided by
a certain understanding of these processes, which is characterized by the central
concepts of Widerspiegelung, the social and subjectivity.

However, theorizing about the comprehension of other humans is not only about
the understanding of Widerspiegelung, the social and subjectivity. Other theories
take different paths – in whole or in part – and arrive at different results accordingly. In this subchapter, ideas about empathy as part of social cognition and about
the Theory of Mind are introduced; the presentation of the Theory of Mind in turn
fans out into a presentation of considerations with a background in cognitive psychology and results from neurobiological research. The aim is to provide an overview of such theoretical approaches. These theoretical approaches provide food for
thought about the complex processes that take place when humans perceive other
humans. However, as will be shown, these approaches have weak points that should
be critically noted.

Empathy and Social Cognition

Doris Bischof-Köhler begins her considerations with hominization. She assumes,
"(…) daß die Hominiden zu einem relativ frühen Zeitpunkt, sicher schon vor 2
Millionen Jahren, dazu übergegangen waren, einen Hauptbestandteil ihrer
Ernährung durch Jagd auf Großwild zu bestreiten (…)".[2] Bischof-Köhler concludes from the changed nutritional behaviour assumed by her that in the realisation of this new demands had to be met by early humans: they had to cooperate in
the hunt for big game as well as share the prey after a successful hunt with those
who were not involved in the hunt, i.e. for example with women and children.
Bischof-Köhler concludes that "(…) die Lösung der in Frage stehenden Probleme

---

[2] Bischof-Köhler (1989, p. 11). Two comments need to be made: Bischof-Köhler still uses the
designation of hominids or – in Latin – *hominidae* for humans and their predecessors; this
has since been superseded by the designation as *hominini*. Whether early humans actually
derived their sustenance primarily from large game is doubtful and unproven; in this respect,
the historical occasion for Bischof-Köhler's argument is speculative. Cf. on both comments:
Scheu and Autrata (2011, p. 158 ff.).

im Bereich *kognitiver Neuerwerbe* zu suchen (...)"[3] is. The acquisition of food through the hunting of large animals as well as the distribution of the hunting prey also to humans who were not involved in the hunt at all, therefore, Bischof-Köhler postulates, requires the formation of cognitive competences that had not existed before.

If one imagines – with Bischof-Köhler – the situation of the early human division of booty paradigmatically, the two basic moments become recognizable: "Zunächst einmal muß die Möglichkeit gegeben sein, den Mangel bzw. die Notlage des Anderen zu erkennen. Daraus muß die Motivation erwachsen, Abhilfe zu schaffen".[4] Bischof-Köhler refers to the recognition of the plight of others as empathy: in doing so, one recognizes that other humans lack something. In the sequence of booty distribution, this is the insight that one or more other humans have not yet received meat and – as a consequence – will not be able to satisfy their hunger, i.e. will have to suffer hardship. Bischof-Köhler explains this for the relationship to another human being in this way: "Man muß die Situation mit seinen Augen sehen können, wenn man das eigene Verhalten auf seine Intention abstimmen soll".[5] That one can 'see a situation with another person's eyes' must be understood figuratively: In fact, one can only see with one's own eyes.

On the one hand, at the heart of Bischof-Köhler's line of thought is the problem of cognition: how does another person see the situation in which he stands? Referring again to Bischof-Köhler's assumed situation of distributing the spoils of the hunt, humans see it under different assumptions: Those humans who have been involved in the hunt assume that they will receive some of the spoils; those humans who have not been involved in the hunt believe that they will receive nothing. Thinking this further, the humans who did not participate in the hunt will be in need because they will have nothing to eat. This is to be grasped when one 'sees with the eyes of the other person'. One then recognizes, according to Bischof-Köhler's idea, that humans are worried that they might be in need.

This first part of the reference to other humans could end there: It is not a foregone conclusion that the result of recognizing must be that one wants to share the spoils of the hunt. It would be just as conceivable that one egoistically comes to the conclusion that one prefers to keep all the prey for oneself. This leads to the other side of Bischof-Koehler's line of thought, which leads her to postulate "(...)

---

[3] Bischof-Köhler (1989, p. 12; orig. citation).

[4] Bischof-Köhler (1989, p. 12 f.).

[5] Bischof-Köhler (1989, p. 12).

3 Social Widerspiegelung in Humans: Fundamentals 61

Mitgefühl als motivierende Kraft (…)".[6] Since humans, she assumes, are endowed with this compassion, they try to put themselves into the perspective of other humans via empathy.

For Bischof-Köhler, compassion is therefore the motivating force. Compassion is implemented through empathy, with the help of which knowledge about the plight of other humans can be gained in order – this purpose is assumed – to be able to provide relief. In an intermediate evaluation it can be stated that Bischof-Köhler introduces essential conditions of her argumentation as unproven postulates: Is it certain that – all – human beings are guided by compassion? If one looks at the historical development, there are doubts about this. Bischof-Köhler does not present a countervailing motivation to compassion, so it remains inexplicable how competition or exclusion can arise. Another point of view: Empathy is based on compassion for distress, Bischof-Köhler thinks. Is that the only way empathy exists? Is it impossible to have empathy for humans whose lives are succeeding? Empathy, as Bischof-Köhler puts it, is moved into the vicinity of compassion. But there are also humans who pursue common goals and must achieve mutual understanding as far as possible. For such constellations, too, it would be beneficial if humans could gain knowledge about each other's situation.

In any case, Bischof-Köhler wants to clarify the key concept of empathy. In doing so, she relies on an explanatory approach expanded to include emotion, which she fundamentally locates in cognitive psychology. However, the expansion of cognitive psychological thinking that she has undertaken is necessary because the tendency "(…) der kognitivistisch orientierten Psychologie, Erkenntnisleistungen prinzipiell auf rationale Einsichtsmöglichkeiten zurückzuführen (…)",[7] leads to a false assessment. In Bischof-Köhler's view, insights in the field of empathy are not to be classified as rational, but as prerational: "Es handelt sich dabei um Erkenntnisse auf primär *emotionaler* Basis. Emotionen vermögen nämlich ihrerseits, unabhängig von rationalen Denkprozessen, Situationen zu bewerten und das Verhalten adaptiv danach auszurichten; das ist einer durch die Vernunft vermittelten kognitiven Leistung durchaus äquivalent (…)".[8] Bischof-Köhler tries to substantiate the extension of the cognitive-psychological approach with evidence from phylogenesis and ontogenesis: In phylogenesis, the insight capacity of humans had not emerged in a single step, but slowly and with intermediate steps; in this phase

---

[6] Bischof-Köhler (1989, p. 13; orig. citation).

[7] Bischof-Köhler (1989, p. 17).

[8] Bischof-Köhler (1989, p. 17; orig. citation).

62   3 Social Widerspiegelung in Humans: Fundamentals

emotions had to replace the still missing rationality.[9] In ontogenesis, i.e. the development of children, Bischof-Köhler believes that empathy can already be detected before rational cognition is fully developed: there too, i.e. in ontogenesis, rational cognition is replaced by emotion.

So how can empathy be defined? Bischof-Köhler proposes a two-part definition: "*Phänomenal* ist Empathie die Erfahrung, unmittelbar der Gefühlslage eines Anderen teilhaftig zu werden und sie dadurch zu verstehen. Trotz dieser Teilhabe bleibt das Gefühl aber anschaulich dem Anderen zugehörig. (…) *Funktional* betrachtet geht es um die Frage, auf welcher Reizgrundlage und aufgrund welcher innerorganismischen Wirkungszusammenhänge sich das als empathische Erlebnis aufbaut".[10]

Empathy is thus centered on the emotional states of other humans, in which one can participate. Bischof-Köhler adds that one can understand these emotional states in this way. What constitutes understanding, however, and what distinguishes understanding from participation in the feelings of other humans, remains open. The Widerspiegelungen on empathy as a phenomenon are rounded off by statements on what constitutes empathy from a functional point of view: the stimulus bases and inner-organismic interactions that can generate an empathic experience are mentioned. In Bischof-Köhler's definition, empathy thus remains tied to the stimulus-based experience, the induced participation in feelings. This is strongly reminiscent of considerations put forward much earlier and in a different scientific-theoretical context – namely that of hermeneutics – by Dilthey: "Unser Handeln setzt das Verstehen anderer Personen voraus; ein großer Teil menschlichen Glückes entspringt aus dem Nachfühlen fremder Seelenzustände".[11] In Dilthey, as in Bischof-Köhler, it remains unclear exactly how empathy or participation in the emotional states of other humans is to be thought of. Likewise, the question remains open as to how the transition to understanding might take place or whether understanding is to be seen from the outset as secondary to feeling-oriented participation.

Bischof-Köhler does not pursue the question of how understanding is formed within the framework of empathy and what significance understanding would have. She concentrates on tracing the emergence of empathy in the determination

---

[9] For humans, phylogenesis ends with hominization, i.e. becoming human. Phylogenesis is then replaced by social-historical development. In this respect, Bischof-Köhler's account should be criticized or at least expanded. However, this will not be pursued further here: Cf. Scheu and Autrata (2011, p. 141 ff.).

[10] Bischof-Köhler (1989, p. 26; orig. citation).

[11] Dilthey (1990, p. 316); critically, see Autrata and Scheu (2015, pp. 83 ff.).

3 Social Widerspiegelung in Humans: Fundamentals

she makes in the course of ontogenesis. This is to be placed within the associated scientific-theoretical framing, which Bischof-Köhler does not, however, make explicit. Her reference to phylogenesis and the derivation from it of ideas about knowledge about human beings follows evolutionary epistemology. Vollmer, for example, formulates: "Denken und Erkennen sind Leistungen des menschlichen Gehirns, und dieses Gehirn ist in der biologischen Evolution entstanden. Unsere kognitiven Strukturen *passen* (wenigstens teilweise) auf die Welt, weil sie sich – phylogenetisch – in *Anpassung* an diese reale Welt herausgebildet haben und weil sie sich – ontogenetisch – auch bei jedem Einzelwesen mit der Umwelt auseinander setzen müssen".[12] Bischof-Köhler also adopts the second part of the considerations presented by Vollmer: She traces the emergence of empathy in the course of ontogenesis.

Bischof-Köhler sees the development of empathy for ontogenesis in a close connection with the recognition of one's own Widerspiegelung: According to her, it is fundamental for the development of empathy that humans are able to recognize themselves. Behind this is the assumption that the basis for empathy is the distinction between oneself and other humans. Only those who can make the distinction between themselves and other humans can subsequently provide empathy. Bischof-Köhler has tested the existence of the ability to recognize oneself with various experimental arrangements in young children. This is evidenced with what is known as the Rougefleck experiment. The design of the experiments varied the fact that a blush stain or a small sticker was applied to the faces of the small children as unnoticeably as possible. Subsequently, it was tested whether the children notice two things when they look into a mirror: Can they recognize themselves in the mirror and can they recognize that they have a stain or sticker on their face? As soon as children try to remove the stain or sticker, this is considered experimental evidence that they have recognized themselves.

Children's empathic behaviour was investigated via the fact that one child's teddy bear – supposedly – suffered damage, for example losing an arm or a leg. If the second child in the experimental situation, for example, tried to repair the damaged teddy, offered his own undamaged teddy as a replacement, or remained comfortingly close to the child mourning for the teddy, this was evaluated as empathic behavior.

The result of Bischof-Köhler's research is that the ability to recognise oneself and to empathise begins at the same time as early as 16–24 months of age. Bischof-Köhler states that "(…) Empathie in der menschlichen Ontogenese erstmals auftritt, wenn die einsetzende Vorstellungstätigkeit es dem Kind ermöglicht, ein

---

[12] Vollmer (2003, p. 18; emphasis in original).

64 3 Social Widerspiegelung in Humans: Fundamentals

Selbstkonzept auszubilden und sich im Spiegel zu erkennen. (…) Die Selbstkonzeptbildung wiederum dürfte weitgehend von Reifungsvorgängen abhängen, die zwischen dem 16 und 24. Monat zum Abschluß kommen (…)".[13]

Three things should be noted about Bischof-Köhler's approach to testing her hypotheses through experiments: First, the operationalization of empathy takes over the determination that empathy is compassion in distress. Participation in other humans's emotional states is also experimentally limited to distress. The counterpoint that empathy could also be participation in joy or success is omitted. Secondly, experimental arrangements that deceive or otherwise mislead the humans involved in the experiments – in this case: children – about the actual circumstances are ethically problematic. Participants in experiments have human rights, they must not be abused as test subjects. Third, the evidential value of experiments is questionable. Holzkamp says: "Der Umstand, dass bei experimentellem Handeln die Realität durch unseren Eingriff verändert wird, ist in der gegenwärtigen Wissenschaftslehre wohl allgemein anerkannt".[14] In the case of experiments, therefore, the manufacturing realization undertaken in the process[15] implements what is subsequently established as a supposedly assured result. Holzkamp pointedly says: Thus "(…) wurde der Umstand, dass die im Experiment erforschte 'Realität' in wesentlichen Hinsichten von uns 'gemacht' ist, in der empiristischen Lehre über die Geltungsbegründungen von Theorien der experimentellen Wissenschaft quasi wieder 'unterschlagen' (…)".[16]

After these critical interim remarks on Bischof-Köhler's methodology, we must return to the presentation of her results. As a result of her experiments, she stated that a self-concept, as evidenced by the Rougefleck experiments, and early forms of empathy, as evidenced by the experiments with supposedly damaged teddy bears, are formed at around 2 years of age and are the result of maturation processes. She states that "(…) anlagenbedingte Unterschiede im Entwicklungsprozess (…)",[17] but also environmental influences play a role in this maturation process. Bischof-Köhler points to two different environmental influences: This is, on the one hand, a "(…) gezielte Förderung einer Leistung durch das Bereitstellen der Möglichkeiten für bestimmte Lernerfahrungen (…)"[18] and, on the other hand, the provision of sufficient nutrition, attention and protection, i.e. everything that is

---

[13] Bischof-Köhler (1989, p. 148).

[14] Holzkamp (2005, p. 43).

[15] cf. Holzkamp (2005, p. 42 ff.).

[16] Holzkamp (2005, p. 43).

[17] Bischof-Köhler (1989, p. 151).

[18] Bischof-Köhler (1989, p. 151).

3 Social Widerspiegelung in Humans: Fundamentals 65

indispensable for the "(...) optimalen Entfaltung der Anlagen des Kleinkindes unverzichtbar ist".[19] If one follows the maturation-specific concept presented by Bischof-Köhler, then all children – provided they grow up under 'normal' conditions – would have to develop a self-concept in the course of their development and then, subsequently, empathy. Practice shows that this is not so clearly the case: Not all children show empathy in the form of compassion outlined by Bischof-Köhler.

Bischof-Köhler assumes that empathy is the result of a maturation process. This in turn follows the principles of evolutionary epistemology: ontogenesis is the reenactment of phylogenesis. Empathy, according to the understanding of evolutionary epistemology, emerged in the course of phylogenesis and is later reproduced in ontogenesis. Despite this assumed linearity, the process of empathy formation does not occur independently of socialization influences, Bischof-Köhler also acknowledges. She writes: "In der Arbeit von Zahn-Waxler et al. (1979) finden sich interessante Hinweise darauf, wie sich Unterschiede im Erziehungsstil bereits beim ersten Auftreten der Empathie in der zweiten Hälfte des zweiten Lebensjahrs bemerkbar machen. Die Autoren stellten fest, daß Empathie reifungsabhängig ist, allerdings unterschieden sich die Kinder individuell im Ausmaß dieser Reaktionsbereitschaft, und dieses korrelierte positiv mit einem *induktiven, einfühlsamen* Erziehungsstil der Mutter".[20] It is not necessary at this point to pursue further what exactly is meant by an inductive and empathetic parenting style of the mother and how this could be determined.[21] It should be noted that Bischof-Köhler does not exclusively assume the biological heritability of empathy, which then only has to unfold in ontogenesis, but assumes a modifiability of maturing empathy: "Nun kann natürlich kein Zweifel darüber bestehen, dass das Empathievermögen im weiteren Entwicklungsverlauf Einflüssen unterworfen ist, die sich sowohl auf seine *Äußerungsformen* als auch auf sein *Fortbestehen* überhaupt in unterschiedlicher Weise fördernd oder hemmend auswirken und schließlich auch in einer manifesten Empathieverkümmerung resultieren können".[22] Empathy therefore does not – exclusively – develop through maturation processes, but can also be further shaped by influences from outside. This can lead to a change in the form of empathy, but can also lead to the disappearance of empathy that has already been formed.

Not mentioned and not considered by Bischof-Köhler is the dimension of one's own intentions and resulting activities: Is the unfolding of empathy in ontogenesis or overall in the course of life only dependent on what is biologically inherited,

---

[19] Bischof-Köhler (1989, p. 151).

[20] Bischof-Köhler (1989, p. 153 f., emphasis in original); cf. Zahn-Waxler et al. (1979).

[21] cf. e.g. Ainsworth in: Grossmann and Grossmann (2003, p. 102).

[22] Bischof-Köhler (1989, p. 153, orig.).

which unfolds in maturation processes, or on external influences? Is it not possible to exert any influence on it oneself? Bischof-Köhler writes that empathy is all about "(…) die Absicht des Anderen zu erkennen".[23] But with which intentions does one enter oneself? Is it a foregone conclusion that all humans always and to the highest degree want to recognize other humans's intentions, especially if the connotation of compassion is added to this? It seems conceivable that humans themselves intervene in the process of the development of empathy, i.e. that they do not just wait and see what maturation and external influences do to them. The dimension of one's own activity as well as one's own intentionality does not play a recognizable role in Bischof-Köhler's work. However, if one assumes that there are intentions in other humans that can be grasped through empathy, it should be inevitable that humans themselves also bring such intentions into the development and realization of empathy. Do I always want to be empathic, do I want to be empathic to all humans to the same degree? The answer to such questions is not possible with Bischof-Köhler.

Bischof-Köhler found a connection between empathy and self-knowledge: Children who recognized themselves in the mirror had a higher willingness to help in experiments, from which she concludes the presence of empathy. However, "(…) Selbsterkennen ist zwar eine notwendige, aber nicht auch hinreichende Bedingung für Empathie".[24] Empathy thus conceived refers to the fact that feelings of others can be perceived on the basis of self-knowledge. For a better understanding, one could add: Only when one can recognize oneself, can one set other humans apart. One must be able to make out the difference between oneself and other humans in order to be able to assign existing feelings accordingly. One step on the way to this differentiation is the concentration of attention on fellow human beings. It arises a "(…) Artgenossenschema (…). Dieses Schema ist zunächst ganz allgemein und führt dazu, dass Säuglinge alle menschlichen Gesichter bevorzugt anlächeln (…)".[25] However, a distinction between faces is not yet possible.

The continuation of this scheme, which generally allows to distinguish faces of conspecifics from other faces, to self-recognition in the mirror, requires interaction. This was found by Bischof-Köhler in primates as well as in human children: If they grow up without interaction with other conspecifics, the process of self-recognition in the mirror is limited or more difficult. Conversely, it is the case that the development of self-recognition becomes possible after social contact. She writes: "Bei normal verlaufender sozialer Entwicklung kann das Kind (…), das 'Material' von

---

[23] Bischof-Köhler (1989, p. 12).

[24] Bischof-Köhler (2011, p. 268).

[25] Bischof-Köhler (2011, p. 274).

3 Social Widerspiegelung in Humans: Fundamentals 67

seinem Artgenossenschema für eine erste 'Ausstaffierung' seines Selbstbildes heranziehen (…). Und die erste Form eines Identitätsbewusstseins, die es erlaubt, das eigene Spiegelbild zu erkennen, lässt sich wohl am besten als 'Artgenossenidentität' charakterisieren (…)".[26] Thus, on the basis of social contacts, the self-image, which in turn allows one to recognize oneself in the mirror, gradually unfolds via the conspecific schema via the conspecific identity to the final self-image. The self-image, which Bischof-Köhler saw as a necessary, if not sufficient condition for empathy, thus emerges in a mixture of a maturation process and development in the context of social contacts. Both are necessary for the self-image to develop in children.

The development of the self-image, which in turn is a prerequisite for empathy, is thus extended by Bischof-Köhler beyond biological maturation: in addition to maturation, social contacts are necessary for such a self-image to emerge. Other extensions concern the actualization of empathy: In the experimental arrangements presented, which Bischof-Köhler employed, the other humans – in this case: children – were directly present and their feelings could be inferred from observation: If a child cries after his teddy bear has lost an arm, it suggests itself that he is sad. Empathy can also begin, however, when the feelings cannot be directly observed, but perhaps result from narratives – i.e. situation-mediated, Bischof-Köhler believes. This is when the process of identification sets in. "Wenn ich (…) identifikatorisch an der Situation des Anderen teilhabe, erlebe ich sie so, als wäre ich an seiner Stelle (…)".[27] It is therefore not necessary in every case to experience other humans's expressions of feeling through one's own eyes; the formation of empathy is also possible after narratives, thus the linguistic reproduction of experiences: Here, Bischof-Köhler assumes, a process of identification begins; humans experience the feelings of other humans vicariously and can thus make these feelings their own.

Similarly, Walter is concerned with empathy. In a publication based on the theoretical background of neurobiology, she examines the connection between empathy and altruistic behaviour: She assumes "(…) dass die Empathie die zentrale Motivation zu altruistischem Verhalten ist".[28] It remains unclear with Walter whether empathy is still mental acquisition or rather behaviour. For example, she writes: "Empathy can be viewed as interaction between two individuals, whereby one individual feels and shares the feelings of the other".[29] Is empathy interaction

---

[26] Bischof-Köhler (2011, p. 274).
[27] Bischof-Köhler (2011, p. 272).
[28] Walter (2014, p. 44).
[29] Walter (2014, p. 44).

68　　　　　　　　　3 Social Widerspiegelung in Humans: Fundamentals

or is empathy the grasping of other humans's feelings? The *individuals* brought into play by Walter will be discussed in more detail later in their conceptual definiteness.[30] It should be noted that for Walter, too – similar to Bischof-Köhler – empathy is participation in other humans's feelings and above all in other humans's distress.

Feelings are at the heart of Walter's definition of empathy. As she points out, "Empathie kann betrachtet werden als Interaktion zwischen zwei Individuen, wobei das eine Individuum die Gefühle des anderen fühlt und teilt."[31] While it remains somewhat obscure how one feels intentionally and to what extent intentional feeling points beyond sharing feelings. Similarly, it does not further explain how one can actually transform another person's feelings into one's own feelings. What seems to be indisputable is that empathy in Walter's version – but also that of Bischof-Köhler – has a lot to do with feelings and little with understanding.

Walter further emphasizes that empathy requires the ability to communicate emotions verbally or nonverbally. This statement complements the definition of empathy as the taking on of feelings: these feelings are passed on or taken on through communication. Communication, after all, has two sides: Someone communicates something through communication, another person takes in that information. Walter means both sides of communication: so it is about communicating emotions to others as well as recognizing and sharing other humans's emotions. For ontogenesis, Walter thinks that verbal communication of emotions is possible from the age of 2 years, while non-verbal communication is already possible in newborns.

For Walter, empathy and emotion move so closely together that they form an almost indistinguishable unit: "Die Empathie ermöglicht eine schnelle und automatische Reaktion auf die emotionalen Zustände anderer und liefert so eine Grundvoraussetzung für soziale Interaktionen, gemeinsame Aktivitäten und kooperatives Verhalten (…)".[32] Emotional states, passed on through communication and grasped through empathy, are the basis of all social activities. Humans have thus adopted the feelings of other humans and then, Walter is to be further reasoned, feel the same as the humans from whom these feelings originate. It could be further assumed that after a certain period of time all humans feel the same: Only existing feelings or emotions are adopted via empathy; new feelings obviously cannot arise. Even a complementary relationship of feelings is not conceivable under the auspices of the mode of action of empathy, let alone contradictory or mutually exclusive feelings.

---

[30] cf. Sect. 3.5 in this volume.

[31] Walter (2014, p. 47).

[32] Walter (2014, p. 48).

3 Social Widerspiegelung in Humans: Fundamentals 69

Walter, like Bischof-Köhler, also makes reference to evolution and phylogenesis. Walter assumes: "Es ist sehr wahrscheinlich, dass sich die Notwendigkeit der evolutionären Entwicklung einer schnellen emotionalen Verbundenheit zwischen Individuen schon lange vor der Entstehung der menschlichen Spezies im Kontext der elterlichen Fürsorge entwickelt hat".[33] This will not be discussed further here. It is significant, however, to note that empathy is understood by Walter as biologically rooted rather than specifically human. At no point in Walter's work does empathy undergo a specifically human elaboration or over-formation. Empathy, as the transmission of feelings, remains significant for closeness and connectedness, but these feelings do not recognizably derive from a human context.

Walter differentiates between three forms of empathy, which in turn are based on different forms of communicative transmission of emotions. The first form is emotional contagion: "Emotionale Ansteckung wird definiert als Angleichung eines emotionalen Zustands eines Subjekts an den eines Objekts".[34] In defining emotional contagion as a form of empathy, it is subjects who come into contact with objects, not individuals. What distinguishes subjects from objects and those from individuals is not explained by Walter. It is also left open what emotional state a subject held before becoming aligned with the object, whether this earlier emotional state disappears completely or returns later. What remains to be noted is the certainty of emotional contagion, that in it one's own emotional state is aligned with the state of the other.

A second form of empathy is called compassion and concern and "(...) ist definiert als das Mitgefühl mit beziehungsweise die Besorgnis um den Zustand eines anderen Menschen und daraus resultierende Versuche, diesen Zustand zu verbessern".[35] Again empathy oscillates between mental apprehension and activity, again the topos of helping in distress is central element. Walter refers once again to evolution in this second form when she writes that this "(...) Form der Empathie kann als weiterer evolutionärer Schritt der Empathieentwicklung (...) angesehen werden (...)".[36] In characterizing this form of empathy, compassion and concern, the original determination, arguably valid for all forms, that empathy is the assumption of other humans's feelings, is abandoned: Compassion and concern are clearly different feelings from those felt by the humans to whom the compassion and concern are directed. The humans whose condition is in some way unfavorable feel threatened by hunger, thirst, or loneliness, for example. Complementarily, obviously, following

---

[33] Walter (2014, p. 48).
[34] Walter (2014, p. 48).
[35] Walter (2014, p. 49).
[36] Walter (2014, p. 49).

Walter, compassion and concern can form in other humans. In any case, however, these are different feelings from those felt by humans in a threatening state. To grasp this new expression of feeling states that form in the compassionate and concerned humans, Walter names it as "(...) kognitive Empathie (...)".[37] Thus, under the guiding concept of empathy, cognitive moments are obviously necessary after all; it cannot be exclusively a matter of transmissions of feelings.

For Walter, the third form is empathic perspective-taking: "Empathische Perspektivenübernahme wird definiert als die Fähigkeit, die Perspektive eines anderen zu übernehmen – beispielsweise durch das Verstehen seiner spezifischen Situation und Bedürfnisse in Abgrenzung zu den eigenen – in Kombination mit einer nachempfundenen emotionalen Erregung".[38] What is at stake here, then, is the ability to access other humans's perspectives and continue to adopt them as one's own. Perspective taking, as presented as a form of empathy, has even stronger cognitive parts than the second form, compassion and concern. At the same time, it is also the first time that something like a subject standpoint is adopted: There is the situation and needs of other humans that one can try to understand; in contrast, there is one's own situation and needs that are different from those of the other person. It remains unclear whether perspective-taking means that the perspective of another person is actually made one's own, or whether perspective-taking merely means understanding the perspective of another person. It would have to be asked what happens in cases in which one's own perspective and the perspective of other humans do not coincide or even contradict each other: Is the subject's point of view then abandoned altogether or at least modified? Walter does not explain in detail by what means the existence of the emotional arousal subsumed under perspective-taking and to be felt is inferred: Does a person's perspective on his situation and his needs always include emotional states of arousal?

For the theorization of empathy, it can be summarized and critically appreciated that it provides important clues: A grasp of other humans is significant, and it also begins at an early age. So it is obviously already possible for humans in ontogenesis to relate to other humans in a grasping way and to recognize what other humans do. It is also important to point out that the grasping of other humans does not just remain on the surface: That a teddy bear is damaged is certainly secondary in a larger horizon of observation. But that exactly this damage of the teddy bear decisively affects the well-being of a child can only be detected with a fine sensorium. Such a sensorium is to be found less in special sensory forms of reception than in the possibility of understanding what is going on in other humans.

---

[37] Walter (2014, p. 49).

[38] Walter (2014, p. 51).

3   Social Widerspiegelung in Humans: Fundamentals

However, when the keyword of understanding is brought into play, the omissions of theorizing on empathy are conspicuous. For long stretches, the reference to understanding is omitted. Empathy is characterized on the one hand as a mixture of feelings, and on the other hand as the taking over of these feelings. Are human beings reduced to feelings, in other words, is the comprehension of feelings alone adequate to what constitutes human beings as a whole? If one thinks only about the participation in feelings, one has deprived humans of the breadth of their existence. This emphasis on feelings results from the fact that empathy addresses one part of humans as victims who suffer distress and develop feelings accordingly. The other part of humans develops compassion for the suffering humans through empathy. If, for example, humans are in a cooperative relationship and work together on tasks, something like empathy would be quite desirable: empathy would then not be so compassionately charged, however, but would be a component of cooperation between humans. An example from sports and music may illustrate this. If fellow players are empathic for what the other players will do in the next moment, this increases the chances of the project succeeding: the ball lands in the goal after the empathically anticipated pass, the orchestra takes up the conductor's tempo instructions empathically and in unison. However, in order for these examples to be appropriately conceptualized as empathy as well, the sacrificial ductus of empathy must be abandoned.

The most relevant omission from theorizing about empathy is the extensive absence of subjectivity. Before the empathic process of taking over other humans's feelings, what was the empathic person's situation and feeling state? Can we really assume that every feeling situation is adopted and then what happens to one's own feelings? The modelling of empathy, on the other hand, is normative and depicts what is desired: a child's teddy bear loses its leg, and the child is sad about it. Who would not want to take pity on the child? In reality, however, it is usually the case that humans have different interests and follow their own ideas. When one encounters other humans and perceives what they do and perhaps feel, it is a meeting of subjects. One part of the perception is the comprehension of what other humans do or have done, the other part is directed towards the comparison with one's own subjectivity: Does this fit with one's own interests or are discrepancies to be found?

The conceptualization of empathy becomes plausible in formations made in experiments: That empathy presupposes the ability to recognize oneself is understandable. If one is not yet able to recognize oneself in the mirror, one cannot grasp the difference between oneself and other humans. However: this is in substance a sober statement, it is about recognition and not about the adoption of feelings. In theory-building terms, this is also access to one's own uniqueness and the possibility of distinguishing and recognizing this uniqueness from other humans.

Recognizing oneself means, on the one hand, recognizing oneself – for example in the mirror – as a person with unique characteristics. But this in turn is also the starting point for recognising oneself, one's own interests and preferences. The possibility of self-recognition arises and takes place – as Bischof-Köhler points out above all – in the context of the social, in that – in this case the child – receives 'feedback' with regard to uniqueness. Recognition is therefore not only the look in the mirror, it is also essential to be recognized, i.e. the Widerspiegelung by other humans.

Theory of Mind

Another school of thought is gathered under the guiding English term of Theory of Mind (abbreviated: ToM). What exactly Theory of Mind is and what it is not is difficult to define. Förstl, for example, formulates Theory of Mind as "(…) die Fähigkeit bzw. der Versuch eines Individuums, sich in andere hineinzuversetzen, um deren Wahrnehmungen, Gedanken und Absichten zu verstehen".[39] Linguistically, it would first be necessary to examine what is meant by *theory* and *mind:* what humans commonly do is not a theory. Only when scientists deal with what humans do, can this lead to theory formation. The debate on Theory of Mind, however, has adopted the concept of theory in the definition of its object: What is meant here, however, is not a theory in the scientific sense and the determinacy of theory. What is meant is theory as everyday theory. Thus Theory of Mind is to be seen as a conception of how humans arrange and connect their perceptions, thoughts and intentions towards other humans. With regard to the terms used, it should be noted that more detailed determinations of the content of perceptions, *thoughts* and *intentions are* not given from within Theory of Mind: Thus, if for the account of the Theory of Mind these terms used by it are employed, their lack of definiteness is to be taken into account.

This would characterize Theory of Mind as the ability or attempt to put oneself in the place of others. If one follows this, Theory of Mind is not the perception of others, but the attempt at introspection that follows perception: one wants to grasp the perceptions, thoughts and intentions of others. Perceptions, thoughts and intentions are not objects; if one wants to grasp them, this is a mental operation directed at mental-internal processes in others. Representatives of the Theory of Mind call this process *theory.* Two conceptual remarks are necessary: Theory of Mind in a scientific context would then have to be understood as Theory of Theory of Mind,

---

[39] Förstl in: Förstl (2012, p. 4).

3 Social Widerspiegelung in Humans: Fundamentals 73

i.e. as a theory of how humans conduct their thinking about other humans. By doubling Theory, it becomes clear that this makes a theory in the scientific sense linguistically indistinguishable from any other human thinking. This softening of the understanding of theory is regarded as false and misleading by the authorship of this paper.[40]

Förstl continues to speak of an individual who directs his efforts towards understanding the perceptions, thoughts and intentions of another. The term individual should not lead to the assumption that the others who are to be understood are in any case human beings. Occasionally, individual is used to refer to a single person, but individual also stands for a single living being.[41] It becomes clear that Förstl uses individual as a designation for a single living being of whatever kind, through the following quotation: "Neben dem Menschen gibt es aber auch andere Lebewesen, die ihren Erfolg durch interindividuelles Verhalten optimieren können".[42] Whether the optimisation of interindividual behaviour could be explained by Theory of Mind, Förstl does not explain.

Förstl further states: "ToM ist die Grundlage sozialen, 'sittlichen' Verhaltens. Ohne Interesse am anderen, ohne Gefühl für dessen Bedürfnisse und ohne differenziertes Verständnis seiner Perspektiven entwickeln sich weder Mitgefühl noch Rücksicht noch Respekt".[43] Theory of Mind thus obviously embraces a strongly normatively charged connotation. If one had perhaps hastily concluded from the provision quoted above that Theory of Mind is the attempt to understand the perceptions, thoughts and intentions of others, that this understanding is open-ended, this is corrected: Theory of Mind is even more strongly oriented towards desirability than the considerations of empathy. As a consequence, the debate on Theory of Mind negotiates deficits and disturbances in great breadth.[44] Theory of Mind is thus on the one hand an analytical theory, but on the other hand also the normative prescribing of values such as respect and consideration.

Theory of Mind, however, is not a closed theoretical edifice with exactly one scientific-theoretical framing. Theory of Mind is rather a catch-all for different approaches that deal with the broad question of whether there is a conception of how mental processes occur in others. The initial publication for the beginning of the debate on Theory of Mind is an essay by Premack et al. from 1978, entitled: "Does

---

[40] cf. Autrata and Scheu (2015, p. 139 ff.).
[41] cf. Sect. 3.5 in this volume.
[42] Förstl in: Förstl (2012, p. 4).
[43] Förstl in: Förstl (2012, p. 4).
[44] cf. e.g. Förstl (2012, p. 225 ff.).

74 3 Social Widerspiegelung in Humans: Fundamentals

the chimpanzee have a theory of mind?"[45] Premack et al.'s considerations do not refer to humans, but to chimpanzees. Do chimpanzees already have, would be the question thereby raised, an idea of what others intend? These others can be chimpanzees, but also keepers of the chimpanzees kept in the zoo. The answer to the question is that such ideas can indeed be found experimentally in chimpanzees. Chimpanzees can identify the fact that the hose must be connected to the water tap so that the keeper can spray water with it as the correct solution by photo selection. The conclusion from this is that chimpanzees can develop a Theory of Mind, i.e. an idea of the intentions of others, according to Premack et al.

In the context of primate research, the results of Premack et al. do not exactly open up completely new territory: Goodall's observations, which also have the methodological advantage of not being experiments,[46] already indicate that chimpanzees exhibit complex social behaviour.[47] However, it is not chimpanzee research that is the focus of interest here. Rather, it should be noted that a decisive impulse for the debate on Theory of Mind stems from chimpanzee research. What needs to be put into perspective for this version of Theory of Mind, however, is that it involves the scientific embedding of common insights. According to Bischof-Köhler, "Theory of Mind wird üblicherweise als 'Psychologie des gesunden Menschenverstandes' definiert (*commonsense mentalism*), oder auch als 'naive Theorie über die Ursachen des Verhaltens'".[48] In contrast to how Förstl above all emphasizes the normative significance of Theory of Mind almost effusively,[49] Bischof-Köhler sees Theory of Mind merely as a superstructure to 'common sense'.

Bischof-Köhler subsequently expresses scepticism about the delimitation and closer definition of Theory of Mind: "Das Problem einer Definition von Theory of Mind als Alltagspsychologie besteht nun allerdings darin, dass sich alle möglichen Formen von Kognition darunter subsumieren lassen, die in irgendeiner Weise auf die mentale Verfassung einer anderen Person Bezug nehmen".[50] It is therefore difficult to grasp, according to Bischof-Köhler, exactly what Theory of Mind is and where it sets its own and distinctive scientific accents. To repeat: Theory of Mind is a catch-all for Widerspiegelungen from very different sources.

---

[45] Premack and Woodruffv (1978, p. 515).

[46] On the critique of experiments, cf. Holzkamp (2005).

[47] cf. Lawick-Goodall (now: Goodall) (1971).

[48] Bischof-Köhler (2011, p. 327); Herv. i.. Orig.

[49] cf. Förstl in: Förstl (2012, p. 3 ff.).

[50] Bischof-Köhler (2011, p. 327).

3 Social Widerspiegelung in Humans: Fundamentals 75

Bischof-Köhler has already been mentioned in the context of the account of empathy and social cognition.[51] Subsequently, one could take her insistent references to flattenings, which are to be stated with reference to the affiliation with Theory of Mind, to mean that she distances herself from Theory of Mind and ascribes herself to a research direction focused on empathy. However, this is not the case. Rather, Bischof-Köhler also accentuates strengths that arise from Theory of Mind: "Theory of Mind erlaubt, die Absichten der Anderen zu durchschauen, ihre Glaubwürdigkeit einzuschätzen, ihre Sichtweise, ihr Denken, ihre Wünsche und Bedürfnisse aus ihrer Perspektive zu verstehen – und zwar in einer Weise, die im Unterschied zur empathischen Identifikation über den eigenen Erlebnishorizont hinaus auch der Andersartigkeit des Anderen Rechnung tragen kann".[52] The first observation is that Theory of Mind allows a more differentiated and discriminating reference to other humans than is possible with empathy. Bischof-Köhler here conceptually chooses the composite of *empathic identification:* empathy, which she elsewhere brings into the field with great conviction,[53] is thus to be thought only as comprehension and subjectless. Regarding Bischof-Köhler's scientific position, it should be noted that in her later publication she reveals a rather critical view of empathy; in her earlier publication on this subject, no such criticism of empathy was to be found.[54]

In the publication from 2011, Bischof-Köhler at any rate acts over long stretches as an apologist for Theory of Mind: Theory of Mind, Bischof-Köhler explains, allows the cross-check against the direct detection of other humans: One can see through intentions or assess credibility. One can even account for the otherness of others. The conceptualization of the difference between oneself and other humans is significant, she emphasizes. This can be explained with the help of the Theory of Mind: "Theory of Mind erlaubt nicht nur das Nachdenken über die mentale Verfassung anderer Personen, sondern auch über die eigene".[55]

Bischof-Köhler thus makes the double claim that it is important to distinguish oneself from other humans and that this distinction is possible with the help of Theory of Mind. Theory of Mind, so the claim goes, not only allows one to recognize, think about and reflect on the mental, cognitive condition of others, but also makes it possible to determine this in oneself. The proof that and how Theory of Mind wants to capture this differentiation between oneself and other humans,

---

[51] See above i. d. Kap.
[52] Bischof-Köhler (2011, p. 354).
[53] cf. Bischof-Köhler (1989).
[54] cf. Bischof-Köhler (1989 and 2011).
[55] Bischof-Köhler (2011, p. 354).

76   3 Social Widerspiegelung in Humans: Fundamentals

however, remains missing. Bischof-Köhler, on the other hand, brings into play the segment of the understanding of time, which in her view can explicate very significant aspects of the recognition of oneself: It is a matter of comparing assessments that one had earlier with those that one reaches later.

It is therefore about the "*(...) Verständnis für die Zeit (...)*".[56] According to Bischof-Köhler, the ability to reflect on oneself and others also requires comparing the present with the past. One will certainly have to agree with this unreservedly. However, her experimental design seems to correspond more to the commonsense mentalism she criticizes in the Theory of Mind: Children had to estimate what contents were in a chocolate lentil tube; this was classified as a past mental state. It turned out that in fact there were no chocolate lentils in the chocolate tubes, but a pencil; this was rated as a mental state of the present. Bischof-Köhler explains the experiment as follows: Man muss ja den gegenwärtigen mentalen Zustand – das Wissen, was das Röhrchen enthält – mit dem vergangenen – was man erwartet hat – vergleichen, sich letzteres also vergegenwärtigen, aber eben mit der Zeitmarke 'vorher'".[57]

Bischof-Köhler concludes from such experiments: The ability to visualize time is reserved only for humans. In contrast to humans, she states that apes do not have this ability.[58] And further: Humans are thus able "(...) *zukünftige Motivzustände* zu vergegenwärtigen (...),"[59] they can thus anticipate what needs and wants they will have in the future. Apodictically Bischof-Köhler formulates: "Diese Art der Zukunftsvoraussicht ist eben dem Menschen vorbehalten, er allein ist in der Lage, auf *mentale Zeitreise* zu gehen".[60]

Bischof-Köhler repeats her initial assertion: Humans are to be distinguished from this. Humans and only humans are not forced to realize their needs and desires immediately, they are able "(...) gegenwärtige Bedürfnisse zugunsten *zukünftiger* oder *vergangener* Bedürfnislagen außer Kraft zu setzen und diese handlungsrelevant werden zu lassen".[61]

Two objections can be raised against Bischof-Köhler's postulate that only humans are capable of an understanding of time that allows for anticipation. The first objection is directed against the validity of her claim. This may be explained by the reference to the constellation of hunter-driver cooperation: the driver has

---

[56] Bischof-Köhler (2011, p. 354; highlighting in original).

[57] Bischof-Köhler (2011, p. 354).

[58] cf. Bischof-Köhler (2011, p. 355).

[59] Bischof-Köhler (2011, p. 355 f.; highlighting in original).

[60] Bischof-Köhler (2011, p. 356; highlighting in original).

[61] Bischof-Köhler (2011, p. 358; highlighting in original).

3 Social Widerspiegelung in Humans: Fundamentals

"(…) das Ziel, die Tierherde zu erschrecken, um sie anderen Jägern zuzutreiben, die im Hinterhalt lauern. Damit ist seine Arbeit vollendet; alles übrige erledigen die anderen Jagdteilnehmer".[62] If one separates the activities of hunters and drivers, their sense is doubtful: "Das Wild von sich weg zu treiben, hat keinen erkennbaren Sinn; an einer beliebigen Stelle auf vorbei kommendes Wild zu warten, wie die Situation der Jäger ohne die Aktivitäten der Treiber zu beschreiben wäre, scheint auch eher aussichtslos. Erst in der Kombination der beiden Aktivitäten und der Erwartung, dass hinterher das erlegte Wild aufgeteilt wird, führt Koordination und Intentionalität zu einem gemeinsam antizipierten Ziel."[63] Hunting according to the hunter-driver model exists in humans. But lions also often hunt this way. If lions hunted according to the principle of immediate need satisfaction, all lions would chase after prey, which would probably not be crowned with success. Using the hunter-driver model, chimpanzees, for example, also hunt after smaller, nimble monkeys. Anticipation, while indicative of phylogenetically higher evolution, is by no means exclusive to humans.

The second objection is aimed at the argumentative significance of the understanding of time. In introducing the understanding of time, Bischof-Köhler responded to her own requirement of Theory of Mind that it allows Widerspiegelung on the mental state of other humans as well as on one's own mental state. Theory of Mind, according to Bischof-Köhler's thesis, is capable of enabling a differentiation of other humans in comparison with oneself. The evidence for this cannot be provided with the introduced understanding of time. Understanding of time plays a role in the processes of perceiving other humans. Once again, Eurykleia is to be remembered: she recognized Odysseus, which implies that her understanding of time can distinguish between past and present, but also build bridges between them. The recognition itself with the additional question from which point of view Eurykleia has recognized Odysseus, however, is not clarified with this: with point of view is not meant whether she was sitting or standing on a chair during the recognition; what is meant is her point of view as a human being. Was she happy about the recognition, what hopes and perspectives did she unfold? In order to be able to grasp this, however, the introduction of a subject standpoint would be indispensable, among other things. But Bischof-Köhler does not address subjectivity.

Thus Theory of Mind remains for long stretches – partially – evident, but limited in its theoretical conclusiveness, and above all in its explanatory power. The basic assumption that humans develop an idea of how other humans think is understandable: How else would humans be able to relate to it with some prospect of

---

[62] Leontjew (1980, p. 204).
[63] Scheu and Autrata (2011, p. 162).

success? Whether the designation that is a theory is successful or not is questionable: Theory as a term is reserved for particular forms of scientific knowledge.[64] Theory of Mind apparently does not denote a theory in this way. Theory stands for considerations or estimations of humans, but they do not have the dignity of theory. The conceptual equation of scientific theory and everyday understanding does not bring clarification, but rather mixes dissimilarities under a levelling term.

Theory of Mind is plausible, but does not go beyond the plausible and commonplace. When Bischof-Köhler marks the objective that the mental difference between oneself and other humans must be able to be grasped by humans, this is justified: Humans must be able to grasp what they themselves are or do and what other humans are or do in order to deal with other humans. This is more substantial as a requirement than the emotion-centered participation in other humans's plights that results from theorizing about empathy. What is missing, admittedly, is the similarly substantive determination of how humans grasp the difference between themselves and other humans. The normative attributions proposed by Förstl on the meaning of Theory of Mind do not help decisively on the way to theory formation either.

Theory of Mind and Neurobiology

Theory of Mind has gone beyond theorizing based on psychological, and especially cognitive-psychological, explanatory patterns to strongly received results with reference to neurobiology. It is the mirror neurons and their mode of action that has gained great influence on the scientific theory on Theory of Mind. According to Förstl, the "(…) Spiegelneuronensysteme stellen wahrscheinlich ein wesentliches Substrat für grundlegende Mechanismen der ToM dar".[65]

Mirror neurons are "(…) eine spezialisierte Zellpopulation, die während der Ausführung und der Beobachtung einer zielgerichteten motorischen Handlung feuert. Dies ist die definierende Eigenschaft eines Spiegelneurons".[66] Mirror neurons are specific forms of cells that are in turn found in specific areas of the brain. These cells 'fire' concurrently with motor activity, i.e. they are active: this phenomenon, being cellular and occurring in the brain, is difficult to access and track via elaborate forms of investigation such as functional magnetic resonance imaging (MRI).

---

[64] cf. Autrata and Scheu (2015, p. 39 ff.).

[65] Förstl in: Förstl (2012, p. 8 f.).

[66] Walther and Förstl in: Förstl (2012, p. 104).

3 Social Widerspiegelung in Humans: Fundamentals

Similar to the mirror neurons, the spindle neurons, which are also named Von Economo Neurons (abbreviated: vEN) after their discoverer, are thought to have a functionality for the social: The receptors of the vEN secrete the hormone vasopressin, "(...) das mit sozialer Bindung in Verbindung gebracht wird (...)".[67] The connection can be thought of in terms of its mode of action in this way: certain neurons are significant for what happens in the social via the release of hormones. The spread of such modes of action, which presupposes the presence of specific cells and the release of corresponding hormones, is by no means limited to humans. For spindle or Von Economo neurons, "vEN wurden in den letzten Jahren auch bei sozial lebenden Tieren wie den Menschenaffen (...), Elefanten (...), Delphinen und Walen (...) nachgewiesen (...)".[68] Spindle neurons as a particular cellular formation are thus also found in the highly evolved socially living animals.

As a result of neuroscience, it can thus be stated that mirror and spindle neurons, which in turn act via the release of hormones into the organism, are present in humans as well as in many highly developed social animals. That there are such neurons – and others – thus seems to be proven. But what do these neurons do about hormones? Walther and Förstl state for the mirror neurons: "Ihre Grundfunktionen scheinen im humanen und im Primatenhirn gleich zu sein. Im menschlichen Gehirn können sie an komplexeren sozialen Prozessen beteiligt sein, die vom Imitationslernen zum Handlungserkennen des Vis-a-Vis (...) und seiner Intention reichen (...) sowie zur interpersonellen emotionalen Kognition (...)".[69] The mirror neurons in particular are thus said to have far-reaching functionality and performance, ranging from imitation and recognition to 'emotional cognition'.

However, before these attributions for mirror neurons are translated from a formulation that is to be understood as subjunctive into the indicative, the postscript by Walther and Förstl should be noted: "Die Spiegelneuronen sind zweifelsfrei Helden der modernen neurowissenschaftlichen Populärliteratur; die ihnen zugewiesene Funktionalität ist jedoch größtenteils spekulativ und empirisch noch wenig untermauert".[70]

Two things should be pointed out: The study of neuroscientific phenomena faces the problem that the connection between neuronal processes and perceptions or activities is difficult to access. Neurons are part of the brain, i.e. an intracorporeally situated organ. What takes place in the brain and – more precisely – in which brain segments what takes place, must be accessed via special forms of investigation.

---

[67] Walther and Förstl in: Förstl (2012, p. 106).
[68] Walther and Förstl in: Förstl (2012, p. 106).
[69] Walther and Förstl in: Förstl (2012, p. 108).
[70] Walther and Förstl in: Förstl (2012, p. 108).

For example, reference is made to a study that proceeded as follows: "Mithilfe von Magnetoenzephalographie zeigten Nishitani et al. (2004), dass die Imitation von Gesichtsausdrücken spezifische Areale mit Spiegelneuronen aktiviert".[71] Magnetoencephalography uses sensors attached to the head to measure magnetic signals from the brain, which in turn are caused by electrical current pulses from active neurons. Complex measuring procedures must therefore be carried out with extremely large devices to which test subjects are connected in order to be able to draw conclusions about processes such as the imitation of facial expressions from the measurement of electrical current pulses. Such experiments depend on a setting that has little to do with normal human life. It is questionable to what extent such experiments can still produce meaningful results.

On the other hand, it is quite plausible that in the course of phylogenesis, in which the social arose and developed, corresponding brain areas also developed as a counterpart to the modes of perception and activities of the social. This is the second point of view to be pointed out. If spindle and mirror neurons are found in many highly evolved social animals as well as in humans, this may be the result of a phylogenetic process that led to similar neuron types. Neuron types such as mirror or spindle neurons are thus not a singular human development, which in turn is consistent with hominization: in humans, phylogenesis ends with becoming human; after becoming human, phylogenesis can no longer take effect because it can no longer provide a survival advantage.

Social perceptions or activities in humans may thus have their organ of control organically in the mirror and spindle neurons. This must be assumed with caution, since the evidence in this regard still has clear weaknesses. Much more than the organic location, however, cannot be established with certainty for the neurons. At the time Eurykleia recognized Odysseus, her mirror neurons may have triggered violent electrical impulses and released appropriate hormones. But does that say much about the feelings she was experiencing? In any case, the connection between subjectivity and mirror neurons cannot – yet – be established conclusively.

In conclusion, it can be stated that Theory of Mind shows interesting intellectual approaches, but on the whole it is too striking and its considerations remain on the periphery. For example, Sommer et al. opine: "Die Fähigkeit, sich und anderen mentale Zustände zuschreiben zu können, stellt die Voraussetzung für ein erfolgreiches Navigieren durch die soziale Welt dar".[72] Admittedly, it is not just a matter of attributing something to oneself and others: navigating through the social world is not as simple as Sommer et al. think. If one contrasts this with the process of

---

[71] Walther and Förstl in: Förstl (2012, p. 105).

[72] Sommer et al. in: Förstl (2012, p. 90).

3 Social Widerspiegelung in Humans: Fundamentals 81

Widerspiegelung, one must conclude that Theory of Mind thinks it can do without Widerspiegelung: Attributions do not presuppose Widerspiegelung, they do not presuppose perception and processing of objective reality. In other words: Theory of Mind and also theorizing about empathy are not sufficient to make the process of Widerspiegelung clear in its breadth.

To sum up: Widerspiegelung is more fundamental than empathy and Theory of Mind, which becomes clear if one reconsiders the results on Widerspiegelung presented so far.[73] Widerspiegelung is not limited to the Widerspiegelung of other humans, Widerspiegelung starts with the Widerspiegelung of the world as a whole. A part of this reflected world is other humans, an even smaller part of what is reflected is the emotions of these humans. Now it would hardly be purposeful to separate out only the side of the emotions from the whole of the Widerspiegelung of other humans. Thus, the process of Widerspiegelung does not only include the recognition of the emotions or emotional states of the other person, but also his or her intentions. To put it simply, it is important to recognize, for example, whether the other person is well-disposed towards me or not. However, Widerspiegelung of other humans does not begin or end there: the recognition of the intentionality of the other person is an essential characteristic in the context of Widerspiegelung, which, however, presupposes that the person reflecting also knows about his or her own intentions. But how is the intentionality of the other person (and one's own) to be recognized? In a first step, the recognition of intentionality is described as a process of recognizing one's own intentionality. What intentions does the reflecting person pursue, is the question, and how does he recognize his intentionality? Recognizing intentionality generally means recognizing the goal that I myself or the other person is pursuing. In most cases, this is a matter of assumptions and/or societal knowledge, which goal the other person is pursuing at this moment. Such assumptions can of course also be subject to deception.

Widerspiegelung aims to recognize the other person in his or her uniqueness, but in turn to relate this uniqueness to one's own uniqueness: Odysseus is always Odysseus and is thereby the only and unique Odysseus. For Eurykleia, however, there are characteristics of Odysseus, combined with memories of incidents they have been through together, that stand out from this uniqueness. So it is a mixture of information drawn from memories of incidents as well as feelings felt by the former nurse at the moment. Both belong together, you cannot take feelings out of context.

But even this is not enough to make the process of Widerspiegelung clear. There is also the question of how Widerspiegelung is socially framed. Odysseus is the

---

[73] cf. Chap. 2 in this volume.

ancestral ruler on his island of Ithaca, Eurykleia was once a nurse and at the time of the reencounter with Odysseus was one of the servants. The Widerspiegelung also includes the dimension of social framing, which results in Odysseus and Eurykleia standing in a hierarchical relationship to each other: He is king, she servant. But the social framing also includes the fact that they both use the Greek language, which they presumably acquired in their respective childhoods. If one wanted to speak here of Eurykleia putting herself in Odysseus' mental state or ascribing a mental state to him, this remains superficial and speculative.

Theorizing about empathy or theory of mind cannot close these gaps. The reappraisal of sociality is missing, as is the reference to the subject. For humans this must mean that social Widerspiegelung means the gnostic apprehension of other humans and oneself. This process of social Widerspiegelung results in activities that can be understood as social action, i.e. action with and towards other humans.

Thus, after reviewing theories on the perception of other humans, which was carried out for the theory on empathy such as the Theory of Mind, it can be stated that these theories are not sufficient to adequately capture the Widerspiegelung of other humans. Thus, the answer to the question of how the process of social Widerspiegelung takes place in humans must be continued. What features and components does the process of Widerspiegelung in humans consist of in correspondence to social action and social relations?

3.2 The Social as Framing

In the previous subchapter, results of other authors on how they want to grasp perception between humans or parts of it were introduced. In the following parts of this Chap. 3, however, the view of the authorship of the present publication will be introduced. The authors use the concept of social Widerspiegelung for the perception of and between humans: The basics of Widerspiegelung have already been introduced in Chap. 2; the explanations of social Widerspiegelung will be unfolded in the following subchapters.

However, before social Widerspiegelung can be explained as part of the social, the social as a whole must be briefly and summarily explained.[74] On the way to an analytical breakdown of Widerspiegelung between humans, determinations and delimitations must be made: Widerspiegelung, as was the definition given at the end of the last chapter, is the representation of objective reality from the subject

---

[74] See in more detail: Scheu and Autrata (2018).

3 Social Widerspiegelung in Humans: Fundamentals 83

standpoint.[75] The Widerspiegelung of other humans must also correspond to this definition insofar as it is also a process that attempts to ascertain objective reality from the subject standpoint with the aim of producing a Widerspiegelung in the process. The Widerspiegelung of other humans is also carried out from the subject standpoint and pursues the goal of achieving an adequate Widerspiegelung. The delimitation starts with what is being reflected, i.e. the object of the Widerspiegelung. In the presentation in the second chapter, the introduction of examples suggested that Widerspiegelung refers to inanimate objects: A piano or the contents of the refrigerator were given as examples. But as the reference to the legendary Odysseus shows, there is also Widerspiegelung of and by humans: Odysseus must first have reflected his old nurse in order to know that the person reflected is precisely the Eurykleia in question. Vice versa, Eurykleia reflected someone who was not known to her at first glance: it was, she thought, a not too handsome beggar. At second glance she noticed, after obviously intensified Widerspiegelung, that the object of her Widerspiegelung was the returned Odysseus. As the recapitulation of the sequence of recognition around Odysseus shows, then, Widerspiegelung is also something directed at humans. Widerspiegelung is thus by no means only intended as the depiction of objects or facts; Widerspiegelung is also directed at other humans and in this case can be described as social Widerspiegelung.

In order to be able to grasp this analytically and conceptually precisely, recourse must be made to the general principles of Widerspiegelung. Widerspiegelung, as has been explained, can also be realized by many animals.[76] Even in the case of those animals that can reflect their environment, there is, in the whole of Widerspiegelung, the sub-area of Widerspiegelung of animals of the same species. For example, chimpanzees can reflect their environment, they also reflect from it the subdomain of other chimpanzees. Chimpanzees can and do reflect humans as well. However, chimpanzees and humans are not of the same species: for humans only humans are of the same species, for chimpanzees only chimpanzees are.

The species affiliation of humans and chimpanzees still needs some clarification: There is only one recent – i.e. still living – species of humans, namely humans with the biological designation Homo sapiens. On the other hand, there are two species of chimpanzees: the common chimpanzee (Pan troglodytes) and the bonobo or pygmy chimpanzee (Pan paniscus). There are significant differences in appearance and lifestyle between the two chimpanzee species: Common chimpanzees do not mirror bonobos – and vice versa – if only because their respective habitats are separated by the Congo River, which is almost impossible for them to cross.

---

[75] cf. Sect. 2.4 in this volume.

[76] cf. Sect. 2.2. in this volume.

84   3   Social Widerspiegelung in Humans: Fundamentals

The explanations of species and of belonging to a species were given in order to introduce the concept of the social. For living beings, what they do towards other living beings of the same species is part of the social. So, for example, what bonobos do towards bonobos is social: for bonobos, other bonobos belong to living beings of the same species. What humans do toward other humans is also social. When humans walk dogs, that is not part of what is social: humans and dogs are living beings of different species. Humans can reflect dogs, just as dogs can reflect humans. Such Widerspiegelungen between living beings of different species exist, but they do not belong to the social. So when humans reflect other humans, this area of Widerspiegelung belongs to the social. Generally speaking, Widerspiegelung of other living beings of the same species is part of the social.

Thus, the Widerspiegelung of other humans is located in a context: it belongs to the social. The decisive factor in determining whether something belongs to the social or not is species affiliation. When humans reflect each other, they belong to the same species and therefore their mutual Widerspiegelung is social. At the same time, a new conceptual classification has been made for this special segment of Widerspiegelung, namely the Widerspiegelung of other humans: Widerspiegelung, insofar as it is directed at other humans, is in turn part of the social in humans. Widerspiegelung of humans is thus on the one hand part of the total Widerspiegelung of humans: But when humans reflect a piano or the contents of their refrigerator, that has nothing to do with the social. On the other hand, when humans reflect other humans, that is part of the social of humans. Widerspiegelung of humans is therefore not social in every case, but it can be.

Before the Widerspiegelung of other humans, i.e. the Widerspiegelung as part of the social in humans, is further elucidated, specifics of the social have to be named. We should begin with the concept of the social and its definition. This definition reads: The social in humans is Widerspiegelung and activity towards other humans. This definition of the social applies in principle to all living beings that possess the social. Accordingly, the definition of the social, formulated for all living beings, is: The social includes all forms of Widerspiegelung and activities towards living beings of the same kind. This is true for humans, but it is also true for animals such as dogs, spiders, or chimpanzees. The social includes the area of Widerspiegelung as well as the activities of living beings of the same species.[77]

The supposedly inconspicuous concept of the social is thus defined. It should be pointed out that although there is an exuberant use of the social in everyday language as well as in science, this does not refer to a clarified content. The authors of

---

[77] cf. in detail: Scheu and Autrata (2018, p. 145 ff.).

3 Social Widerspiegelung in Humans: Fundamentals 85

the present publication have already pointed out the often found conceptual vagueness of the social: The social appears as an object in various academic disciplines, but remains conceptually indeterminate. In social work, for example, there is extensive discussion about the design of the social that is to be striven for, without, of course, explaining what it is that one wants to design.[78] It also remains open whether the social, about which scientific social work is debating, is the same object that is dealt with in biology. At this point, the weaknesses of the scientific discussion on the social can only be recapitulated without going into detail.[79]

In this context, it should be emphasized that the precise definition of the term can provide a remedy for the vagueness of the discussion about the social. Common notions of scientific work also suggest this: central concepts are to be determined and defined. A definition in science basically has the goal of clearly defining a concept and thus making it understandable and comprehensible to others. Brun and Hirsch Hadorn put it this way: "*Definitionen* sind Aussagen, die die Bedeutung eines Begriffs so bestimmen, dass jemand, der diesen Begriff nicht kennt, aus der Definition erfahren kann, was seine Bedeutung ist. Definitionen gehören also zu einer besonderen Klasse von Aussagen, die sich dadurch auszeichnen, dass sie etwas über die Bedeutung eines Begriffs sagen."[80]

One can also formulate it in such a way that definitions of – apparently – common terms hypostasize a meaning that has not been discernible so far in the sea of meanings bobbing side by side and on top of each other. If we consider this again in relation to the small section introduced on the legendary life of Odysseus, it becomes clear that phenomena of the social defined above – i.e. Widerspiegelung and activities in relation to other humans – were already described more than 1000 years before the turn of time.[81] The term anagnorisis, which denotes a recognition based on certain features as a key passage in a drama, is already found in Aristotle, i.e. in the fourth century before the turn of time.[82] Such phenomena have therefore been known and discussed for a long time: Nevertheless, a scientifically precise reappraisal of these phenomena has not been found for a long time.

This indicates that the definition of a term, which on the one hand establishes the meaning of the term beyond doubt and on the other hand thereby determines

---

[78] cf. Scheu and Autrata (2018, p. 64 ff.).

[79] See Scheu and Autrata (2018).

[80] Brun and Hirsch Hadorn (2009, p. 155, orig. citation); see also Autrata and Scheu (2015, esp. p. 195 ff.).

[81] cf. Brommer (1983).

[82] cf. Fuhrmann (1994).

86   3 Social Widerspiegelung in Humans: Fundamentals

the object designated by the term, is not and cannot be a product of chance. The definition of a term stands at the end of the scientific clarification of an object and is to be seen as a condensed summary of the results achieved in the process.

What the social is has been outlined above. It should be further explained *how* this understanding of the social was obtained in earlier publications.[83]

This raises the question of the way in which the definition of the social as an object introduced above was achieved. This leads to a consideration of the scientific-theoretical foundations that were used to achieve this result, namely the establishment of an inferred definition of the social.

Let us begin with a quotation from a publication from a context that seems remote from social work, but also from a debate on the social. In a book entitled *The Mathematics of Mathematics*, Roth formulates the following: "One affordance of Marx's presentation is that it allows apprehension of the distinction that he, as well as the cultural-historical psychologists that employ his method – e.g., Wygotski, Leont'ev – make in differentiating the *social* from the *societal*".[84] Roth thus states that an explicit distinction between the social and the societal can already be found in Marx and that psychologists who follow his method – better: methodology – also make such a distinction.

This seems doubtful. Roth is to be followed unreservedly when he calls for a distinction between the social and the societal: "A distinction between the two terms is theoretically necessary – though frequently not made (…)".[85] Roth refers elsewhere to the differentiation of the social and the societal made by the authorship of the present publication: "There are suggestions in social work and sociology that the social and the societal need to be understood as different and distinguished theoretically, especially for doing appropriate empirical work (Scheu & Autrata, 2011)".[86] But is it really possible to find a definition that grasps the social and the societal separately and differentiates them from each other already in Marx, Wygotski and Leontjew?

It seems questionable, above all, whether there is such a determination of the social in the authors mentioned. A discussion of the social or of societies does exist

---

[83] cf. Scheu and Autrata (2018, esp. p. 145 ff.).

[84] Roth (2017, p. 18). Roth prefers a different spelling for the author Leontjew, already mentioned in the present publication, but means the same psychologist. Likewise, there are also different spellings for the psychologist Wygotski, who also belongs to the cultural-historical school.

[85] Roth (2017, p. 18).

[86] Roth (2018, without page numbers. [p. 2]; emphasis in original).

3 Social Widerspiegelung in Humans: Fundamentals 87

in Marx, but also in Leontjew and Wygotski. Here, production is at the centre of the determination: in short, for Marx the development of material production is "(...) die Grundlage alles gesellschaftlichen Lebens (...)".[87] Similarly, in Leontjew we find the statement "(...) die menschliche Arbeit [war, author's note) von Anfang an ein gesellschaftlicher Prozeß".[88] In contrast, the concept of the social in Marx is already not to be found in the accurately kept keyword indexes to the Marx-Engels works: What the social is and constitutes, therefore, finds no expression there. The search for the social in Leontjew and Wygotski is similarly inconclusive: no explicit understanding of the social can be found.

Thus, at the very least, it can be ruled out that Marx, Leontjew, and Wygotski developed a viable determination of the social. A further question follows from this: Would this have been possible on the scientific-theoretical basis of historical-dialectical materialism alone? It should be recalled that, in terms of the philosophy of science, historical-dialectical materialism was consulted in order to grasp matter in the context of Widerspiegelung.[89] Could this be continued without circumstance to derive social Widerspiegelung from it? This is a question that discusses potentialities and in this respect it is difficult to come to a completely unambiguous conclusion. It should be noted that – in contrast to Roth's assessment – from the point of view of the authors of the present publication, it has not yet been possible to sufficiently theoretically determine the social solely from what Marx and Engels have unfolded on historical-dialectical materialism.

The fact that the social can only be derived with difficulty from historical-dialectical materialism in terms of scientific theory is due to the social as an object: the social exists in many animals as well as in humans. A well-founded breakdown of the social must therefore be able to grasp the totality of the social from a scientific-theoretical point of view and thus be able to shed light on interrelationships. The necessary scientific-theoretical means for this are not provided by historical-dialectical materialism alone. An extension is necessary. This extension was found with the historical approach and the shaping into categorial analysis. The historical approach and categorial analysis provide additional means of knowledge and, more importantly, an operationalization of the knowledge to be found. The historical approach with categorial analysis was, however, only conceived and extensively elaborated in the twentieth century by the aforementioned

---

[87] cf. e.g. Marx and Engels (1977, MEW 23, p. 195).
[88] Leontjew (1980, p. 202).
[89] cf. para. 2.1 in this volume and Scheu and Autrata (2018, p. 84 ff.).

cultural-historical psychologists Wygotski[90] and Leontjew,[91] as well as by the founder of subject science, Klaus Holzkamp.[92]

With regard to the historical classification of science, it should be said that the historical approach continues historical-dialectical materialism with categorial analysis: However, historical-dialectical materialism is thereby deepened and elaborated as a scientific-theoretical basis for theory formation in disciplines such as psychology, sociology and ultimately social work. Obsolete thus became science-theoretically inadequate connections of – for example – psychoanalysis and historical-dialectical materialism to the so-called Freudo-Marxism.[93] It should also be noted, however, that the scientific-theoretical continuation of historical-dialectical materialism to the historical approach with categorial analysis was not yet available during the lifetime of Marx and Engels. Marx and Engels, had they actually been concerned with the social as an object, would therefore not yet have had access to these scientific-theoretical means. Wygotski, Leontjew as well as Holzkamp developed the historical approach with the categorial analysis, i.e. they made the essential scientific-theoretical intermediate step of continuing historical-dialectical materialism accordingly: They have done the preliminary work in the theory of science that forms the basis for the theoretical grasp of the social.

The considerations on the scientific-theoretical justification of the recording of the social are to be rounded off with the recapitulation of Roth's statement: It is theoretically extremely necessary to determine the social precisely.[94] This determination must be based on an explicit scientific-theoretical foundation. This creates clarity compared to a consideration of the social without a theoretical foundation.

One cannot simply claim, that is the background of these explanations, via a definition that the social is this or that. At least for the field of science it is true that knowledge about an object must be derived and its dignity secured by means of scientific procedures. Admittedly, it must be noted that even in the practice of scientific work, the acquisition of knowledge often remains dubious and unexplained. Thus, in an earlier publication, statements from scientific social work on the social were reported, which all lack the presentation of their scientific-theoretical framing and the derivation of their results.[95] The fact that many authors consider a scientific-

---

[90] cf. Wygotski (1985).

[91] cf. Leontjew (1980).

[92] cf. Holzkamp (1985).

[93] cf. e.g. Braun (1979).

[94] cf. Roth (2017).

[95] cf. Scheu and Autrata (2018, p. 37 ff.).

3 Social Widerspiegelung in Humans: Fundamentals

theoretical framing and derivation to be dispensable, however, only proves that mistakes are also made in science, but not that the principles of scientific work are suspended.

The process of scientific knowledge acquisition is – to put it in very basic terms – the path via the presentation of the scientific-theoretical framing to the single-theoretical comprehension of an object. The scientific-theoretical framing of the theorization of an object as well as the derivation of the theorization of the object from the scientific-theoretical framing has the task of making theory comprehensible and verifiable. Whether a theory does justice to the object it explains can be measured by the way in which it frames its explanation. The scientific-theoretical framing and derivation of a theory thus serve to make the process of knowledge acquisition transparent and comprehensible. This leads into the truth test that theories must undergo, with the resulting decision as to whether these theories are true or false.[96]

Thus, for the analytical breakdown of the social as an object, such a scientific-theoretical framing must be established as well as a theorization of the social derived from it. This was done earlier by the authorship of the present publication. To this end, the first step was to introduce and review the schools of philosophy of science. In the résumé, it was concluded that the historical approach appears to be the most appropriate school of scientific theory to guide a scientific breakdown of the social: "Die historische Herangehensweise unterscheidet sich insofern von anderen wissenschaftstheoretischen Rahmungen, als in ihr auch Verfahrensbestimmungen enthalten sind. Der Unterschied zu vielen anderen wissenschaftstheoretischen Rahmungen wird durch den Vergleich deutlich: Aus der historischen Herangehensweise folgt logisch eine Fixierung des wissenschaftlichen Erkenntnisweges, auf dem dann eine Theorie gefunden werden und ein Gegenstand bestimmt werden kann: Das ist die Kategorialanalyse. Sie wird für die Aufklärung dessen, was das Soziale ist, als wissenschaftstheoretische Rahmung benutzt werden".[97]

The principles of the historical approach and its implementation in a categorial analysis have already been introduced.[98] The historical approach with its development into a categorial analysis was used by the authors for the breakdown of the social. On the basis of a categorial analysis the already mentioned definition of the social was found: "Zum Sozialen gehören alle Formen der Widerspiegelung und

---

[96] cf. Scheu and Autrata (2018, p. 121 ff.).

[97] Scheu and Autrata (2018, pp. 112 f.).

[98] cf. Sect. 2.2 in this volume.

der Aktivitäten zwischen Lebewesen der eigenen Art".[99] The social can thus be identified as a category or basic concept of life that occurs in many species and in many forms. The social exists in the – simple and less complex – basic form as well as in the – very complex – final form in humans.

The definition derived from categorial analysis implies presuppositions that need to be explained. The formula that the social is all forms of Widerspiegelung and activities between living beings of the same species is based on the fact that such living beings have possibilities of Widerspiegelung and differentiation at their disposal. In other words, if living beings cannot reflect their environment, they cannot be social as a consequence. Differentiation into living beings of the same species and of a different species is not possible for them; activities based on Widerspiegelung are also not possible.

The prerequisite for the formation of the social, then, is the possibility of reflecting the environment and of translating this Widerspiegelung into activities. The general possibility to reflect the environment and to transform this Widerspiegelung into activities lies in the psyche. Psyche is thus the characterizing term for the totality of these capabilities. If these abilities are realized, if the environment is reflected and the Widerspiegelung is converted into activities, these are processes that result from the psyche, i.e. mental processes. Psychic processes begin phylogenetically with simple creatures that can, for example, reflect differences in brightness and move toward the light in order to be more likely to find food there. Psyche is also a category that ranges from simple basic forms to the final form found in humans.[100] Psyche, in turn, is not possible without appropriate organic equipment. Schurig states, "(…) *daß von den mehrzelligen biologischen Systemen nur Organismen mit Nervenzellen bzw. einem Nervensystem als Träger psychischer Prozesse in Frage kommen*".[101] Thus, of all living beings, only multicellular organisms, and of these only those with nerve cells and a nervous system, can be considered as carriers of mental processes. Without the psyche, on the other hand, social life is not possible.

Summarizing, one can thus exclude that living beings other than multicellular animals can exhibit sociality: Plants or fungi are indeed multicellular living beings, but they have no nerve cells. Only from the formation of mental processes, for which the organic endowment with nerve cells and a nervous system is indispensable, is the condition for the social given, that a Widerspiegelung of the same kind as well as activities resulting from the Widerspiegelung are possible. So it is only

---

[99] Scheu and Autrata (2011, p. 172).

[100] cf. Scheu and Autrata (2011, p. 147 ff.).

[101] Schurig (1975, p. 84; emphasis in original).

3 Social Widerspiegelung in Humans: Fundamentals

animals and humans, who biologically belong to the animals, in which social can be found. Although psyche is the indispensable prerequisite for sociality, there are differences even among animals that are capable of mental processes: some have little or no social life, while others have highly developed social behavior. Snails (Gastropoda), for example, have antennae with which they can orient themselves, i.e. psychic processes. Many snails are hermaphrodites, which leads to different forms of reproduction with and without actual mating. However, Roman snails do meet for mating with other Roman snails: For mating, they apparently have to find other Roman snails and move towards them; mating of Roman snails is preceded by extensive mutual palpation with their respective antennae. More social is not ascertainable with them, however. The other pole with dense and lifelong social behavior is taken, for example, by the dogs (Canidae), to which, among others, the wolves and – as a domesticated form – the domestic dogs belong.

Note the stipulation that the social includes all forms of Widerspiegelung and activity towards creatures of the same species. There are plenty of forms of Widerspiegelung and activities towards animals of other species in nature: for example, predators sometimes spy on prey animals for a long time before they try to overwhelm them with a surprise attack. There are also forms of symbiosis in which animals of different species benefit from each other, as occurs, for example, in oxpeckers and rhinoceroses. Here, too, forms of Widerspiegelung and resulting activities can be detected, but it is not social. The social is bound to the limits of the same species. It should be emphasized that the social is phylogenetically derived from bisexual-sexual reproduction. The social has become developmentally sexually attached to this core, namely, bisexual-sexual reproduction. Not all forms of the social subsequently center on reproduction; there is also social coexistence of sexual equals. But even these evolved forms of the social take place between animals of the same species. In general, it can be postulated that such forms of social cohabitation also increase the probability of survival: If even a single specimen of the species is killed by a predator, for example, other animals have survived under the protection of the group.

In order to define the category of the social for humans, a second criterion must be introduced: Although the social is phylogenetically based on bisexual-sexual reproduction, it has – proceeding from this – developed into quite other areas. Thus, according to the second criterion, the social is malleable and, as a consequence, by no means remains limited to the functional circle of reproduction. In its malleability, the social continues to follow the biological principle that developments and changes that occur in phylogenesis must contribute to increasing the probability of survival: If developments and changes did not do this, they would not be able to solidify and pass into the biological endowment. The social thus

92   3 Social Widerspiegelung in Humans: Fundamentals

contributes to increasing the probability of survival, but does not do so – after phylogenetic reshaping – exclusively in the segment of reproduction.

The aforementioned categorial analysis of the social has been carried out and presented in previous publications.[102] It should be underpinned with the reference to the scientific-theoretical framing and the single-theoretical execution that the introduced understanding of the social and its definition stems from a derivation process: The given definition of the social, that it includes Widerspiegelung and activities towards living beings of the same kind, is not a speculation or arbitrary assertion. Rather, this definition is the result of scientifically validated work.

Humans therefore, and this is also a result of the derivation process mentioned above, do not have a unique position with regard to the social: many animals have a partially highly developed social system. Humans, however, have a unique selling point in another respect: the social in humans is specific and reserved for them alone. By transcending immediacy, humans have gained a developmental context peculiar to them, namely, social-historical development. The fact that human beings have been able to make the developmental leap to the historical-social way of life has become possible through the attainment of this transgression of immediacy.[103] What is meant by this? All living beings other than man live in immediacy to nature, have to accept the conditions of nature. Humans, on the other hand, have succeeded in stepping out of immediacy with nature: Humans are able to influence and shape nature. Thus, the social in humans also stands in this social-historical context: the social in humans is framed by the social existence of humans.

With this, one can return to the categorial analysis introduced[104]: the social in humans belongs to the category of the social and represents within this category – so far – the final form of development. The transgression of immediacy represents an enormous leap that endows the social in humans with new qualities. Nevertheless, the social in humans remains part of the category of the social insofar as the basic determinations of the social – Widerspiegelung and activities towards other living beings of the same kind – are preserved. Thus, for example, when a human walks his dog, both the human and the dog may reflect each other and engage in activities; but these are not forms of the social, since the human and the dog are not of the same species. Widerspiegelungen and activities between humans, on the other hand, are social, since they take place between living beings of the same species. For a better understanding of why only Widerspiegelungen and activities between living beings of the same species belong to the social, it is necessary to recall the

---

[102] cf. Scheu and Autrata (2018, esp. p. 145 ff.).

[103] cf. Scheu and Autrata (2018, p. 176 ff.).

[104] cf. Sect. 2.3 in this volume.

3 Social Widerspiegelung in Humans: Fundamentals

emergence of the social in the context of phylogenesis: the phylogenetic achievement of the social was able to increase the survival probability of a species and arose in the context of bisexual-sexual reproduction. Widerspiegelungen and activities between creatures of different species do not have such a connotation of strengthening the probability of survival.

A further deduction must be made: Humans live in the context of society that is specific to them. It has been explained and illustrated that this leads to the specific way of life of humans[105]: Humans live in social spaces of possibility, so that their activities are to be seen as a relation of possibility to the world. This is fundamentally and always true for human beings. Human life is therefore always social, but by no means always social. Only that part of human life which – following the definition of the social – directly reflects other humans or represents activities towards other humans is social. So, for example, when humans read a book or a newspaper or ride a bicycle, this is always an outflow of the social form of human life: A book or newspaper must be available as a social source of information and a bicycle must be produced in the social labor process; books, newspapers, and a bicycle are in turn based on societal knowledge. The enumerated examples demonstrate the social embeddedness of these activities, but they are not social. Only when the exemplary activities are related to other humans would they be social: thus, when a newspaper article or a book is discussed and when the bicycle ride is undertaken in a group, this belongs to the social.

So, on the one hand, humans's lives are always social, but not all humans's activities are social. On the other hand, the social aspect of humans's lives is always socially framed. When humans meet or encounter each other, it is always under social conditions: Whether they meet in a restaurant, on the street, or on the train, the location of the social that can unfold there is socially predetermined. The social aspect of humans is not outside, but within the social framework.

The social is thus positioned in the possibility structure of humans's relationship to the world. Possibilities are available that can be used to realize the social. It should be noted that the social is a category that is analytically conceived. To use an example, when humans encounter each other in traffic and disagree about the applicable right of way, it can lead to nasty looks or name-calling. They may even get out of their cars and get physical. All of these actions are social: they are mutual Widerspiegelungen and reciprocal activities; moreover, that they are living beings of the same species is indisputable. But: social is not to be unilateralized as prosocial and not to be normatively exaggerated.

---

[105] cf. Sect. 2.3 in this volume.

94   3 Social Widerspiegelung in Humans: Fundamentals

What needs to be explained is the dimension of the sociality of the social in humans. This sociality of the social has two sides, which must be analytically separated from each other. One side is that the social inevitably takes place in the context of a social framework. Humans's lives always take place in a social context, and so does the social. Even among dropouts, who form only a small cohort in terms of numbers anyway, objects and products that have been socially produced are used: Circumnavigators use a socially produced sailboat and socially produced knowledge about navigation. Humans can use the social framing of their lives as a structure of possibilities, they can thus choose among possibilities. However, one cannot completely leave behind the social framing of human life.

This means that the social must also expect to be permanently framed in the context of society. The places where the social takes place are socially created places. Even if one thinks of places that are largely natural, that is, little socially processed or planned, the question arises as to how humans reach these places: It is then the means of transportation or the travel enterprise that entails the social framing. Looking further at what humans do in such places where they meet other humans, other aspects of social framing come into play: such places might be workplaces, a school, or a recreational meeting place. What humans do in such places remains within the possibility structure of humans to the world: humans can choose between possibilities. Humans can choose – in sweeping terms – to be engaged or bored at school, for example. But the social framing is given and exists: a school is a school. Social that emerges in school is framed by the circumstances of the school.

A specific social framing of the social can also be found, for example, in rural areas. Characteristic for rural areas is the necessity of working outside the village or of attending educational institutions for adults or for children, adolescents and young adults outside the village. This results in the necessity of commuting and mobility: inhabitants of rural areas have to spend a considerable part of their time for travelling. Especially for the younger inhabitants of rural areas it is the case that they cover such distances to a large extent by public transport. This in turn has the consequence that the social takes place in the social framing of the commute: Humans meet at bus stops, on buses or on trains, contacts and appointments take place in this context. The social framing of commuting is predetermined, since corresponding workplaces or educational institutions are located in the city, i.e. not in the place of residence. But how the social is shaped within the framing condition of commuting is open: Who you sit next to on public transport or who you make contact with at bus stops is part of the social.

From the situation outlined for rural areas of at least two places where one spends one's life, the necessity arises to deal with different circumstances. This

3 Social Widerspiegelung in Humans: Fundamentals

already starts with the language: In rural areas, the linguistic form of dialect is more widespread and differentiated than in the city. Language as a whole is an important means of passing on and using societal knowledge. Thus, for example, the fact arises that societal knowledge is acquired at school. If, however, pupils originally acquired their language in dialect, this results in breaks between high level language and dialect. This in turn radiates into the social sphere: Conflicts can arise from the fact that dialect speakers feel misunderstood; conversely, an eager adoption of the standard language in the village can lead to criticism that one is adapting to the customs of the city.

Such differences in social framing can be thought further for the broad field of traditions and rules. Such traditions and rules, which – especially in rural areas – are of great importance, are supposed to provide orientation as socially developed and traditional guidelines. However, such traditions and rules can quickly lead to internal and external conflicts in the social sphere: For example, should humans be greeted on the street? In rural areas this is often still a valid rule; if one does not adhere to the rule, this quickly leads to reprimanding looks or corresponding words. In the city, on the other hand, someone who greets oncoming humans is likely to cause irritation.[106]

What has been illustrated by examples could be continued and made explicit for further situations. It is sufficient at this point to note the fact of the fundamentally given social framing of the social in humans. The sociality of the social, however, does not remain external to the social only as a framing, but also permeates humans themselves. Thus we must continue with the second side of the sociality of the social.

The social in humans consists of Widerspiegelung and activities towards other humans. Widerspiegelung and activities are socially framed, which has already been explained, and are influenced by this framing, though not determined. Sociality, however, does not only remain external to humans, but also penetrates into them. Taking school as an example, school is the social framing of the social that occurs within it. Further, it is the case that humans who meet in school live socially: Humans relate to the social space of possibility – in this case: school – and choose possibilities. This is also true of the social. Widerspiegelung and activities towards other humans take place and relate to these humans. In turn, however, sociality is inherent in these humans. This concerns, among other things, societal knowledge that is passed on and absorbed: Teachers, according to their social function in school, are there to pass on knowledge, students, according to their function, are in school to absorb such knowledge. But whether teachers or students perform such social functions with pleasure or rather reluctantly is not said. Both, the social

---

[106] cf. on social framing in rural areas: Scheu and Autrata (2011, p. 236 ff.).

96 3 Social Widerspiegelung in Humans: Fundamentals

function as well as the corresponding emotion, are in turn significant for the social that arises from it: teachers reflect pupils and come to activities on the basis of the Widerspiegelung, likewise pupils do this with regard to teachers. This should make it clear that sociality permeates humans and thus becomes an important reference point for the social. However, the provision that humans have the possibility to choose is still valid and unbroken: They are not victims of sociality, but can decide between given possibilities of action or even develop new possibilities of action.

3.3 Social Widerspiegelung as a Unique Process

If one considers social Widerspiegelung for humans systematically, one must start with the simplest form. Social Widerspiegelung is always the Widerspiegelung of another human being by a human being. The simplest form of such a Widerspiegelung is a social Widerspiegelung without any repetition or deepening.

In order to illustrate how such a thing can turn out, the following example is to be explained: One enters a department store in which one has never been before. You have not visited the department store to pass the time, but with the aim of acquiring something. But since you do not know the department store, you don't know where to find certain goods. So you look for someone from the staff to ask the location of the goods you are looking for.

A process of Widerspiegelung is therefore necessary in the situation exemplified. Since it is already certain that the target of the Widerspiegelung is a human being, it is – over long distances – a process of social Widerspiegelung. The restriction that it is not only about a social Widerspiegelung has to be made because the whole of the found objective reality in the department store has to be reflected first in order to get closer to the goal of the social Widerspiegelung of an employee. Thus, it is perhaps better to first sound out via signposts in which department the sought-after product can be found: it is likely that contacting the staff in the food department is not very purposeful if one is looking for a product that belongs to clothing. The process of non-social Widerspiegelung is not to be pursued further at this point. It should be pointed out in general that non-social Widerspiegelung in the context of the example touched upon follows the general purpose of grasping objective reality and in doing so has to go through the steps of Widerspiegelung, i.e. it carries out sensory perception with active control, compares this in a gnostic process with existing knowledge as well as one's own subject standpoint and ultimately arrives at a Widerspiegelung[107]: In this way, non-social Widerspiegelung is

---

[107] cf. Sect. 2.4 in this volume.

3 Social Widerspiegelung in Humans: Fundamentals 97

used to delimit where the sought-after product is likely to be found and, accordingly, contact with the personnel appears promising. The subject's point of view always enters into the Widerspiegelung: One will usually not reflect the offer of the fish stall more accurately if one is looking for a new belt. But these are all just Widerspiegelungen that address probabilities: There are also humans who like to roam around department stores and take in the range of goods on offer. The subject standpoint in this case could be described as bipolar: One is looking for a certain object, but one also enjoys the variety of the range of goods on offer. In any case, however, the elements of Widerspiegelung that have been presented remain, i.e. even in the case of different forms of subject standpoints: each subject standpoint forms itself in the face of actively controlled sensory perception of objective reality and a gnostic working through of what has been grasped, in order to result in an image.

Whether, thinking the example further, one looks for knowledgeable personnel right at the entrance of the department store or first looks around in the corresponding department on the basis of factual Widerspiegelung, the first step of social Widerspiegelung is sensory perception. If one wants to reflect humans, one has to find them. The essential sensory impressions are likely to be obtained through vision. It is unlikely that errors will occur in this process. However, for reasons of systematics alone, it is worth mentioning: social Widerspiegelung begins with the fact that one must determine where humans are, whom one then reflects further and more precisely. A mannequin may look similar to a human, but it is not one. Via sensory perception, it will probably be quickly noticed that the mannequin does not move and also only resembles humans in external appearance.

It becomes more difficult when it is a question of finding the person in a department store who is the suitable contact person for one's own concern: it can be assumed that a large number of humans are present in such a department store. It must be remembered that one has never been in this department store, i.e. one does not know anyone: one cannot therefore look for a particular salesperson with whom one has had good experiences. Rather, the process of Widerspiegelung is first directed at the totality of the humans present, among whom one must make a selection.

At this point, the societal knowledge that one acquired earlier comes into play. Societal knowledge has its location in Widerspiegelung not only ex post, by comparing impressions of sensory perception with such societal knowledge in the gnostic process. Societal knowledge directs Widerspiegelung also ex ante: One knows that shop assistants usually wear work clothes that make them recognizable in their function. This can be clothing in a colour that signals that they belong to the department store staff. Common are also name tags, which also reflect the name of the wearer. One is thus, if one has this knowledge, in the position to determine on the basis of such characteristics whether someone belongs to the personnel of the department store or not. If there were no such features, which can also happen, one would have to try to determine by Widerspiegelung, whether someone, for example, puts goods on the shelves or makes eye contact with the customers: But these are again rather hints and not indubitable features. Whether someone is filling up a shelf or perhaps just looking for something on it and whether someone makes more eye contact with the customers than others is difficult to decide and by no means unambiguous.

Sensory perception is therefore likely to be directed first towards spotting such more meaningful features as professional clothing or name badges. This can possibly be done while standing. But perhaps the humans sought, together with their features, are hidden by shelves or other humans, and one must first reach such a position, by actively controlling the locomotion, that one can make out the existence of the features.

Once one has found out via sensory perception – in this case: seeing – whether someone with the sought-after characteristics is present, the gnostic process will enter a second stage[108]: One checks sensory perception against societal knowledge. Has one actually found someone from the sales staff or does someone just happen to be wearing clothes in the color the department store has chosen for its staff? If one is convinced to have found someone from the staff, next steps of social Widerspiegelung are initiated.

It remains to be stated that up to this moment – mentally following the unfolding of the example – the social Widerspiegelung is referred to facts that are due to the social existence of humans.[109] One has not yet looked into the face of the person to whom one may now direct one's steps, nor does one know anything about his preferences. In the social context in which the exemplary social Widerspiegelung takes place, this is not necessary, and would probably also be counterproductive: if all customers in a department store were so interested in sales assistants, sales would probably come to a standstill. It should be noted that social Widerspiegelung is by no means always accompanied by intensive rapprochement or understanding. Social Widerspiegelung not infrequently remains within the boundaries of the given space of possibility: in order to be able to buy something in a department store, one must be able to find it and may need help to do so. Social Widerspiegelung follows such functional contexts. In this way, however, social Widerspiegelung can contribute to the realization of subjective quality of life only within the limits of the

---

[108] cf. Sect. 2.4 in this volume.

[109] cf. Sect. 2.3 in this volume.

3 Social Widerspiegelung in Humans: Fundamentals 99

given: in the case that social Widerspiegelung has succeeded, one has found the sought-after goods after assistance from the sales personnel and can take them with one. Social Widerspiegelung as a Widerspiegelung of other humans has thus taken place, but has not left the socially given space of possibility. This is the end of the introductory reference to the social integration of social Widerspiegelung and the return to the exemplary description of the situation in the department store.

If one has clarified via sensory perception and by assigning the results obtained to societal knowledge via a gnostic process that one has someone from the sales staff in front of one, the Widerspiegelung continues. If the determination of whether someone belongs to the sales staff or not was about the recording of social characteristics, now it is about the preparation of the question about the sought-after product. The assumed goal here is to ask a question that will be understood and lead to an answer that will help. Again, societal knowledge and experience go into the Widerspiegelung: One knows that it is one of the tasks of salespersons to advise customers. But one probably also knows that salespersons are also entrusted with other tasks: For example, a shop assistant may not have time to look after customers at the moment and may have to restock goods. Sales assistants in general often have stressful working conditions and may therefore be inclined to avoid contact with customers.

The social Widerspiegelung must therefore go further and provide clues as to whether and how an approach to the found salesperson can be promising. This involves determining which prerequisites are given for taking up the question that one wants to ask. If the found salesperson is already talking to another customer or is balancing a stack of fragile dishes, it is probably advisable to wait with the question. Concerning the Widerspiegelung taking place, it has to be said that processes are recorded via sensory perception and compared with societal knowledge: When humans are intensely busy, their attention is likely to be focused entirely on these preoccupations; questions are likely to be received as disturbing at this moment. Thus, Widerspiegelung is used to check whether one's own concern – the question about a product – has a chance of being received positively. The facial expression or body language can also be the object of Widerspiegelung: Does the facial expression or body posture suggest that the counterpart is willing to answer a question? Again, societal knowledge and personal experience are consulted for this purpose: One assumes that humans who do not make eye contact and do not show a smile when making contact are less willing to respond to a question. Similarly, one might assume that humans who are constantly moving restlessly and give the appearance of wanting to leave right away are not ready to respond to a question. However, such features as facial expression or body language are by no means always unambiguous in their meaning: humans may have a facial expression that is interpreted as 'scowling' or 'aloof', but may not themselves actively want to display such a facial expression.

The subject-relatedness of social Widerspiegelung in such a context of unique encounter still needs to be addressed. The subject standpoint can be found in the goal of the Widerspiegelung process: The goal in the example described is to find a product in the department store; an intermediate goal here is to find someone who knows the location of the product and can give this information to facilitate one's search. However, the subject standpoint also enters into the shaping of the search and the shaping of the social Widerspiegelung in the process. Thus, from the subject's point of view, the most careful social Widerspiegelung possible, which can also be described as respectful, may appear to be called for: one looks closely to see whether a question might not be perceived as disturbing at the particular time, and one checks through social Widerspiegelung whether the person addressed might not be otherwise occupied. The subject standpoint as the basis of such social Widerspiegelung is that one does not want to annoy other humans or, said from the subject standpoint, one wants to avoid having to feel the annoyance of other humans. Another form of the subject standpoint is that one does not want to waste time on social Widerspiegelung of the situation of the department store personnel and – without further social Widerspiegelung – loudly shouts out one's question from a distance: the subject standpoint in this second form leans on the societal knowledge that department store personnel are there to answer questions. This is extended by the attribution that the department store personnel must comply with this without delay. Social Widerspiegelung thus also has implications via the underlying subject standpoint, which are realized in the process of Widerspiegelung.

This in turn can be condensed into the principle of the image, which is the result of Widerspiegelung as well as social Widerspiegelung. At the end of the process of social Widerspiegelung in the department store, there is an image of the person to whom one wants to ask the question about the location of the product one is looking for. On the basis of characteristics, one has found someone whom one considers to belong to the department store staff. Further one has gained the further impression from the social Widerspiegelung of the person that the willingness to answer the question is given. Thus, it seems promising to be able to implement the subject standpoint in the sense of realizing subjective quality of life: Subjective quality of life can fan out into wanting to be able to find and later buy a certain product; at the same time, wanting to be treated kindly – in everyday language – by the staff of the department store in the context of the contact. However, subjective quality of life can also be limited to finding the product one is looking for; one reduces the social Widerspiegelung to the most necessary and is not interested in the good behaviour of the staff. At the end of the social Widerspiegelung there is in any

3 Social Widerspiegelung in Humans: Fundamentals 101

case an image of the person with whom one has had to do. This image can be more multifaceted or reduced to a few characteristics: One can be content with being able to say that one had contact with a salesperson; one did not want to know more and also set up the social Widerspiegelung accordingly. But it can also be that the image has more depth of field: One can remember the face, for example, or has noticed linguistic peculiarities such as a certain dialect.

In summary, it can be said that Widerspiegelungen of humans whom one has not seen before and does not know, as a rule, have to make do with little information and, above all, with little confirmed information. To add: Social Widerspiegelung can get by with little information about each other in many situations where humans meet once. When humans meet on the street, they have to choose walking paths in such a way that they do not collide; for this purpose, social Widerspiegelung must be used to determine the direction of movement and speed of other humans. However, more sophisticated social Widerspiegelung is not necessary. Similarly, for many other situations where humans are encountered once, it is also the case that in-depth social Widerspiegelung is not necessary. However, it is also the case that social Widerspiegelung in such one-time encounters is often conducted on the premise that high meticulousness is unnecessary. What then the facial expression of the person you are socially mirroring actually means goes unnoticed. If one has found someone from the sales staff in the department store, this, i.e. the affiliation to the sales staff, can be reliably determined by social Widerspiegelung. But whether the person one has found is particularly committed or less committed as a salesperson and is satisfied or dissatisfied with his or her work would have to be investigated more closely. In this respect, social Widerspiegelung of the kind presented builds up only a very partial level of information.

Social Widerspiegelung has all the principles of Widerspiegelung even in the case of a unique process between humans who have never met before: it includes sensory perception, active control, the gnostic process, subject-relatedness, and finally ends with the image. What the unique social Widerspiegelung lacks are the dimensions of personalizing cognition, recognition, and consequent individuality. This will be addressed in the next subchapter.

3.4 Cognition, Personalised Cognition and Recognition

An essential dimension of social Widerspiegelung is that social Widerspiegelung is connected with processes of cognition: the basis of both Widerspiegelung and social Widerspiegelung is always sensory perception. In terms of social Widerspiegelung, this means that one sees, hears, smells or feels someone.

Although this is the basis of social Widerspiegelung, it is not very helpful in itself: Only when one can compare the sensory perception of someone with gnostic processes, can an image emerge – again in connection with one's own subjectivity – which can then be the starting point for goal-directed activities. Thus, for the linking of social Widerspiegelung and social activities, important stations of the connection of sensory perceptions and their gnostic matching have to be introduced. All these stations carry a cognition in themselves. How and what is cognitively recorded and which stages are to be found in this process, will be explained in this subchapter. It is important to keep the connection and the aim of social Widerspiegelung in evidence: Social Widerspiegelung prepares social activities. Social activities are based – grasping the connection in the opposite direction – on the results of social Widerspiegelung: what one has learned about another person via social Widerspiegelung and subsequently has available as knowledge is the basis for subsequent social activities: The specificity of this knowledge can be differentiated and thus provides clues as to which subsequent social Widerspiegelung processes and which subsequent social activities can be based on it.

Coming back to Odysseus, one can state: The recognition and being recognized exemplified for Eurykleia and Odysseus presupposes that they have met before. One can only recognize someone whom one has seen, heard, smelled or felt before. Such recognition was possible between Eurykleia and Odysseus. Recognition is to be distinguished from the cognitive recording of a social position or function: In cognitively recording a social position or function, it is established that a person holds such a position or function. Whether one has met this person before or not is of secondary importance: It may be that one is actually meeting for the first time; but it may also be that one has met before without realizing it. The cognitive recording of a social position or function in a person occurs through social Widerspiegelung. In cognitively recording the social position or function, one only wants to establish this position or function.

The cognition of a person's social position or function via social Widerspiegelung takes place in a certain space of possibility, which is contoured, for example, by the setting in a department store: One wants to buy something and needs the help of appropriate personnel to do so. In order to be able to realize this, one has to find out via social Widerspiegelung who belongs to the staff and who is available for such assistance. Similar processes can be imagined for an administrative institution. However, societal knowledge is always necessary in order to be able to carry out social Widerspiegelung adequately.

The desired cognition, which is to be achieved through social Widerspiegelung, however, remains limited: The result of cognition must be that one has ascertained the social functions or positions and has ascertained whether the humans who hold

3 Social Widerspiegelung in Humans: Fundamentals   103

these positions or functions are reachable in order to be available in the attainment of one's goals. Thus, it is not necessary for social Widerspiegelung to capture more than what is situationally important. One does not necessarily have to recognize salespersons in a later encounter: It is enough to be able to distinguish salespeople from non-salespeople and to find out which salespeople are willing to address one's own concerns.

If one addresses the differentiation of social Widerspiegelung from recognition, one can state: Recognition and being recognized have two preconditions. First, there must have been at least one previous encounter so that one can later recognize someone or be recognized by someone. Secondly, the Widerspiegelung must have been focused in such a way that recognition is possible. One can also put it this way: Recognition presupposes the cognitive recording of a person as a specific person. This is different from the fact that, for example, one passes the same person several times in a crowd without noticing that one is meeting the same person. Recognition, then, presupposes a recognizing Widerspiegelung that has grasped the specificity of a person. One cannot recognize someone whom one has never seen. Likewise, one cannot recognize someone whose specificity and characteristics one has never grasped in detail.

A key concept for characterizing this quality of cognition is that of personal specificity. Personal specificity is to be distinguished from the concept of personality. According to Leontjew, "(…) unabhängig von der Erfahrung, von den Ereignissen, die das Leben eines Menschen beeinflussen, und unabhängig von den physischen Veränderungen bleibt der Mensch als *Persönlichkeit* sowohl in den Augen der anderen Menschen als auch für sich selbst ein und derselbe".[110] Personality – at least as Leontjew understands it – is obviously invariant: personality always remains the same, not subject to change through experience or physical development. Personality as Leontjew understands it stands apart from the everyday language view that sees only outstanding humans as personalities. Klaus et al. argue similarly to Leontjew in setting themselves apart from the everyday understanding of personality. They assume that "(…) im umfassenden Sinn jeder Mensch, der durch sein produktives, politisches, geistig-kulturelles und sittliches Handeln auf die gesellschaftliche Entwicklung einwirkt"[111] is a personality. Although this further develops the concept of personality beyond the everyday understanding, it imposes on personality a dubious independence from experience and change.

---

[110] Leontjew (1982, p. 176; orig.).

[111] Klaus and Buhr (1976b, vol. 2, pp. 920 f.).

Personality, then, in everyday understanding means only outstanding humans; in Leontjew's understanding personality acquires a speculative constancy. Thus, the concept of personality is burdened with determinations that are not adequate. Thus, the authorship prefers another concept, namely, personal specificity. The basis of this concept – person specificity – is, on the one hand, the fact that humans are unique, i.e. specific.[112] On the other hand, humans are persons. The term person derives from the Latin *persona*. In Latin, *persona* was the term for the mask with which actors appeared. In a figurative sense, a person is cognitively recordable through a characteristic – as the mask originally was. The concept of the personal specificity of humans thus grasps that humans are unique and at the same time cognitively recordable by characteristics. The personal specificity is admittedly – unlike personality – not to be understood as a constant, but – in the sense of matter[113] – as being in permanent motion. The personal specificity oscillates between continuation of the previous, change of parts and addition of something new. An aid for grasping the meaning of personal specificity can be found in the *persona*, i.e. the mask that actors used to wear: If one could not cognitively record which actor is currently acting, one would probably not be able to understand the meaning of the play's plot. It is the cognitive recording of the persona specificity that makes it possible to grasp and assign what is happening in the social.

Personal specificity is used to grasp the totality of a person's characteristics. Cognitive Recording based on personal specificity, which is achieved through social Widerspiegelung, must go beyond the cognition of social function or position: Since many humans may perform the same or at least similar social functions, they cannot be distinguished by this alone. The social position or function enters into the personal specificity of a person, but is only a part of it. A person is more than his position or function.

Thus, in order for recognition to be possible, a personalizing cognitive recording must have taken place beforehand, which has determined the personal specificity of a person via social Widerspiegelung. As a definition, one can state: Personalizing cognitive recording determines the personal specificity of a person by means of social Widerspiegelung. What remains open in personalizing cognition, however, is which characteristics result from social Widerspiegelung and form the personal specificity. Social Widerspiegelung is subject-related, as has been explained[114]: In this respect, personalizing cognition is also influenced by the

---

[112] cf. Chap. 1 in this volume.

[113] cf. Sect. 2.1 in this volume.

[114] cf. Sect. 3.6 in this volume.

3 Social Widerspiegelung in Humans: Fundamentals 105

subject standpoint of the reflected. That which is cognitively recorded as personal specificity corresponds on the one hand with the reflected person, but also corresponds with the subjectivity of the reflector. Thus, different reflectors can see different characteristics as characteristic of a personal specificity, which in turn does not always have to coincide with what someone sees as his or her personal specificity.

Personalizing cognition is the prerequisite for recognition, but not every personalizing cognition must be followed by recognition. Personalizing recognition goes beyond the mere cognition of social positions and functions and aims at grasping the specificity of a person. It may be, however, that personalizing cognition is not followed by a second encounter with the personalized person: In this respect, recognition remains absent. Personalized cognition remains as a potential, as assignable knowledge about the specificity of a person: whether this knowledge is later implemented in renewed social contacts, however, is an open question.

Before recognition, therefore, there must have been personalized recognition: Personalized recognition in the context of the Widerspiegelung of other humans is the grasping of specific characteristics and properties of a person as well as the assignment to exactly this person. Thus, the dimension of knowledge is also decisive for the Widerspiegelung of other humans: if one has knowledge about the so-being of a person that provides precisely fitting information about this person, this is the indispensable core component for recognition – as a central process of the Widerspiegelung of other humans: only because Eurykleia knows that Odysseus has a scar on his thigh and that this continues to be an unmistakable scar, can she recognize him, although he otherwise appears completely different from what he used to be.

Recognition follows as the third mode in the process of social Widerspiegelung: the first two modes of social Widerspiegelung, namely cognition and personalizing cognition, have already been presented. In order for recognition to be possible, two preconditions must be fulfilled: as a first precondition, there must have previously been personalizing cognition, which has been condensed into knowledge about characteristics that allow a person to be distinguished as a personal specificity from other humans who also exhibit personal specificities. The second prerequisite is that there is a renewed encounter with this person and that recognition is achieved in this encounter via social Widerspiegelung. If renewed encounters do occur, but recognition does not take place, personalizing cognition remains, but with one restriction: Obviously, personalizing cognition was not sufficient to ensure recognition. This is by no means just a fictional mention: if one makes an effort of one's own memory, one will probably be able to quickly recall encounters with humans whom one knew very well 'in the past' but recognized only with difficulty 'later', or perhaps not at all. This is what happened to Penelope, who could not recognize her husband Odysseus at first sight after decades of separation.

Parallel to the differentiation of cognition, personalizing cognition and recognition, the embedding of the processes of Widerspiegelung underlying cognition in the totality of the social is to be grasped: Through the social as a whole, personalizing knowledge about other humans emerges, which in turn represents an important variable for later processes of Widerspiegelung into which this knowledge enters. In principle, the differentiation of the social into Widerspiegelung and activities vis-à-vis other humans must be emphasized. A further concept is to be introduced: as soon as Widerspiegelung and activities are repeated between the same humans and the determination is added that these other humans are cognitively recorded in their specificity and later recognized again, these are social relations. In social relations, too, the social remains in its determinateness, namely, that it is a matter of Widerspiegelung and activities vis-à-vis other humans. In social relations this is extended by the fact that one has knowledge of the other person on the basis of previous encounters and knowledge of what took place in these encounters between the two humans.

Social Widerspiegelung is a component of the social and can only unfold in the context of the social as a whole: One can realize processes of cognition, personalizing cognition and recognition only towards humans with whom one comes into contact in such a way that Widerspiegelung and activities become possible. This can be unique or repeated more or less frequently. For the cognition of social function and position, one-time contact should usually suffice, which is often not yet sufficient for personalizing cognition. Recognition presupposes social relations, since recognition is only possible with more than one contact.

The social can be accomplished without and with social relations. In order to make clear the differences between the social in itself and its specification into a social relation and furthermore the resulting preconditions for recognition, personalizing cognition and recognition again, this is to be explained in more detail by way of example: If one meets someone at a narrow place in a pedestrian zone, one may notice that not both humans can pass the narrow place at the same time. One person has to wait so that the other person can go on without problems. As a rule, it should be sufficient to try to determine who is giving way to the other person by means of Widerspiegelung. Widerspiegelung is usually not carried out with the intensity that leads to a recognition of the specifics of the other person and later to a recognition. In the example described, the social has fulfilled all the determinations of the social: It was reflected and there were interrelated activities. If humans who already knew each other had met in the same narrow place, recognition would have set in via the Widerspiegelung. With recognition, in turn, knowledge from

3 Social Widerspiegelung in Humans: Fundamentals 107

previous encounters about the other person would be actualizable: one knows, for example, where this person lives and what profession he or she has. In this respect, there are points of reference and knowledge about the other person. One would then presumably not simply have passed each other by, but perhaps would have greeted each other and had a short conversation. Thus the characteristics of the social relation would have been realized: It is now a matter of socials between humans who have had several dealings with each other and who know each other. In this case, the Widerspiegelung takes over the sounding out of the dimension of recognition, of personalizing recognition and recognition: What kind of person is this that I am meeting, where and how have I already had dealings with him?

Widerspiegelung of other humans thus stands in a context, but remains open in its result. Before the Widerspiegelung of other humans begins, for example when they enter the field of vision, one does not yet know what results their Widerspiegelung will produce: If it is only a matter of recording a situation, as was explained for the example of the bottleneck in the pedestrian zone, the Widerspiegelung of other humans ends quickly and does not deepen the recording of information any further. If the Widerspiegelung reveals that one has met someone one knows, this is to be extended to the rapid working through of the previous social relationship: Where and how has one already met this person, does one have good memories of these encounters or were they rather unpleasant? But these are only the first differentiations that need to be developed further.

It is clear, however, that the process of Widerspiegelung within the framework of the social has a reference value that can vary: This is the dimension of experience and knowledge of the other person with whom one is in contact via the social. It may be that one has knowledge about the personal specifics of the other person, i.e. that one is familiar with all of his or her characteristics.[115] But it can also be that one sees someone for the first – and perhaps only – time, so that the Widerspiegelung in this case cannot be based on previous experiences with this person. Knowledge about this person cannot exist from the context of the social, since contacts with this person have not yet existed. Knowledge about the person, however, can come from the context of societal knowledge: If, for example, one can cognitively record via Widerspiegelung and the gnostic process inherent in it that someone wears the professional clothing of a salesperson or the corresponding uniform signals that this person works for the police, one knows something about the objective meaning of this person. However, direct experiences with these humans in the way that one has already reflected them and carried out social activities towards them have not yet existed: Thus, as a result of such encounters, one does not yet have any

---

[115] cf. Leontjev (1982) as well as Sect. 3.4 in this volume.

knowledge about whether these humans are to be classified in their actions, for example, as – in everyday language – friendly or less friendly. Such classifications, if it were possible to make them, would rather belong to the subjective meaning. This brings the second reference value of social Widerspiegelung into view, namely the subjectivity of the person being reflected: From this point of view, it is to be examined what subjective meaning the reflected has or could have. Social Widerspiegelung thus moves in relation to the two poles of experience and knowledge about the reflected and the subject standpoint of the reflected.

If one considers the possible forms that social Widerspiegelung can take, one must begin with the fact that there is as yet no knowledge or experience about the person currently being reflected. First-time or one-time social contacts have to be carried out without knowledge about the former course of such contacts: Since there were no contacts, no knowledge can have been gained from them. Here, too, there is a subject standpoint, but precisely none that can be based on earlier experiences and thus on knowledge derived from them. Alternatively, societal knowledge can be generalized to assumptions that, for example, shop assistants are always or never friendly. It is obvious that social Widerspiegelung in such forms entails an immanent probability of error. In contrast, repeated social contacts can build on knowledge about previous contacts: One knows what other humans have done in the context of such social contacts, and further knows how one used to evaluate it. This brings into play a subject standpoint that is not only currently formed, but can also take into account earlier stages. Did the other person, who is facing one now, contribute in any way to the increase of one's own subjective quality of life in former times or was the opposite the case? Widerspiegelung of other humans is thus related to topicality, but it can also take into account longitudinality if the conditions for this are met.

Widerspiegelung of other humans is thus related to the activities towards other humans, which can fail once or repeatedly. On the one hand, Widerspiegelung is a sequence in itself in humans's lives. On the other hand, Widerspiegelung is also the preparation of activities, which in turn are based on the acquisition of the situation. Widerspiegelung in general and also the Widerspiegelung of other humans is thus closely related to activities.

3.5 Social Widerspiegelung and Individuality

When humans reflect other humans, i.e. a social Widerspiegelung takes place, recognition plays a central role: Have you met the person you are now facing before? What kind of person is this that you are dealing with? On the one hand, these are

3 Social Widerspiegelung in Humans: Fundamentals 109

questions that arise in practical life, but they are also questions that require a theoretical breakdown. What can be said about the process that leads to the recognition of a person?

At its core, recognition is about distinguishing between humans by means of Widerspiegelung. Social Widerspiegelung does not have methods at its disposal such as the forms of fingerprint comparison or genetic analysis known from criminology. Social Widerspiegelung operates with the possibilities of human beings, which must make do with the already introduced components of Widerspiegelung, namely sensory perception, active control and gnostic processing up to the creation of an image. For the time being, the subject standpoint, which will be deepened later, remains excluded.[116]

The core of the process of recognition in social Widerspiegelung is the differentiation of humans. This distinction is possible because humans are not completely alike, but have recognizable differences. These differences between humans result in humans being unique: They are individuals, thus distinguishable from all other humans.

What constitutes an individual and individualization in humans is often recorded. For a better understanding of individualization in humans is therefore used with individualization in animals: Individualization and subsequently the emergence of an individual or individuals is already found in the phylogenetic process. The basic understanding of individualization in turn facilitates the understanding of the specifics of human individualization.

In the phylogenetic process, therefore, the possibility of individualisation arose in some more highly developed animals: such animals can recognise other animals on the basis of characteristics and thus gain orientation for their social behaviour.[117] An individual is thus recognizable on the basis of characteristics. The essence of the individual is that it is recognized by other animals of the same species. Accordingly, the animal is unique in that it can be individualized by other animals of the same species through Widerspiegelung. Out of – possibly – a multitude of animals of the same species, which are similar because of species identity, a single animal can be extracted: Only this one single animal exhibits the constellation of characteristics by which it can be recognized. This is again to be classified as a process that follows the pattern of *genus proximum et differentia specifica*[118]: Recognition and recognition have two poles. Firstly, membership of the same spe-

---

[116] cf. Sect. 3.6 in this volume.

[117] In the case of animals, we speak of behaviour; in the case of humans, we speak of action: Cf. Sects. 2.2 and 4.1 in this volume.

[118] cf. Chap. 1 in this volume

cies, i.e. the *genus proximum*, is established. Secondly, the *differentia specifica*, i.e. the uniqueness of the currently reflected animal, is determined.

Individualizability – i.e. recognizability – can refer to a few facts which are characteristics in the sense presented, i.e. which result in easily distinguishable and easily remembered characteristics. It should be noted that the differentiation of such characteristics depends on the reflective abilities of animals: Thus, for canine animals (Canidae), it is the respective scent that enables individualization as a trait. This in turn requires the possibility of a very differentiated sensory perception in the olfactory segment. However, such individualization is not immune to errors and deceptions: If a dog's own scent is overlaid by another, strong scent, recognition is no longer possible. In contrast to individualisability via one trait, individualisation via several traits is more secure: This form of individualisability refers to several or many traits and can thus accommodate the complexity of an animal. Such individualizability is found in more highly developed animals such as primates.

Individualizability at such a high level refers to many characteristics. These include not only physical characteristics, but also peculiarities that show up in the social: Individuals can be identified as supporters or as competitors, for example. Social behaviour based on individuality is differentiated and can thus more adequately accommodate the intentions of the animals, which can be based on individualisation.

An essential element of individualization, insofar as it has developed higher, is reciprocity. Recognition does not only run in one direction, recognition and individualization are reciprocal. This provides orientation for two or more individuals as to how reciprocal social behaviour is to be applied. Individualization, however, is not to be regarded as fixed for all time: Individuals are recognized because they exhibit familiar characteristics; but such characteristics can also change, and with them the individuals. For example, individuals grow up, become sexually mature and age. Social behavior must accordingly adapt individualization or adapt social behavior to the changed individuality. In the process, social behavior may change in basic orientation: If at times individuals were cooperated with, this may change to competition to driving other individuals out of the social structure. Individualization is the finding that other animals can be recognized and that orientations for social behavior result from such recognizability. Widerspiegelung is thus facilitated, resources can be saved: One does not have to sound out in every encounter what exactly constitutes the counterpart in the context of the social and what behavioral options are given. For example, the laborious and energy-consuming sounding out of hierarchies is no longer necessary: it has already been clarified in previous encounters who is higher in rank; through Widerspiegelung and individualization, this is updated and brought into the next contact as a prerequisite.

3 Social Widerspiegelung in Humans: Fundamentals 111

If one continues the analysis of the emergence of individuals and individualization in animals, the location is that individualization originates from the social: Individualization is to be grasped as the givenness of recognizability. To the individual belongs a life in the context of the social, in which on the one hand unique characteristics are formed, which on the other hand are recognized. This is to be embedded in the consideration of individualisation and the associated recognition in the social as a category, which can already be found in animals.[119] As long as recognition is not possible, the social remains limited: Differentiated activities towards other animals of the same species presuppose that these animals can be distinguished. Such a differentiating Widerspiegelung then allows activities to be individually tailored to other animals of the same species.

The important qualitative leap made in phylogenesis takes the social from contacts between animals that remain anonymous to each other to contacts between animals that can recognize each other and are thus individualizable to each other. For animals living in a social association, it is usually sufficient if they can differentiate whether other animals they encounter belong to the same species or not; this is the starting point for activities that constitute a social association. Further and individualizing differentiation is usually not necessary. Non-individualized social life becomes plastic in schools of fish, which often form the shape of a social association.[120]

The ability to individualize is thus a criterion that shapes and differentiates the social: Of all the animals that possess the social, some possess the capacity for individualization, others do not. Individualization can be defined as the recognition of uniqueness. Inherent in individualization is that individualization as a criterion results from the interaction of two or more animals: An animal must be unique in the sense that it stands out from other animals of the same species, that is, it must have significant differences. Another animal of the same species must be able to sustainably make distinctions between other animals of the same species: Individualisation only succeeds if the distinction between animals of the same species can be repeated and – at least in normal cases – leads to the same result.

The above account of individualization in animals is to be noted as a result and applied to the question of the extent to which individuals and individualization also exist in humans and – above all – what it implies when one speaks of humans as individuals. In terms of the development of the category of the social from the basic form to the final form, humans take individualization as a high developmental stage of the social. Human beings categorically represent the final form of the social and

---

[119] cf. Sect. 3.2 in this volume

[120] cf. Scheu and Autrata (2011).

thus carry within them the higher developments of the social, including individualization. Humans are thus potentially individuals for other humans: they can be recognized by other humans, which in turn provides orientation for the later social. Individualization and thus the constitution of individuals is based on Widerspiegelung.

It should be noted that individual and subject are not synonyms: The differences between individual and subject will be discussed below. In the meantime, however, the concept of the individual, with its origins in the social, needs further explanation: Individuals or individuality have nothing to do with particular idiosyncrasy or 'stepping out of line'. Individuality merely makes it possible to recognize other humans and, on this basis, to orient oneself as to how the social is to be applied to them.

This is the bridge to recognizing and being recognized: Through recognition, another person can be reflected in such a way that – through the recognition of characteristics – the uniqueness of the recognized person is established. In order to be able to determine the uniqueness, the recognized person must be linked with knowledge about this person. This is part of the gnostic process, which is part of the Widerspiegelung. It was stated that the gnostic process in the context of Widerspiegelung is a cognitive process in which societal knowledge about the nature of reality is related to and compared with sensory perceptions.[121] This was the general definition of the gnostic process in the context of Widerspiegelung. For Widerspiegelung in the context of the social, this specifies that known knowledge about a person is related to sensory perceptions to and about that person. Thus, when Eurykleia, the former nurse, recognizes Odysseus by means of the old boar scar, she can connect the knowledge that Odysseus was once wounded by a boar when he was young and has retained a scar from it with the person sitting in front of her, who has the same scar in the same place.

The individualisation and identification of an individual is realised in this case through being recognised by another person. Individualisation is therefore a two-sided process: for individualisation to be possible, on the one hand there must be a unique person who stands out from other humans and can be distinguished from them. On the other hand, individualization is the process that draws from the fact that recognition or anagnorisis takes place.[122]

Since the definition and conceptualization of the individual, individualization and individuality in the present publication do not coincide with the often used, but mostly very fuzzy understandings in this regard, it is necessary to explain this once

---

[121] cf. Sect. 2.4 in this volume

[122] cf. Chap. 1 in this volume

3 Social Widerspiegelung in Humans: Fundamentals

again in summary for humans: An individual is a person who has been recognized through social Widerspiegelung. One thus becomes an individual through recognition by others, who – since this process is part of the social – must belong to the same species, i.e. are also human beings. One thus becomes an individual as the *result of* recognition. Individualization is the *process* of recognition, that is, of establishing the specificity of another human being. Individuality denotes the *prerequisites* for recognition, i.e. the totality of all characteristics which distinguish the individual human being from all other human beings. Individuality, however, is complemented by the ability of other humans to distinguish between humans on the basis of their different characteristics: This would also be called individualizability.

These conceptual explanations are to be applied to an ancient hero who has already been mentioned several times: Odysseus is unique on the one hand. Only he is exactly this person with these characteristics and qualities. Eurykleia did not 'make' him this person, he was already this person before he met Eurykleia on his return to Ithaca. However, on the other hand, the recognition is incumbent on another person. It was Eurykleia whom Odysseus recognised via the combination of sensory perceptions and the gnostic process. This second side of individuation is done by another human being. One is an individual in such a case only through the involvement of another human being. But this can again be influenced by a human being through actions: Odysseus disguises himself as a beggar in order not to be hastily recognized. He has reasons for delaying individualization and recognition. On the other hand, he could promote recognition by others by immediately giving his name: even if, after years or decades, a person looks different from before, giving his name can facilitate and promote recognition. But it is also conceivable and common that humans change their names: Such a thing occurs, for example, when a person marries; the change of surname indicates a new family affiliation, but in the process may well make recognition more difficult. In other cases, the name is changed intentionally: The name as a permanent feature thus experiences a break. After the name change, the same person no longer 'trades' under the same name. This shifts the recognition: The person is now recognized because of a new name, the old name loses recognition.

Another way of recognition already mentioned is looking in the mirror,[123] at photographs or films. In this case, one recognizes oneself again, perhaps one can notice in old photos that one used to look different. Looking in the mirror, one may notice that one has grown older. Despite changes, you will probably recognize

---

[123] cf. Chap. 1 in this volume

yourself as the unique person you are. Recognition and individuation in this case is a gnostic process that one does alone and for oneself. The gnostic process in such forms of reference to individualization may also have the connotation of asking oneself whether one is already or still suitable as an individual for something. Thus Odysseus may also have had doubts as to whether he – having grown older – still had the heroic strength of younger years to defeat the suitors in his palace. Individualization in this sense, i.e., with a scrutinizing look at oneself, is conceived as self-reflection: How do I look, do I notice changes in myself?

Individuality in humans has biological sides, but also takes on the sociality of humans. Odysseus has a height or a hair colour, which are biological characteristics of his individuality. But hair can already be dyed, so the characteristic of hair color can also be socially overformed. Odysseus' disguise as a beggar again uses socially produced clothing as a means of disguising his individuality. In general, it is often the knowledge of certain facts that makes humans recognizable as individuals. Penelope only doubts and recognizes Odysseus as her husband when he shares that he knows how their marriage bed is constructed: namely, it is built on the trunk of an olive tree that was left standing when the house was built. Recognizing humans, then, also refers to features that come from humans's social lives.

Individuality and individuals are formed through recognition: Individuals are recognized either by other humans or by humans themselves through the use of aids. In recognition, the finding of known characteristics plays an important role. Individualization and the identification of a person is contrasted with the change that humans undergo throughout their lives: While they remain unique individuals, they change many of their characteristics. The key to dealing with the unique but changing individual is knowledge about the person in question: On the basis of this knowledge, humans can assign current results of Widerspiegelung and take adequate – social – actions.

The above determination of individuals and individuality results from the application of the scientific-theoretical methodology of the historical approach with the categorial analysis: individuals and individualization belong to the category of the social. In simple forms of the social, other animals can only be recognized as belonging to the same species, no further differentiation is possible. At this level of development, the formation of social associations is possible, such as fish or birds joining together to form swarms. Individualisation begins with the recognition of individual specimens of the same species in animals. Individualization becomes possible through appropriate social Widerspiegelung and allows the differentiation of activities from other animals of the same species. Individualization continues to

3 Social Widerspiegelung in Humans: Fundamentals 115

the final form in humans, which can incorporate into recognition the specificity of humans: What constitutes the specificity of humans in terms of recognition will be further explained below. For the determination of individuals and individuality made so far, it should be noted methodologically: It is a closed and verifiable derivation of what constitutes individuals.

For humans, it is the case that with them individuality also absorbs the social framing: Characteristics of humans by which they are recognized can be biological or social. Biological characteristics are, for example, height and figure; characteristics from the social framing of human existence are, for example, knowledge of a language or knowledge of a subject. Some characteristics of social provenance are used specifically to emphasize individuality: These include, for example, clothing that is intended to emphasize the uniqueness of the wearer. Body jewellery such as tattoos or piercings have a social origin, but permanently change the nature of the body.

There are, of course – this is not to be discussed in detail, but at least to be mentioned – also other understandings of individuality. Thus, the individual is often seen, admittedly without a derivation of this understanding of the term, as an individual who stands out from the masses. Beck, for example, has postulated that developments of the 1960s, such as rising prosperity, the increase in leisure time, as well as competition in educational institutions and at work, have since led to humans having to act more individually than in the past. According to Beck's thesis, in the absence of binding guidelines, humans have to stand out from the crowd and lead their lives individually. An individually led life is characterised by the fact that it differs from the lives of other humans. Beck calls the development away from predefined to self-selected forms of life individualization.[124]

An individual in such an understanding is only characterised by the fact that it differs from other humans. It should be critically reconsidered whether there were no individuals before the 1960s, i.e. whether individualisation only began there. Individualisation in the version found in Beck's work is essentially the transformation of a critical view of – supposedly established social developments – into a diagnosis of the resulting problematic or erroneous developments in individual humans.

It must also be questioned whether, before such social changes, there were actually forms of coexistence in which individuality was unnecessary. Beck states the social changes that caused connections to disintegrate in the 1960s. Tönnies states already for the end of the nineteenth century that there communities, which gave

---

[124] cf. Beck (1986).

humans support, disintegrated.[125] Consequently, individualization as a necessary separation from the masses should have already begun at the end of the nineteenth century.

Thus such conceptions of individuals and individualization are of dubious relationality: Is it conceivable that within the framework of communities individuals do not yet exist at all? Is it conceivable, in continuation, that individuality is formed only under the influence of social changes or social crises? This is not plausible, nor is it justifiable. Thus the reference to further views on individuals and individuality has to be left again. Still to be done, however, is a more precise account of subjects and subjectivity within the Widerspiegelung of other humans, as well as the demarcation from individuality.

3.6 Social Widerspiegelung from the Subject Standpoint

To be distinguished is subject from individual. This distinction is often not considered necessary: Walter, for example, speaks of the individual where, from the point of view of the authorship of the present publication, the term subject should be used.[126] This can be explained by distinguishing the two terms, individual and subject.

If one recalls once again Odysseus, who obviously returned to Ithaca for reasons that can essentially be attributed to the social,[127] the question arises as to what was at the centre of this: was he an individual or a subject? Odysseus himself probably did not ask himself this question: He wanted to see his wife and son again, probably also to resume his position as king, and thus to resume contact with the rest of the humans at court. These goals are understandable and comprehensible; for Odysseus, the necessity did not arise to link his goals with analytical terms in a gnostic process: it is typical that a gnostic process does take place; it is not usual, however, for the gnostic processes to be provided with analytical terms in the process of self-reflection. Odysseus, then, on his return home to Ithaca, was quickly able to ascertain via Widerspiegelung that the situation at his court had changed considerably: men were present as suitors who wanted to marry Penelope, Odysseus' wife, and thus also become rulers of Ithaca. Whether Odysseus was actually dead and whether Penelope wanted to marry again was of no concern to

---

[125] cf. Tönnies (1963).

[126] cf. Walter (2014); cf. Sect. 3.1 in this volume.

[127] cf. Sect. 3.2 in this volume

3 Social Widerspiegelung in Humans: Fundamentals 117

the suitors. These men ate and drank what the supplies of the court could provide. The situation found was certainly cause for a gnostic trial: how was Odysseus to deal with the situation? Could he trust the humans he knew from before if he wanted to take revenge on the uninvited suitors? These are questions that arose for Odysseus in the gnostic process to be assumed. But he probably did not bother to seek or find a theoretical classification for his situation.

If, on the other hand, one approaches Widerspiegelung in the context of the social analytically, as this publication does, such theory-related questions do arise: when humans move in the context of the social and thereby reflect other humans, they first do so as humans. Ulysses, then, is Ulysses when he mirrors other humans or acts towards them. Analytically, however, it is necessary to fan out further and to break down what is hidden beneath this determination on the surface.

It is necessary to take up the fundamental determination introduced, according to which Widerspiegelung is the depiction of objective reality from the subject's point of view.[128] This determination remains the same for the Widerspiegelung of other humans. The Widerspiegelung of other humans also begins with sensory perceptions. These include seeing, hearing, smelling and, on certain occasions, touching. For example, it is reasonable to assume that when Eurykleia washed Odysseus' feet, she discovered the scar on his thigh by touching it while washing it. The gnostic process, that is, comparison with existing knowledge, led her to conclude that the man with the scar must be Odysseus, who had once received such a scar as the result of a wound. The corresponding result of her Widerspiegelung, then, is that she has Odysseus before her: Though he is changed by the long time and the adventures he has had in the meantime, he is still the same man.

Other humans who have the knowledge that Ulysses has such a scar would also come to the same result of Widerspiegelung. Widerspiegelung, however, is influenced by the subject standpoint, which in turn results from reference to one's own quality of life. If any of the suitors who were at Odysseus' court had been able to recognize the scar as a feature and had then similarly concluded that the seemingly strange beggar was Odysseus, the outcome of the situation would have been different: This suitor would have seen his subjective quality of life, along with his life, as highly threatened and probably would have thought about appropriate steps. Options such as fleeing quickly or getting rid of the disagreeable ruler of Ithaca would probably have been conceivable. Into Widerspiegelung as a statement of objective reality-is it Odysseus or not? – enters via the gnostic process of comparison with the subject standpoint: If it is Ulysses, what are the consequences for my

---

[128] cf. Sect. 2.4 in this volume

subjective quality of life? Widerspiegelung in general as Widerspiegelung of other humans does not end as contemplation, but is the starting point for action.[129]

What this means is made clear by the comparison to the subject standpoint of Eurykleia in the same Widerspiegelung. Eurykleia is likely to be closely attached to her former foster child even after years and decades. Likewise, she is indebted to Penelope, the ruler beset by suitors. For Eurykleia, the surprising appearance of Odysseus is likely to open up the prospect that conditions at the court of Ithaca could change again: she is likely to hope that Odysseus will once again ascend the throne and that this would put an end to the harassment by the unpopular suitors. For Eurykleia, then, entirely different options open up as a Widerspiegelung result: She has the prospect of regaining a position of influence at court as the king's former long-time and close confidante. Eurykleia, full of joy, wants to rush to Penelope to deliver what Eurykleia sees as good news, but is prevented from doing so by Odysseus. In any case, from Eurykleia's subjective point of view, the realization that Odysseus has returned is a turning point that promises a positive turn for her subjective quality of life.

Following on from the concept of the *turning point*, the specificity of subjectivity for the Widerspiegelung of other humans is to be explained. The fact that humans are subjects is based on the fact that, on the one hand, they have a choice among possibilities and that, on the other hand, they can make this choice according to their subjective quality of life. The realization of these possibilities takes place through action. What constitutes action towards other humans, i.e. social action, will be pursued in more detail later.[130] The preparation of action prepares the decision between possibilities and includes the consideration of what exactly could be beneficial for the subjective quality of life. This preparation for action can be found in the Widerspiegelung: It is about the determination of the situation and the options that arise in relation to the situation.

If one analyses the sequence of Eurykleia's recognition of Odysseus from such points of view, it becomes clear that another option than the one chosen later would have been at least conceivable: Eurykleia could, for example, also have considered betraying Odysseus to the suitors in order to receive a reward. Likewise, she might have pretended not to recognize Odysseus at all: This could have been due to the fear of being involved in Odysseus' anticipated revenge plans, which was an undertaking with an uncertain outcome. Despite all emotional closeness to Odysseus, Eurykleia might have thought that – regardless of whether the suitors or Odysseus were victorious – she would have to continue to lead an existence as a maid.

---

[129] cf. Sect. 2.5.

[130] cf. Sect. 4.1 in this volume

3 Social Widerspiegelung in Humans: Fundamentals 119

Widerspiegelung remains on this side of the turning point between weighing and the decision that leads into action. Widerspiegelung of other humans thus comprises the sequence from sensory perception to the gnostic process involving the subject's point of view. What should be emphasized here is what is typically human: the dimension of the relationship of possibility to the world and thus also to other humans already enters into the Widerspiegelung. Humans have alternatives open to them between which they can choose. What these possibilities are essentially results from the societal knowledge about the space of possibilities. This knowledge allows us to anticipate which possibility can lead to which consequences for our own quality of life. Reflecting other humans therefore does not end with looking at other humans and coming to an identification: reflecting other humans happens from the subject's point of view with the aim of sounding out options for possible actions that benefit one's own quality of life or at least do not harm it.

Both subjectivity and individuality can be influenced by humans: it is possible to intervene in one's own subjectivity, for example to modify preferences, interests and the view of quality of life. Although such changes in subjectivity are often difficult, since there are long experiences behind subjectivity, they are nevertheless possible. One can also try to influence individuality in the sense of recognition: One can change one's own hairstyle and clothing in order to perhaps not be recognized or not be recognized so easily. Again, this is opposed by the fact that recognition – apart from one's own recognition in the mirror – is something that is carried out by other humans. Individuality, since it is based on recognition, is thus strongly located in other humans, is based on the selection of characteristics and corresponding mirroring performances. Thus humans who do not want to be recognized at all are recognized in spite of a different hairstyle and clothing; in the case of others a new hairstyle and clothing are overlooked, although they may have made an energetic effort to correct the individuality they have formed up to now. Individuality can therefore only be influenced by one's own efforts in correspondence with what other humans do, and thus remains in a relational relationship.

In summary, one can say that individual and subject are not synonyms, but refer to two different circumstances that both exist in the lives of humans. On the one hand, one is an individual in the sense of recognizing and being recognized in a social context, i.e. when one is recognized by other humans. On the other hand, one can also recognize oneself with aids such as a mirror or photos. One is a subject with and without a social context: subjectivity is the specifically human relationship to possibilities. On the one hand, the social is embedded in the structure of possibility as a specifically human relationship to the givenness of society. On the other hand, the possibility structure is opposed by subjectivity as a counterpart: Dealing with the possibility structure is guided by human subjectivity.

For Widerspiegelung as a whole, it is the case that one can only speak of Widerspiegelung from the subject standpoint. Only in a Widerspiegelung of other humans do individuals come into consideration at all who can recognize each other. Thus, for the question raised at the beginning of the subchapter, whether Odysseus returned to Ithaca as an individual or as a subject, one can give the Solomonic answer: He was both individual and subject. The two terms individual and subject are not synonyms, however; rather, they denote different dimensions of human beings, both of which are of importance to the social. The analytical separation will have to be kept in mind when looking at the shaping of the social.[131]

For the debate about the Widerspiegelung of other humans, it is to be noted that only the reference to the subject standpoint creates stringency: the Widerspiegelung of other humans or factual circumstances is to be determined uniformly in such a way that it is carried out from the subject standpoint. The subject standpoint is the center of human Widerspiegelung.

---

[131] cf. Chap. 6 in this volume

Social Widerspiegelung in Humans: Shaping

4

It needs to be explored in more detail how for humans – under the influence of social life – social Widerspiegelung and social activities are connected with each other. Conceptually, it should be pointed out that for humans all activities, including social ones, are actions. Accordingly, in the further argumentation for human beings, the concept of activity(ies) will no longer be used, but that of action and – individual – actions. What constitutes acting and actions will be explained in more detail.[1] First of all, however, the connection between social Widerspiegelung and social action has to be established: Social Widerspiegelung, after all, does not end with the creation of an image via Widerspiegelung, but this image is the starting point for social action. Again, social actions of other humans are important objects of social Widerspiegelung: social Widerspiegelung fathoms what these actions are and how they are to be evaluated. This interweaving of social Widerspiegelung and social actions is to be analytically broken down in this chapter.

We should remember the already well-known protagonist from Greek history, namely Odysseus. He probably had very close and frequent contact with Eurykleia during the time when she was his nurse. Although nothing is reported about this in the Iliad and Odyssey, it can be inferred from the fact that Eurykleia was Odysseus' nurse. The incident of Odysseus being wounded by a boar must have been later: thus Odysseus was a youth or man, but Eurykleia must have been in closer contact with him. How else could she have known about the scar on his thigh? During the time Odysseus was in the Trojan War and later completed his long journey back from Troy, Odysseus and Eurykleia were demonstrably not in immediate social

---

[1] cf. Sect. 4.1 in this volume.

© The Author(s), under exclusive license to Springer Fachmedien Wiesbaden GmbH, part of Springer Nature 2023
O. Autrata, B. Scheu, *Subjective quality of life and social work*,
https://doi.org/10.1007/978-3-658-40400-0_4

122   4 Social Widerspiegelung in Humans: Shaping

contact. Whether they occasionally thought of each other is again not recorded. It is not until Odysseus returns to Ithaca that Odysseus and Eurykleia meet again after many years.

In general, one can say: the social, which is composed of actions and Widerspiegelung, pervades human life. However, as the example of Odysseus and Eurykleia shows, it can vary: At some stages, encounters are frequent, humans see each other every day, and in some circumstances later on they do not see each other at all for years. In some phases of life social Widerspiegelung and social actions towards some humans are frequent, in other phases of life social Widerspiegelung and social actions towards the same humans are rare or do not take place at all. There are also humans whom one meets only once in life and accordingly reflects and acts towards them only once.

The first distinction that needs to be made is whether a form of social interaction has taken place at all: one has never come into contact with many humans in the sense of social interaction, one has not reflected these humans and has not become active towards them. This may be because the respective places of life are too far apart, or it may be pure coincidence. In fact, however, it is not at all the case that one comes into social contact with all humans who live in the same country or at the same time as oneself: there is no social Widerspiegelung and there are no social actions towards these humans.

One has contact with other humans in the sense of the social: So there is social Widerspiegelung and social action. But it remains with one-time encounters, one does not meet again later. A variant of such one-time encounters is that one actually does meet again later, but is not aware of it. This has already been illustrated for the example of contact with a salesperson in a department store.[2] The first basic constellation in which social Widerspiegelung and social action correspond with each other is thus that of one-time or at most rare encounters. Two things can be said about this: Social Widerspiegelung with its principles takes place in the process, but is usually limited to features that are important for the situation. It is therefore a matter of determining whether the person reflected is a salesperson, i.e. whether he or she holds a social position or function. Characteristics that lie outside the situational possibility space are often not reflected at all or only superficially. The second observation is that social Widerspiegelung and social action correspond even in such unique encounters: Social Widerspiegelung prepares social actions, social actions are based on social Widerspiegelungen. The sequence of the social, which includes Widerspiegelung and action, is given.

---

[2] cf. Sect. 3.3 in this volume.

4 Social Widerspiegelung in Humans: Shaping

The second basic constellation to be highlighted is the one in which one repeatedly comes into contact with humans in the sense of the social. The definition of this constellation includes the fact that humans not only repeatedly come into contact with each other in the sense of the social, but also find out in the process that they have already had contact with the respective other person in the sense of the social. This second basic constellation, in which social Widerspiegelung and social action are interwoven at least repeatedly, but often permanently and throughout life, is found in social relationships.

4.1 Social Widerspiegelung and Social Action

In this subchapter, the explanation of the connection between social Widerspiegelung and social actions is to be provided. These forms of social Widerspiegelung and social actions, which are yet to be explained, are present in all forms of the social in human beings. In the context of one-time encounters or encounters that do not lead to mutual recognition, these determinations of the formation of social Widerspiegelung and social actions remain. In the context of frequent and repeated contacts between humans that lead to mutual recognition, the basic determinations that always apply to the shaping of social Widerspiegelung and social action expand: This will be argued in the next subchapter. It should be noted that social Widerspiegelung and social action are always intertwined. Social Widerspiegelung prepares social actions, social actions are in turn based on the social Widerspiegelung of other humans's social actions: This connection is always present, regardless of whether one is just meeting the other person with whom one is dealing for the first time or has known him for a long time.

The first step is to break down action towards other humans as part of the social: The specifically human form of activity is action. Action is based on the possibility relation of humans to the world, thus it is an activity under the condition that possibilities of actions are available for choice.[3] For humans, this is to adapt the definition of the social: For human beings it is that they relate to other human beings by Widerspiegelung and action. So it is social action that is realized as activity between humans. For humans, then, we no longer have to speak of activity, but of social action or of individual social actions.

What constitutes action and structurally distinguishes it as a peculiarity found only in human beings must be determined in more detail: Humans have to deal with the possibilities that are available to them. It is obvious that possibilities require

---

[3] cf. Sect. 2.3 in this volume.

decisions as their counterpart: If humans lived in a determinate environment, they could not and would not have to make choices. However, since humans live in an environment of possibilities, the question arises as to how they make decisions in this respect. This is to be explained in terms of fundamental dimensions.

In order to be able to deal with possibilities, the first necessary step is to be able to recognize and distinguish them. In principle, such processes belong to the Widerspiegelung of the environment:[4] Widerspiegelung of the environment serves to grasp the structures relevant for one's own life. For human beings it is the case that the world confronts them – after and on the basis of transcending immediacy – as a field of possibilities. In order to be able to deal with these possibilities, i.e. to choose one for one's own actions and to reject others, it is first a matter of being able to recognize them as possibilities: As long as the environment exists as a space of possibilities, it is a compilation of potentialities. Only the transformation of one of the possibilities into action realizes a part of this potential. Widerspiegelung, then, is directed precisely at the compilation of possibilities and the identification of the potential inherent in them. It should be obvious that a potential cannot be directly sensory perceived: The potential is only revealed in the gnostic processes that follow sensory perception. In humans, therefore, the apprehension of the given structure of possibility as well as the subsequent preparation of actions encompasses the entire sequence of Widerspiegelung, ranging from the sensory perceptions and active control via the gnostic process of apprehension to an image of the given, taking into account the subject's point of view.

The particularities of being human become evident for Widerspiegelung at two points: first, this is the gnostic process of apprehension that begins after the sensory perception of the world or parts of it. In order to be able to recognize in the sensory-perceived parts of the world the structure of possibility inherent in them, there must be societal knowledge of their generalized meaning, which comes into play in the gnostic process: one can recognize a generalized meaning, and thus its possibilities, only by involving societal knowledge in this regard. This was explained in detail in an earlier publication of the authorship using the example of a hammer: if one does not know the generalized meaning of a hammer, namely that it is a tool with which one can hammer a nail into the wall, for example, even the most careful sensory perception will not help. One must have fundamentally grasped the generalized meaning of the hammer, which is inherent in it and is passed on as societal knowledge, in order to bring this to bear via Widerspiegelung in the case of an object that one gets to see on occasion: One can then establish, via the connection

---

[4] cf. Chap. 2 in this volume. and Scheu and Autrata (2011, p. 147 ff.).

4 Social Widerspiegelung in Humans: Shaping

between sensory perception and gnostic process, that one has a hammer in front of one and that such a hammer carries a specific generalized meaning.[5]

The second side of the Widerspiegelung is again also a gnostic process, which, however, is directed towards the comparison with one's own subject standpoint. The fact that something has a generalized meaning and is thus given as a possibility for corresponding action remains largely irrelevant if this cannot be linked to one's own subject standpoint. Widerspiegelung thus provides the answer to the question of what the quintessence of things or – for the social – of humans is for the reflecting person via the image that emerges at the end of the Widerspiegelung process: what is to be done, what actions are appropriate?

Human action is thus to be characterized as a selection among possibilities from the subject's point of view; Widerspiegelung prepares action and permits verification of whether action has produced the result that has emerged as a goal from the image. In this connection of Widerspiegelung and action, however, directional determinations and potentialities still enter in, which are to be explained in more detail: These are presuppositions that will also be ascertainable for the reference to other humans via the social. In order to make this comprehensible for the social, these determinations of direction and potentialities must first be determined in general terms: The relation of possibility of human beings to the world, as well as the subjectivity that enters into it, make possible and require decisions that are made by human beings under certain premises.

The starting point is what has been explained under the guiding concept of being a subject:[6] What humans see as beneficial for their own interests and needs is closely tied to their respective view of quality of life. Whether someone sees the realization of one or another possibility for the maintenance or increase of the own quality of life as appropriate, is to be decided only by her_himself. Quality of life is thus not something that is objectively given and the same for all humans. Quality of life is rather subjective and varies. Thus, attempts like Nussbaum's to fix quality of life as a catalogue of demands that turns out the same for all humans do not do justice to their object[7] : quality of life is not objective, but subjective; thus one has to speak of subjective quality of life. There is not only one possibility to realize quality of life for each person, but several, often even many possibilities. Thus, it is still impossible to determine from the outside what constitutes the increase or maintenance of quality of life for a person: this is only possible from the horizon of

---

[5] cf. Autrata and Scheu (2015, p. 123 ff.).

[6] cf. Sect. 3.6 in this volume.

[7] cf. e.g. Nussbaum in: Douglass et al. (1990).

subjectivity. Humans's quality of life can therefore only be adequately grasped as subjective quality of life.

For subjectivity, it is thus to be noted that it has unfolded in relation to the context of humans's relation of possibility to the world. Subjectivity is the measure of how humans shape the unfolding of quality of life in relation to socially given possibilities. Subjectivity, then, is – in the Latin sense of the word – what underlies humans's decisions vis-à-vis possibilities that present themselves. It is about quality of life that is to be maintained or achieved.

It is to be noted that both the grasping of the given possibilities and of one's own subjectivity is carried out via Widerspiegelung: Both the outward gaze and the inward gaze are part of Widerspiegelung. In this context, the gaze referred to is to be understood not only as a sensory perception, but above all as a gnostic process. In other words, there are no objectified inventory lists that provide a list of the given possibilities as well as one's own subjectivity, and perhaps even classify them hierarchically. Rather, Widerspiegelung is the process that attempts to break down the world as well as one's own subjectivity. Widerspiegelung prepares actions by forming an image that unites possibilities and subjectivity in an overall view: Actions, however, are based on this image, they take over the results of the created image with its achievements as well as distortions. Actions are the continuation of the result of Widerspiegelung. Narrowings of Widerspiegelung are found again in action, innovative actions are based on Widerspiegelung in the same way, but with a different directional determination.

This needs to be elaborated further: Humans's subjective quality of life unfolds in relation to possibilities that are available. These possibilities compose a space of possibilities for a person. Humans's lives are diverse and take place in different contexts: They work or do not find paid work, they live, they need food and they have leisure time. These are just a few examples, for different humans other relations can be of importance. However, it is to be noted that humans – considered over their entire life – are confronted with a conglomerate of possibilities. These possibilities outline a space of possibilities that challenges evaluations and decisions: Which of the possibilities is suitable for ensuring subjective quality of life? If one of the given possibilities meets the requirements of subjective quality of life, it can be perceived accordingly.

However, it can also be that the given space of possibilities is not suitable for realizing subjective quality of life. The existing possibilities do not allow the realization of what humans strive for as subjective quality of life. This makes the decision necessary, either to accept the given possibilities, which, however, do not allow the realization of subjective quality of life, or to try to change the given possibilities in order to come closer to the desired quality of life. Thus, the relation

4 Social Widerspiegelung in Humans: Shaping 127

of possibility of human beings to the world becomes a double relation of possibility: a decision has to be made between given possibilities and it has to be further decided whether the given possibilities are accepted or new possibilities are developed.

As soon as humans have made a decision for a certain possibility after Widerspiegelung of the given, they have to realize it by acting. Such an action can be the realization of a given possibility. It is just as much an action when – again acting – the possibility space is tried to be expanded or changed in order to achieve more suitable conditions for the realization of subjective quality of life. After the Widerspiegelung of the world and oneself, an action is chosen that seems promising to achieve subjective quality of life: It should be remembered that already Widerspiegelung of the world as Widerspiegelung of possibility structures is oriented towards potentialities.[8] The Widerspiegelung of oneself complements or corrects this. One's self is also to be grasped as an interplay of circumstances, potentials as well as interests and needs. Widerspiegelung of oneself is thus a process of weighing up which of the available possibilities best suits one's own personal specificity with its characteristics. An example: It would perhaps correspond well to one's own interests and needs if one could act successfully in the field of sport. Starting from the conditions and potentials, however, one may have to realize in the – critical – Widerspiegelung of oneself that the conditions and potentials for this are not, or perhaps not yet, available: One is too untrained or possibly too young or too old. The Widerspiegelung of oneself is an important part of the determination of the situation as well as the weighing of the potentials. The action that follows the Widerspiegelung is always based on the principle of the relationship of possibility to the world: since humans are not determined, but have the freedom to choose between several possibilities, action remains linked to intentionality and freedom of choice. Taking up the example from the world of sport, action can then also be such that one begins a training programme or disregards – supposedly given – age limits.

The fact that action is based on intentionality and freedom of choice should be noted, but at the same time contrasted with what has been said about spaces of possibility: Given possibility spaces offer possibilities, but may well be restrictive and limiting for the realization of subjective quality of life. In short, one has a choice, but none of the available possibilities is really satisfying. Possibilities available to humans result from the social life of humans: Humans's livelihoods are essentially given by their respective societies. Thus, on the one hand, humans are relieved of the contingencies and adversities of securing a livelihood vis-à-vis nature: The

---

[8] See above in this section.

128   4 Social Widerspiegelung in Humans: Shaping

provision of food, clothing or housing, for example, is ensured by social processes. Likewise, the transmission of knowledge is socially built in. Thus, essential possibilities that frame humans's lives derive from sociality. On the one hand, such social possibilities can promote and support humans's lives, but they can also restrict and hinder them. Humans are therefore faced with the decision as to which of the opportunities offered they will take up. If one has chosen a constricting possibility, this was intentional and voluntary, but nevertheless it also implies the acceptance of the restriction. Acting with such a determination of direction is restrictive acting: The restrictions of the possibility space are accepted in action and thus change their reference point. Possibilities and possibility spaces are social, action is bound to humans and thus subjective. Originally social restrictions are taken over into the sphere of humans through restrictive action.

Restrictive action includes – necessarily – self-hostility. By limiting their actions to restrictive spaces of possibility, humans cement such spaces of possibility. In this way, humans themselves contribute to fixing and perpetuating restrictive spaces of possibility. In this way, humans become enemies to themselves, but also to other humans: the perspective of realizing subjective quality of life is thwarted by settling into restrictive possibilities. At the very least, it is accepted that restrictive spaces of possibility are also established for other humans. Restrictive action, however, still has the additional value that it is realized competitively: Restrictive action is directed towards one's own advantage with the perspective of achieving such advantages at the expense of other humans.

The opposite directional determination shows generalized action. If humans have to determine that the possibilities available to them are not suitable for maintaining or improving subjective quality of life, the perspective can also be adopted that such limiting possibilities for action are to be expanded or changed. The limitations resulting from the given possibilities of action are not accepted; rather, humans strive to overcome such limitations: Action in this case becomes generalized action by realizing the quality of human action, namely subjective quality of life through the possibility relation to the world. Human action is generalized when it takes up the double relation of possibility of humans to the world – that is, the realization of given possibilities as well as the overcoming of a limiting space of possibility – in this completeness.

A second provision for generalized action is to be added: Human action is action of a human being in and towards the world. However, already in the explanation of what restrictive action is, it was pointed out that there are other acting human beings besides an acting human being: Restrictive action, it was illustrated, can lead to one person's action curtailing possibilities for other humans. To use a common image: If one person has already cut off the largest piece of a cake, there

4 Social Widerspiegelung in Humans: Shaping

is not much left for the other person(s) who later also want a piece of the cake. This interconnectedness of action between humans is also given for generalized action. Generalized action must include the perspective of generalizing the double relation of possibility of humans to the world, that is, of making it sustainable for all humans. Generalized action must therefore build on the fact that the gnostic grasp of the world – and of oneself – includes the grasp of other humans's interests, which in turn presupposes social Widerspiegelung. Generalized action without reference to the subjective quality of life of other humans cannot exist: That would be restrictive action again.

The relationship between Widerspiegelung and action in humans can be summarized in this way: The chosen option that seems best suited to realize subjective quality of life is translated into action. Action thus sets in after Widerspiegelung: Widerspiegelung captures the possibility space as well as – in comparison – the subjective quality of life. The guiding question here is: Does one of the given possibilities appear to be suitable for realizing subjective quality of life? If this is not the case, the second decision is whether to try to expand the possibility space or to settle in the given possibility space. This second decision is thus the directional decision between the restrictive and the generalized perspective. If this is further analytically separated, an action follows from the image obtained via Widerspiegelung. With the action, the chosen possibility is transformed into activity. In each case it has to be considered that after an action a new Widerspiegelung is carried out: What was achieved with the action, did it actually succeed in maintaining or improving subjective quality of life? This is followed by processes of comparison with possibilities and renewed actions. Thus human life is a sequence of Widerspiegelung and action. The confrontation with the world does not come to a standstill and only ends with the end of life.

Thus, important provisions on the connection between Widerspiegelung and action have been elaborated.[9] Now which of these belongs to the social? Every Widerspiegelung that is a Widerspiegelung of other humans is social Widerspiegelung. Every action that is an action towards other humans is social action. Widerspiegelung and action that do not directly relate to other humans are Widerspiegelung and action, but are not social Widerspiegelung and social action. The following definition was introduced earlier for social action: Social action is the specifically human form of action by and towards other humans.[10] This is to be extended as a definition for Widerspiegelung: Social Widerspiegelung is the specifically human form of Widerspiegelung of other humans.

---

[9] cf. Scheu and Autrata (2011, p. 179 ff.).

[10] cf. Scheu and Autrata (2018, p. 214 ff.).

Social Widerspiegelung and social action incorporate the determinations of Widerspiegelung and action: There are also the components of the structure of possibility and of the double determination of direction into the restrictive and generalized perspectives. Specifically, however, social Widerspiegelung and social action are directly related to other humans. Thus, social action is also based on social Widerspiegelung: the social Widerspiegelung that precedes social action refers to the situation that presents itself as well as to the subject's point of view. Social Widerspiegelung is at most a panoramic study in its approach, but immediately focuses on the determination of the given in accordance with one's own subjective quality of life. Social Widerspiegelung, which underlies social action, prepares action, i.e. it is guided by the intention to obtain information, to weigh this information and to compare it with one's own ideas and interests. For social action, the Widerspiegelung is directed towards other humans.

The social also confronts humans in a structure of possibility. In the case of the social, it is humans who form this possibility structure. If we reflect on the example of someone who is unsure of his way, cannot use his mobile phone with navigation app due to lack of network access, and would like to have relevant advice from other humans, it is the other humans on the street who form the possibility structure in this case. These humans may be knowledgeable about the location, so are able to provide adequate directions. However, they may also be unfamiliar with the place, or not very familiar with it. Then it is a question of whether they try to give directions: In some circumstances, directions so obtained may be more misleading than helpful. But it is also conceivable that humans are not inclined to try to help by giving directions: This may be due to lack of time, but racially motivated reservations are also possible, should the question about the right way be asked by someone who looks different. In order to receive usable directions, those seeking information can make a selection, i.e. specifically address those humans who can be assumed to have knowledge of the local conditions: this would exclude humans who are not themselves familiar with the area. The social Widerspiegelung, which is carried out for the selection among those who presumably know the place and those who presumably do not, concentrates again on relevant characteristics: A postman or a policeman, recognizable by their respective uniforms, could presumably be well suited to provide relevant information. Social Widerspiegelung concentrates on characteristics that belong to the specificity of the respective person, who is not known in his personal specificity with the entirety of his characteristics, but has a characteristic that seems evident for social Widerspiegelung.

It may be that the possibility spaces outlined in the example introduced are sufficient to achieve one's own interests and thus to realize quality of life. One received information that made it possible to find the place one was looking for

4 Social Widerspiegelung in Humans: Shaping

without any problems. In addition, the humans who provided information were friendly and concerned. Thus, one is relieved and has the feeling of being in a neighbourhood where humans care about other humans. However, the opposite can also be the case: information was refused brusquely, and the impression was created that it was not only a lack of time that was the decisive factor, but also reservations and prejudices. First of all, this brings with it a limiting space of possibilities – one cannot realize one's own quality of life because other humans are obstructing it – and secondly, the question of how to behave: Does one accept this nolens volens and comfort oneself that one can literally 'not eat good cherries' with some humans? This would already be close to a restrictive perspective. If one fully draws the lesson from this that one also 'gives strangers the cold shoulder' once in a while when the opportunity arises, one has taken the directional determination of the restrictive even further into one's own subjectivity. Would it be adequate, on the other hand, to react to a harsh or flippant answer to the question of the right way with protest, in order to act in a generalized social way? Presumably, a generalized perspective is likely to need more preparation and detours: One could think of implementing other forms of dealing with humans via a citizens' initiative.

The fact that such detours have to be taken in order to realize a generalized perspective of the social points to the specificity of the structure of possibility in the social: The social, being social, refers to human beings as living beings of the same species. The social, being human, is bound up in a structure of possibility. Putting this together, we find that the possibility structure of the social is incorporated in human beings. It is other humans towards whom it is reflected or acted upon. Thus possibilities for the selection of actions arise from the situatedness of other humans; this situatedness of other humans must in turn be grasped via Widerspiegelung. Reference has already been made to the social framing of the social, which also has an influence on the structure of possibilities.

The possibility structure of the social is to be clarified by an example: When young humans meet in a youth house, the youth house is the social framing of the meeting of the young humans. The youth centre has a spatial offer and is in its setting framing for the social, i.e. Widerspiegelung and action, between the young humans. If one contrasts this with the social framing that is given in a school, the differences become clear: in the youth centre and the school there is also Widerspiegelung and action between young humans, but the social framing is clearly different. But it remains a framing: one can neither act socially with the youth centre nor with the school, the youth centre and the school do not reflect either. The respective framing, however, certainly does not remain without influence on the social that takes place within the framing. Which influence this is in each case is not to be pursued further at this point.

The possibility structure of the social, however, results primarily from other young humans. The social does not refer to an inanimate object, but to other humans with their peculiarities. If one wants to read a book at school, the structure of possibility may depend on whether the book is available. If the book is available, one can engage with it: The book remains unchanged while one is engaged with it, since it is an object. If the desired book is not accessible, one will presumably regard this as a restriction of the possibility space, and – in the sense of extending the possibilities of action – will endeavour to ensure that the book is acquired. In all these options for action, the person acts in the school; the book is the object of the action.

In social Widerspiegelung and social action, humans face each other with the potential for their own Widerspiegelung and their own actions. The possibility structure is therefore not that of a subject to one or more objects, but that of subjects to subjects. If, for example, someone speaks to another person, it is open how the situation will develop. It is possible that a friendly reaction occurs and a conversation develops; it is also possible, however, that distancing or rejection becomes apparent and the conversation quickly peters out again.

In the case of humans, the possibility structure that is given to them enters into the social: they can choose between possibilities and can also change their possibility space. The spectrum of the social is expanded for humans by the fact that they can adopt knowledge and experience from the stock of the social for the social.

For example, when humans have learned to be able to play a musical instrument, playing the instrument is something that is based on societal knowledge about instruments and music in general. If one subsequently decides to not only want to play the instrument alone, one can do so with other humans. How and which humans one seeks and finds for this intention depends again on social framings: There is house music, traditional costume bands, rock groups or large orchestras. How broad in such groupings is the share of the social during music making can vary. One has eye contact in order to coordinate the right use: That is part of the Widerspiegelung. It can also be that one hugs each other after a successful performance: that would be a social act. It can also be that the social is limited to a short greeting at the beginning and end of the music making. However, the social is always related to the space of possibility in which it is performed: The greeting can be a conventional greeting formula or a gesture typical of the scene. Furthermore, the social is the result of the confrontation with the space of possibility: one would not be in the space of possibility of making music if one had not first learned an instrument. Making music together is preceded by decisions for or against a musical form. These decisions may have been under the influence of other humans, but

4 Social Widerspiegelung in Humans: Shaping 133

they always remain decisions that one has made oneself: If one has yielded to influences, that too was a decision made after reflecting and reflecting the situation.

Social Widerspiegelung and social action are thus embedded in the structure of possibility typical of human beings and absorb it. At the same time, the possibility structures of the social are not merely factual: for a person, other humans are the possibility structure of his social Widerspiegelung and social action. What in turn other humans do or are likely to do is important for the social. Are other humans likely to act on one's own intentions, or will they act against them? Again, this is not so easy to anticipate: Intentions are not written on humans's foreheads. On the contrary, it is often the case that it is rather the intention of humans to conceal interests.

4.2 Social Widerspiegelung and Social Relations

In the previous subchapter, the connection between Widerspiegelung and action was introduced in the context of the social in humans as a whole. These introduced determinations of the social apply to all forms of the social. This is to be continued to the circumstances in which one is dealing with humans whom one has already met several times and whom one can recognize.

For example, when you meet someone at the door to a building, you are first stopped in your tracks and must establish the presence of another person. The process of the social begins: The other person is reflected. This mirroring can be done routinely and leads to – first – results: It is a man or a woman, perhaps an age classification is made, and impressions about appearance or dress emerge. At the same time, it is determined whether one knows this other person or not. If one does not know the person, the possibilities for social action are probably not too great: one can smile at the other person, one can hold the door open or quickly push past in order not to lose any time.

Even if the exemplary social that might arise in the encounter at the door is brief, all the conditions of the social are fulfilled: There is a Widerspiegelung, there is a possibility structure, and there is comparison with one's own subjectivity, which then results in action. Even if you push the other person aside so that you can go through the door first, that is a social action: There may be a store in the building that has special offers, and one wants to at least diminish the other person's chances for a cheap purchase. Whichever of the exemplary possibilities for action is perceived, presumably it remains a one-time social Widerspiegelung and a one-time social action: one has looked at another person, one perhaps smiles, one holds the door open or pushes past. It can be further assumed that, should the meeting take place at the door of a building in a large city, the humans involved will not see each other again later, or at least will not recognize each other: The social thus remains unique, occurring between humans who are unknown to each other and will probably remain unknown.

At the door of a building in a big city it might not be the rule, but it is possible that social Widerspiegelung and social actions are in turn answered with social Widerspiegelung and social actions: One also takes in the other person's gaze, may smile back, thank them for holding the door open, or complain to the person who pushed past. Again, in the process, Widerspiegelungen have been made, possibilities recognized and examined, ultimately leading to action. It is questionable whether social Widerspiegelung has reached the level of recognition as the determination of a social function or position or even personalizing recognition:[11] But if, for example, the person reflected at the building door wears a uniform that identifies him/her as an employee of a security company, recognition would be possible. If one memorizes additionally characteristics of this security employee, also personalizing recognition would be conceivable. Recognition would only be possible if the person in question had been encountered before.

At least one piece of information is given by the social Widerspiegelung about the other person at the door: He/she has smiled, held the door open or pushed his/her way past. Social Widerspiegelung thus accompanies the sequence of the encounter at the building door. The assumption in the example described is that it does not remain with a brief and one-off Widerspiegelung, but rather that repeated Widerspiegelungen accompany the encounter. Social Widerspiegelung and social action become reciprocal: the respective second Widerspiegelungen and actions build on the first Widerspiegelungen and actions. The social in the exemplary encounter is based on information drawn from the preceding parts. So one already knows something about how the respective other humans deal with the social. This condenses the structure of the social: initial orientations are formed about what can perhaps be expected from the other person and how one can position oneself in relation to it.

The reciprocity of the social between the same humans marks the beginning of a social relationship. In order for it to become a social relationship, the characteristic of recognition must also be present. If social Widerspiegelung and social actions between the same humans become reciprocal, but the humans involved do not recognize each other, one cannot yet speak of a social relationship. It would be conceivable, for example, that humans repeatedly meet at the door to a large building: Humans look at each other, perhaps greet each other briefly, and possibly even

---

[11] cf. Sect. 3.4 in this volume.

4 Social Widerspiegelung in Humans: Shaping

hold the door open for those following, without, of course, taking any closer note of who they are. Thus, the other person or humans are not recognized; information and impressions from previous encounters cannot be individualized. In this case, the social does not reach the social relation. For social relations, on the other hand, it is constitutive that humans reciprocally and repeatedly reflect each other as well as reciprocally act socially; in addition, for a social relation to come into being, it must be given that the humans involved can recognize each other on the basis of characteristics in their personal specificity. Thus, the following definition can be given for the social relation: A social relation is the consequence of reciprocal social Widerspiegelungen as well as social actions between humans who recognize each other as individuals.

By way of explanation, it should be added that the concept of social relations encompasses a subset of the social as a whole: There are forms of the social, i.e. Widerspiegelung and social action, which are not reciprocal and for which recognition is not given. These would not be social relations, taking into account the above definition. In this respect, the conceptualization of social relations is consistent: the addition of the *relation to* the social distinguishes reciprocal and individualizing forms from non-reciprocal and non-individualizing forms of the social. However, relations between humans are always social: even business relations cannot do without a social component, that is, Widerspiegelung and social action. If one thinks this through further, the extension of relationships by the addition of *social* would seem dispensable. But if one were to speak only of relationships, the connection to the social would not be conceptually recognizable. In order to keep this reference to the social evident, the concept of *social relations* is retained.

If both the reciprocal social Widerspiegelungen and social actions between the same humans and mutual recognition are given, the social can build on information and experience: One knows, as a result of Widerspiegelung, how a particular person acted socially in the past in reciprocity. If, on the other hand, one meets a person for the first time, it is uncertain what he will do and how he will react to a social action: Is the other person pleased about a friendly gesture and returns it in a similar form or does she_he grimace because this is judged by the other person as unwanted closeness? Socializing in a situation where the other humans you meet are completely unknown is often underlaid with uncertainty and apprehension: One does not know what to do and what to refrain from doing. Social relationships, on the other hand, create a climate of familiarity in contrast to such situations of uncertainty: one knows what one can count on. One must add: one at least assumes to know what is to be expected.

Explicitly, it should be noted that social relations, following their definition, are found only in humans. This is derived from the determination that social relations include a sequence of social actions. Social, also reciprocal activities as well as individualization already exist in animals. On the other hand, actions are only given in relation to a possibility structure as well as on the basis of subjectivity: This, in turn, is exhibited only by humans. So it would be wrong to speak of social relations of animals: Animals live in social associations or social structures; social structures are a mode of repeated mutual social activities. But the activities of animals are not actions, since they lack the aspect of choice among possibilities, so that the concept of social relations must remain conceptually reserved for humans.

Social relations create new conditions for social Widerspiegelung in two respects: First, there is the dimension of information and knowledge already mentioned, on which social Widerspiegelung can build. Social Widerspiegelung in the context of a social relationship does not start at a zero point of information, where one knows nothing about the person standing opposite; rather, social Widerspiegelung continues known knowledge about the person standing opposite and supplements or corrects this with updated information. The second dimension that opens up for social Widerspiegelung in social relations is that social Widerspiegelung becomes reciprocal. This is based on the fact that in social relations two or more humans mutually and repeatedly reflect each other. While one person socially reflects another person, the second person does likewise: the second person reflects the first person. This is obvious and evident for the sub-area of sensory perception within mirroring: as long as one person can see, hear, smell or touch another person, so can the other person, as a rule. There are special cases in which, for example, the view is obscured for one of the humans involved or sensory perception is only possible in one direction due to other circumstances; in most cases, however, reciprocity is given for sensory perception.

If you think about this again with the example of Eurykleia and Odysseus, you can see: At their meeting after Odysseus' return, they both see each other again. It can be assumed that they both looked at each other. Sensory perception via vision thus took place simultaneously, albeit reciprocally: Eurykleia saw a beggar, Odysseus saw Eurykleia. Knowledge about their social relationship from earlier days flowed into the Widerspiegelung: Odysseus was obviously able to recognize Eurykleia without any problems, Eurykleia succeeded in recognizing Odysseus only because of the recognition of the scar as an unmistakable feature. However, the social Widerspiegelung does not end there: Odysseus notices that Eurykleia has recognized him and fears that she might announce this joyfully and loudly in the next moment. Social Widerspiegelung in such a context can be captured with the metaphor of a billiard ball: Eurykleia reflects Odysseus, the result comes back like the billiard ball from the gang and triggers in her – at least in the beginning – an action: She wants to express her joy. Vice versa and at the same moment Odysseus

4 Social Widerspiegelung in Humans: Shaping

reflects Eurykleia, again the result of his Widerspiegelung runs back like the billiard ball from the rail and triggers an action: He stops Eurykleia's shouts of joy. The metaphor is, of course, too mechanical, but it is meant to make clear that social Widerspiegelung in social relations is done at the same time by two or more humans, and is thereby directed at other humans involved.

The decisive instance for which results Widerspiegelung leads to is subjectivity.[12] This is also true for social Widerspiegelung in social relations, but it has to be extended: Since in social Widerspiegelung in social relations not only one person appears as a subject, but two or more at the same time and reflect each other, several subjectivities are involved. When one person reflects an object, the subject standpoint is to be assigned precisely to this one reflecting person. If, however, in such a reciprocal and interlocking social process of Widerspiegelung, several subject standpoints can be discerned, the question must be asked as to what connection these subject standpoints enter into. Is there, then, an intersubjectivity and what constitutes it? In order to clarify this question, however, we must once again begin with subjectivity.

It is always one's own subjectivity that guides social Widerspiegelung and the decision between social possibilities for action. In view of the situational circumstances, however, it quickly becomes clear that it is always subjective quality of life that is pursued or can be pursued in different situations. However, it is different aspects of quality of life that come into play in different circumstances: for example, one has preferences and interests that relate to eating and drinking; likewise, one may have ideas about what music contributes to quality of life. Furthermore, subjective quality of life also includes orientations towards educational careers or a desired profession. Subjective quality of life is therefore not to be reduced to a single-goal programme, but is the overall idea of what one strives for and considers good.

If one recalls once again the situational circumstances one encounters at the door to a building, it becomes clear that everyone brings with them ideas about subjective quality of life, which in turn are also socially framed. One might imagine that greeting other humans and smiling at them in a friendly manner is the right thing to do; societal knowledge about encounters with other humans and how they are shaped flows into such notions. In the continuation, one hopes that other humans will react to one's own greeting with a greeting and smile in turn. It is also conceivable that one wants to calmly make one's way into the building in the morning oneself and not spend time on greetings.

---

[12] cf. Sect. 3.6 in this volume.

Humans have such and other ideas of subjective quality of life. They reflect and act accordingly socially on this background: they greet curtly, they smile friendly or they lower their gaze and try to avoid contact with other humans. At the same time, social Widerspiegelung is used to determine what other humans do reciprocally. It is also conceivable that one tries to delay one's own social actions in order to first gain clues about what the other person is doing through Widerspiegelung. Social Widerspiegelung and social action have two kinds of reference values: firstly, the situation and secondly, the subjectivity of the other humans involved in the situation. Thus, inner deliberations, i.e. gnostic processes, are necessary to clarify what is appropriate.

Considering the situation, the question is in what way or dimension is social imaginable and appropriate. For example, is it possible to tug on someone's sleeve at said door to make physical contact and draw the other person into a longer conversation along the way? For one's own subjective quality of life, it might be desirable to find a hearing for pressing problems in such a conversation: One fears to lose one's job or one's partner. One's own subjectivity would thus certainly speak in favor of immediately beginning a social relationship with a social act – tugging at one's sleeve: In the conversation, in the hoped-for close and reciprocal contact, solutions to the problems would perhaps emerge.

On the other hand, the Widerspiegelung of the situation probably advises caution: it could well be that such an unmediated contact is perceived as harassment. A social relationship could develop as a result, but not one that is seen as desirable. A loud conversation could ensue, perhaps beginning with the words: What do you allow yourself! Such a conversation, too, would be a social relation-reciprocal social Widerspiegelung and social action between humans who would recognize each other after such a conversation but would not value meeting again-in the fully valid determinacy of social relations. Whether one's own subjective quality of life would be improved or worsened by such an argument, which would presumably be witnessed by others, depends on the subject's point of view: the general attention one receives can be seen as distinctly unpleasant, but also as the supportive presence of a large audience. One's own subjective quality of life would therefore either judge the unmediated start of the conversation as inappropriate to the given situation or come to the opposite conclusion, namely that it is precisely this and the subsequent scenario that creates the desired public attention in the first place.

The second dimension to which the social refers is the subjectivity of the other person: The social is, after all, addressed by one human being to one or more other human beings. Social Widerspiegelung and social action do not go into the void, but refer to other humans. The gnostic capture thereby refers to circumstances as well as to humans. For the social, the Widerspiegelung of the other person is im-

4 Social Widerspiegelung in Humans: Shaping 139

portant in order to be able to carry out social action appropriately. A simple example: waving at someone who is looking in the opposite direction will not achieve the inherent goal of the action, namely to greet.

Under the premise that the establishment of a social relationship is involved in a first contact, the reference to the subjectivity of the other person becomes important: Does the idea of a social relationship, i.e. repeated reciprocal mirroring as well as action including mutual recognition, fit the idea of subjective quality of life of the other person? Another important question here is: What could be the content of the social relation that is suitable to correspond to the notion of subjective quality of life of the two humans involved? Social relationships must have a recognizable meaning and fit to the subjectivity of the humans potentially involved.

Social relations of the kind described are often the result of voluntary choices and result from compatibilities in subjectivity. Other social relations – such as those in the family – are not originally based on voluntary choice; this will be discussed later. For social relations whose genesis is based on voluntary choices, it can be said that those involved in them have similar or at least complementary conceptions of subjective quality of life, which then flow into a social relation. The beginning of such social relationships must therefore have a meaning for the humans involved: The social relations must contribute – at least in anticipation – to the respective subjective quality of life, otherwise they would not be initiated. In this context, it must be remembered that subjective quality of life is something that contributes to an increase in quality of life *under* the *given conditions*. Subjective quality of life is also in the process of weighing up what can and cannot be achieved.

Other social relations are also based on entangled subjectivities, but in their formation they are not primarily the result of voluntariness. If one thinks back to the beginning of the social relationship of Eurykleia and Odysseus, it should be noted that she was his nurse. Even children are already capable of social relations, but whether Odysseus had a choice among wet nurses is doubtful. Similarly, as a servant at court, Eurykleia is unlikely to have been asked to be the wet nurse. For many social relationships it is true that they are important for the lives of those involved, that intensive social Widerspiegelung and action are essential to them, but the dimension of voluntariness must be considered more closely: as a constituent of the human, it remains the case that humans have a relationship of possibility to the world, i.e. that they can decide between alternatives. But if Eurykleia had refused to take on the task of a wet nurse, which subsequently gave rise to the social relationship with Odysseus, this would presumably have had lasting consequences for her. Such social relations thus involve the fact that humans are to be found in them as subjects who have to come to terms with the structure of framing possibilities.

Social relations thus arise under different premises. What becomes clear, however, is – despite and in spite of all the differences – an essential and constitutive feature that always constitutes social relations: social relations require the participation of the humans involved. In the case of social relations between strangers, it is still possible that the sequence breaks off after the first Widerspiegelungen and the first social action: the person who reflects and greets another person at the door in question may not receive a counter-greeting. The sequence of the social Widerspiegelung of another person and, as a consequence, of the greeting, is directed at a second person, who, however, does not feel obliged to offer a greeting and continues on his way without a greeting. It can be assumed that on the level of Widerspiegelung a confrontation with the greeting took place, but the second person decided not to return the greeting. Thus, the social action of greeting does not find a continuation through further reciprocal social actions. Apparently, social Widerspiegelung, including the gnostic process of comparison with one's own subjectivity, has led to the decision not to give a reciprocal greeting. The step of participation towards social relation is omitted, reciprocity does not take place.

However, social relationships often develop and accompany humans over longer periods of their lives. It is the case that the participation of two or more humans must take place in the unfolding of a social relationship: One person alone cannot have a social relationship; social relationships depend on the participation of at least two humans. It may be questionable to what extent social relations have been entered into voluntarily and an explicit decision has been made for the social relation in question. Social relations are embedded in the process of life and society: for example, social relations between parents and children are not based, at least for the children's side, on a decision to want to start this social relation. Rather, children, as well as parents, are faced with the task of being expected to conduct a social relationship with each other. This can be evaded: Parents have already abandoned their children, children have run away from home. One can critically evaluate families in which children are beaten or otherwise bullied. Analytically, however, it should be noted that such forms of contact are also part of social relations. Again, this demonstrates that the realization of subjective quality of life can deviate from common notions of 'right' or 'wrong': Beating children, for example, secures the power position of the parents who do it; subjective quality of life is thus generated in such ways as well. As long as reciprocal social Widerspiegelung and reciprocal action persist, the existence of social relations is maintained. Whether they always correspond to what is normatively thought about social relations by others remains open.

For social relations, the reference of two subjectivities to each other is necessary. Humans are always and in every case subjects. This means, as a consequence,

4 Social Widerspiegelung in Humans: Shaping

that humans bring their respective subjectivity into the social relationship: Each of the humans involved has ideas about his or her respective subjective quality of life, which is to be brought to bear within the framework of the developing social relationship. This corresponds to the principles of human action: human action is carried out in order to maintain or improve the subjective quality of life.[13] If one acts towards objects, one can deal with them as one sees fit: If one deals with a musical instrument and then puts it away to reach for a newspaper, the musical instrument will not be offended. If, on the other hand, one begins a social relationship with a human being and then engages – primarily or exclusively – with other human beings, the first human being may well be offended and turn away. This is only an exemplary constellation, but it is meant to provide the hint that for social relations the linking of subjectivities is inescapably necessary. This can be grasped with the concept of intersubjectivity.

Social relations are constituted by the reciprocal and repeated social Widerspiegelungen and social actions between the same humans, who thereby become recognizable individuals for each other. Humans are each endowed with subjectivity, which they bring to bear in shaping the social relationship. But since social relations are only possible through the participation of other humans, whereby in turn the respective other subjectivity comes into play, a reference to this other subjectivity must take place within the framework of the social relation. It should be emphasized that a reference to the subjectivity of another person is not to be thought of as merely joyful and gratifying: rather, through social Widerspiegelung, for example, an attempt is also made to recognize a potential threat posed by another person. Is the other person perhaps angry and about to strike? Contributing to the social relation can then mean trying to appease the other person and possibly taking the blame for something without actually being at fault. Social relation is an analytical term that carries no ethical exaggerations: The goal in social relations is – from the subject's point of view – to maintain or increase one's quality of life. However, this may well entail resorting to tactical or strategic manoeuvres that are detrimental to one's subjective quality of life in the long term.[14]

The sequence of Widerspiegelung and action is also found for intersubjectivity in social relations: Before one can act upon another subjectivity, a social process of Widerspiegelung takes place. One's own subjectivity, to begin with, is given to one: Quality of life is always subjective; there is no externally applicable standard for what constitutes quality of life for someone. Of course, this does not mean that one's own subjectivity is completely clarified and gnostically accessible for some-

---

[13] cf. Sect. 2.5 in this volume.
[14] cf. Sect. 4.1 in this volume.

142   4 Social Widerspiegelung in Humans: Shaping

one at any time: there are errors and deceptions; furthermore, subjective quality of life is not static, but can change. Thus there can be no doubt that every human being has subjectivity. Whether, of course, one's own subjectivity can be operationalized without doubt through gnostic processes towards oneself in such a way that subjectively correct actions within the framework of a social relationship are thus clearly evident, is to be questioned.

Involved in social relations is not only one's own subjectivity, but also that of another person: It is equally true for the other person that the yardstick for him within the social relationship is his subjective quality of life. Now, the humans involved in the social relationship do not blindly act socially in such a way that they only strive to achieve their own subjective quality of life. Such a thing may happen, but it brings with it the risk that social relationships will break down. Subjective qualities of life are tied back to subjectivity, i.e. they are not the same for all humans or at least well compatible between humans. Thus, different subjective qualities of life can – at first – be far apart and do not have to be in harmony with each other. If then, within the social relationship, only the respective subjective quality of life is pursued by the humans involved, the thereby – potentially – unfolding diversity of interests can exceed the carrying capacity of the social relationship. In view of the variability of quality of life, the idea that subjective qualities of life are the same between humans, i.e. that any kind of coordination between different ideas of quality of life would be unnecessary, is likely to apply at most to partial areas. Subjectivity of humans is unique, one can postulate: Subjectivity is the result of the complex life process of humans, which humans in turn can actively shape. It is extremely unlikely that this could lead to two identical results.

It is therefore probable that in social relations the subjectivities that come into contact with each other have to be checked for their fit. This happens via social Widerspiegelung, which tries to clarify this and also to connect it with one's own subjective ideas. If one recalls Bischof-Köhler's example of empathy incorporated in an experiment and thinks this through from the theoretical perspective of intersubjectivity in social relations, one can say:[15] The fact that a child cries because its teddy bear has lost a body part is readily accessible to social Widerspiegelung. Sensory perceptions that provide information about the situation are possible. At the very least, social norming is likely to provide essential impulses for comforting action to set in as a consequence. In Bischof-Köhler's example, it is therefore unlikely that social Widerspiegelung will lead to incorrect assessments, i.e. that it will not be recognised how the situation is to be assessed from the point of view of the subjectivity of the crying child; it is equally unlikely that conflicts will arise with

---

[15] cf. Sect. 3.1 in this volume.

4 Social Widerspiegelung in Humans: Shaping 143

one's own subjectivity, i.e. that one will see one's own subjective quality of life impaired if one comforts the crying child.

When humans's subjectivities come into contact with each other in social relations, a comparison takes place: Do they fit together or not? It can often be seen that – at least at first glance – intersubjectivity as the creation of a fit between subjective ideas about quality of life remains a desideratum. However, this cannot be the end, since otherwise social relations would regularly have to fail in view of a non-existent or incomplete fit of subjectivity. Thus, the possibility of an understanding or a reconciliation of interests must exist, at least in principle. This is to be found in intersubjectivity, whereby it should be added that the fact that intersubjectivity exists in principle does not mean that intersubjectivity succeeds in every case.

Intersubjectivity is thus the reciprocal effort to recognize and reconcile subjectivities within a social relationship. Each person carries his or her own subjectivity into a social relationship with the central element of subjective quality of life as a yardstick. Thus, at least two subjectivities are already involved in the unfolding of the social relationship. Since social relations always depend on the participation of the other person, a strict and unconnected coexistence of subjectivities is not possible. Subjectivities in social relations must therefore always enter into some form of connection with each other. This is what is to be called intersubjectivity: one human being with his subjectivity comes into contact in the social relation with another human being and his subjectivity.

Intersubjectivity is tied to social relations as a medium. One can be a subject vis-à-vis objects insofar as one realizes the possibility structure of the world and refers to one's own subjective quality of life when selecting or changing possibilities. But one cannot establish an intersubjective relationship with objects and, more generally, with inanimate nature as a whole. Nor is intersubjectivity possible with animals: intersubjectivity requires, as the opposite of a subject, another subject again. This is only given between humans. However, while all humans are subjects, one does not have an intersubjective relationship with all humans. Intersubjectivity is only possible in and through a/social relation. Intersubjectivity is not possible without the interlocking of repeated reciprocal social Widerspiegelungen as well as social actions and mutual individualization.

The central function of social Widerspiegelung results from the fact that subjectivity is not written on other humans's foreheads. You cannot tell from a person's face what subjective quality of life she or he is pursuing. An image of the subjective quality of life of another person can only be achieved through sensory perception and rarely through unique social Widerspiegelung. An approximation to the subjectivity of another person is possible via reciprocal social Widerspiegelung and social actions: In the inference of social actions that follow one's own social actions, one can infer, after gnostic utilization of the accompanying social Widerspiegelungen, which subjectivity was the basis for this. This is not a procedure that is completely secure and leads to accurate results in every case. But it is the only procedure possible for the production of intersubjectivity. It must be remembered that intersubjectivity in its determinacy is always to be thought of as a reciprocal process. If, for example, one attempts to illuminate the subjectivity of a person in a biography, this is a one-sided process: reciprocally, the person whose life is traced in the biography does not attempt to grasp the subjectivity of the biographer. It is therefore not a matter of intersubjectivity.

The inherent connection between social relations and intersubjectivity must be underlined: social relations are based on intersubjectivity, intersubjectivity is only possible within social relations. This does not say anything about the intensity, direction or even the success of social relations and intersubjectivity: we will come back to this later.[16] What is to be noted is the inner connection that is always given: there is an indissoluble junction between social relations and intersubjectivity. Social relations require the participation of at least two humans. The participation includes two things: One's own subjectivity is brought in and reference is made to the subjectivity of the other person involved in a reflecting and acting way, that is, intersubjectivity is realized. To repeat: this is nothing more and nothing less than an analytical statement. Who benefits from this and to what extent it can be considered successful is still out of the question. With the statement that humans are permanently and inescapably woven into the social relations they have through their own subjectivity and intersubjectivity, another theme, perhaps also a problem, becomes clear: humans are involved in social relations in a reflective and actively acting way; they are not passive and victims.

The second side of the junction between social relations and intersubjectivity is that intersubjectivity is only possible through and in social relations. In this context, intersubjectivity is to be understood in the Latin sense of the word as a connection and reference between two – or more – subjectivities. Intersubjectivity can only arise through social relations: The subjectivity of another person is not obvious and must first be opened up. The basis of this process of development are the social Widerspiegelungen and the social actions in the social relationship. The reciprocal and reciprocal social Widerspiegelungen and actions in a social relation are in turn the bracket that allows intersubjectivity to emerge on the basis of the reciprocal gnostic inference of the subjectivity underlying the actions. Intersubjectivity, then, is not a one-way process in which only one person seeks to

---

[16] cf. Chap. 5 in this volume.

4 Social Widerspiegelung in Humans: Shaping 145

understand another person's subjectivity. Intersubjectivity is necessarily a two-way process, since both humans involved in social relations must gain foundations for their future social via the intersubjective process.

The medium in which intersubjectivity unfolds is the social relations that two or more humans have with each other. Only through social relations is it possible for humans to relate to each other as subjects and thus for intersubjectivity to be formed. Intersubjectivity is thus on the one hand something like a means to an end: social relations require intersubjectivity as a regulative and controlling element. This is the sober and functionally oriented attribution that can be given to intersubjectivity. It must be said, however, that such a splitting off of functions from being a human being has to face the objection that precisely this is not permissible: a human being is a being as a whole, cannot be split up into parts or functions. The consideration of intersubjectivity in its functionality is thus to be classified as an analytical procedure, which, by means of analytical reduction, wants to direct the view to this functional context, but does not want to question the wholeness of a human being. On the other hand, intersubjectivity in social relations is something special in human life: Only in this special constellation, namely in social relations, does the relationship between two subjects, conceived as intersubjectivity, arise. Only in this way is it possible for one's own subjectivity to enter into relation with another subjectivity and for an interaction to occur between the two subjects: One subject reflects and acts socially with the other subject as addressee, the other subject reflects and acts socially with the first subject as addressee. Intersubjectivity can therefore only exist between subjects, but not between a subject and an object.

Intersubjectivity is thus something special in human life: It can only be achieved together with other humans through social relations. This, in turn, has effects on subjectivity and the version of subjective quality of life: insofar as subjective quality of life is directed towards the creation of intersubjectivity and, above all, a certain intersubjectivity that is conducive to one's own subjective quality of life, social Widerspiegelung as well as social action and social relations will be oriented towards it. Intersubjectivity is thus not only a means but also an end of social relations: It is striven for in order to achieve the connection with another subject that is important for one's own quality of life.

In summary, social Widerspiegelung and social action are always embedded in the possibility structure that frames human life. An important consideration here is that in the context of the social, other humans are part of this possibility structure. For social Widerspiegelung, the task is to fathom what the possibility structure offered by and through other humans is like. Are the other humans inclined to support one's options for action, or at least to tolerate them? Are the other humans perhaps more inclined to counter one's own courses of action? This is important information that shapes the outcome of one's social actions. Social Widerspiegelung is the sole and decisive source for this. Of course, social Widerspiegelung must take into account that it is by no means easily accessible and evident what other humans intend.

Through social relations and the possible repeated social Widerspiegelungen, at least more information is available about the other humans with whom one is in social contact. What is important is the intersubjectivity that arises in the process, through which humans are connected with each other as subjects. Intersubjectivity is only possible in social relations; it is based on the interlocking of contacts and, above all, of reciprocal social Widerspiegelungen. It should be noted that intersubjectivity is an analytical concept and not a normative one: intersubjectivity is the quality that arises through social Widerspiegelung and social action in social relations. But whether social relations and the intersubjectivity inherent in them are beneficial or detrimental to the subjective quality of life realized in them by one or more affected humans is an open question. Subjective quality of life in social relations can be realized in essential parts only through intersubjectivity, but it is also possible that intersubjectivity in social relations does not lead to the desired subjective quality of life for the humans involved in the long run.

This makes it clear that the social and especially social Widerspiegelung in its form in relation to social action and social relations carry decisive potential for the success or failure of human life. An improvement in social Widerspiegelung can contribute significantly to realizing subjective quality of life in the context of the social. This in turn provides clues to the question of how an improvement in social Widerspiegelung could be approached. Social work, which as a discipline is concerned with the social, its research and development, or at least should be concerned with it, should be taken into account here.[17]

In the presentation of the shaping of social Widerspiegelung in relation to social action and social relations, which was unfolded in this chapter, it became clear that this is a complex process: precisely the specificity of the social, namely that the socially reflected are in turn confronted with humans who also socially reflect and act, creates potentials as well as problem situations. The intersubjectivity that arises in social relations makes it clear that two or more subjects come into contact with each other through social Widerspiegelung and social action. Humans as subjects are in turn able to act at their own discretion and according to their respective subjectivity in the context of the social: The outcome of a situation is uncertain. On the one hand, this corresponds to everyday experience: one does not know ex ante for certain how an encounter with other humans will turn out. Even if one wants to

---

[17] cf. Sect. 6.1 in this volume and Scheu and Autrata (2018).

4 Social Widerspiegelung in Humans: Shaping 147

head for a certain result by exerting one's greatest efforts, this may possibly coincide with the efforts of the social counterpart or be diametrically opposed to them. This points to the other side, the side of the scientific recording of the formation of the social together with the social Widerspiegelung: the scientific recording of the social, which is composed of social actions and social Widerspiegelung, must also have cognitive possibilities to analytically break down the complex and interwoven of the social.

This will be pursued in the next chapter. Under the guiding concept of reciprocity, of understanding and of determining direction, analytical starting points are provided for being able to grasp the complexity of the social. From the analytical grasp of what part social Widerspiegelung plays in such interweavings of the social, perspectives in turn arise for how a development of the potentials of the social is to be thought.

Social Widerspiegelung in Humans: Perspectives

5

In the previous chapter it was explained that social Widerspiegelung in its shaping is part of the social and is positioned in relation to the second part of the social, the activities: social Widerspiegelung is embedded in social action and thus in social relations. Social Widerspiegelung captures circumstances and prepares action, one can summarize. Although social Widerspiegelung can be analytically broken down into individual processes of Widerspiegelung, it is, in accordance with its task, a permanent process: social Widerspiegelung follows the provisions of matter and is always in motion.[1] As long as humans live, they are in fact always subject to changes and developments, which are in turn captured by social Widerspiegelung. In this respect, the task of social Widerspiegelung is always only temporarily completed after a Widerspiegelung sequence: the next change or development requires renewed Widerspiegelung and the consideration of whether a social action is appropriate and, if so, which one.

Social Widerspiegelung is thus permanently part of the social. However, it is not the case that social Widerspiegelung only carries out the neutral observation of the given and only social action selects a certain direction. Rather, it is the case that the social is an overall process to which social Widerspiegelung and social action jointly contribute. As an example, social Widerspiegelung is used to choose whether to start a conversation and with whom. The conversation is then started via social action. Social Widerspiegelung is then used to check whether the conversation is proceeding satisfactorily and should be continued. Possibly the topic of the conversation has to be corrected or another interlocutor has to be brought in, but

---

[1] cf. Sect. 2.1 in this volume as well as Marx/Engels 1962a, MEW 20.

© The Author(s), under exclusive license to Springer Fachmedien Wiesbaden GmbH, part of Springer Nature 2023
O. Autrata, B. Scheu, *Subjective quality of life and social work*,
https://doi.org/10.1007/978-3-658-40400-0_5

perhaps also another place of conversation has to be suggested: This suggestion would then again be implemented through social action.

Social Widerspiegelung is therefore a permanent process, which must always focus anew on situations and above all on humans. This establishes *that* social Widerspiegelung is permanently and repeatedly in relation to other humans. However, it remains to be explained *how* social Widerspiegelung unfolds in relation to other humans. It is typical for social Widerspiegelung and for the social in general that it takes place in relation to other humans. One can read a book alone or ride a bicycle alone. In contrast, the social is consistently embedded in a relation to other humans. So the question is how to conceive of it: how is the social and the associated social Widerspiegelung created on the premise that other humans are affected by it? Social Widerspiegelung, after all, is not a one-way process in the way that someone sits behind a mirrored glass and observes others. Rather, in social Widerspiegelung and the social vis-à-vis, two or more humans face each other, all of whom are active, or at least can be active. This interlocking of the social and social Widerspiegelung is essential and needs to be explored in more detail. So this chapter is about interactions that can be found in the social and thus also in social Widerspiegelung: It is a peculiarity of the social that it does not have only one subject that reflects and acts, but that several subjects always relate to each other simultaneously or consecutively.

Beyond the provisions of social Widerspiegelung already introduced, specifics of the shaping of social Widerspiegelung in relation to others can be analytically derived: In three subchapters, this is explained via the dimensions of reciprocity, understanding, and directional provisions. In this way, the decisive role of social Widerspiegelung for the interconnectedness of the formation of the social as a whole is highlighted. At the same time, perspectives for shaping the social become discernible.

5.1 Reciprocity

Social Widerspiegelung is reciprocal by nature. Reciprocal, or the related noun reciprocity, refers to the fact that social Widerspiegelung takes place reciprocally: As long as one person socially reflects another person, the other person can equally socially reflect him. The term reciprocity is used to describe the fact that the range of sensory perception possibilities in humans is generally the same or at least similar: if one person can see, hear, smell or touch another person, the other person can do the same; pathogenic limitations are excluded. Thus, if social Widerspiegelung becomes possible for one person via sensory perception, it becomes so for the other person as well.

5 Social Widerspiegelung in Humans: Perspectives

A reciprocity of social Widerspiegelung in the sense of this reciprocity may be possible, but still does not take place: For example, humans can have different lines of sight, which can result in one person seeing the other, but the other not seeing the first. Further, there are also humans with visual or hearing impairments, which in turn limits their sensory perception: The reciprocity of social Widerspiegelung is at least impaired by the fact that mutual sensory perception via the same sense organs is limited or excluded; reciprocity can, however, be established by the fact that, for example, humans with visual impairments reflect their counterpart via hearing.

However, a lack of reciprocity of social Widerspiegelung does not have to stem only from the segment of sensory perception. The cause can also be the subject's point of view: In the example explained in detail, in which a customer looks for a salesperson in a department store in order to ask for the location of a product,[2] two different subject standpoints are recognizable. The customer will reflect socially with high intensity in order to find a salesperson she is looking for. However, the subject standpoint might be different for sales staff: They also have other work to do and will probably not reflect the customer socially with meticulousness in order to possibly be able to take up a request for advice. In such a case, the reciprocity of the social Widerspiegelung will not occur, or at least not immediately, due to different interests and intentions.

There are thus reasons why the reciprocity of social Widerspiegelung does not come into play on every occasion on which humans meet. However, the situations in which social Widerspiegelung is reciprocal predominate. It should be borne in mind that reciprocal social Widerspiegelung does not necessarily have to be intensive and protracted. For reciprocity to be established, it is enough for two humans in a scrum to take a look at each other and thereby – in the very streamlined gnostic process – perhaps come to the following reciprocal conclusion: The other person is not known to me, I do not have an occasion for his more detailed Widerspiegelung.

For social relations it is the case that they are based on reciprocal social Widerspiegelung: a constituent of social relations is that there is multiple social Widerspiegelung and social action between the humans who have such a social relationship, and that humans can recognise each other. Here, too, special cases would have to be taken into account that would affect reciprocity: Thus, while interrelated Widerspiegelung and action might have already taken place several times, recognition is also given, but this only proceeded from one person: The other person may not have noticed this social contact. Something like this would be conceivable, but could also be stored in this way: The other person noticed the multiple

---

[2] cf. Sect. 3.3 in this volume.

152   5 Social Widerspiegelung in Humans: Perspectives

social contact, but did not want to acknowledge that. In fact, there would have been reciprocity of mutual Widerspiegelung, but it was hidden under the consideration of not wanting to be involved in a social relationship. Such a process finds its proverbial expression in the maneuver of looking over someone.

Once one has taken note of the special cases and exceptions to the rule that social Widerspiegelung is generally reciprocal, one encounters another, very significant point of view in the consideration of reciprocity: reciprocity in social Widerspiegelung and thus in the social as a whole denotes an essential fact. Without reciprocity, the social would be gutted. The realization of the social would make no sense if reciprocity did not lead to interconnection in the social. Reciprocity is thus fundamentally based on mutuality. It should be noted, however, that reciprocity must not be simplified as commonality or cooperation: the slap given in response to the preceding slap is also part of the reciprocity of the social.

Such reciprocity Gabriel already states as the "(...) Grundmuster antiker Sozialbeziehungen".[3] As already described in the Gospel of Luke in the Bible, the rich can only experience salvation through the support of the poor: The support of the poor secured one's own salvation. Here reciprocity is treated in terms of exchange: Support for salvation. Whether the focus was not on the rich's own salvation cannot be clarified at this point. According to Gabriel, this form of reciprocity lasted until the fifteenth/sixteenth century and only changed with the establishment of poor relief. Critically, however, social relations of this kind would be more accurately termed social relations: When alms were given to the poor, it was usually not in social relations in which one directly reflected oneself socially and acted socially, but rather from a distance.

From this historically early statement of reciprocity, the determinacy of reciprocity is to be taken up: reciprocity refers not only to the factual, but is also the key term for the normative. Reciprocity is factually – more or less always – part of the social: However, the fact that humans reciprocally reflect each other socially says nothing about the interests that come to bear in the process. The reciprocal social Widerspiegelung includes ideas about what should happen in the social sphere and, above all, what the other humans should do. Reciprocity forms the yardstick here: do the other humans achieve the assumed norm value through their social actions or do they fall short of it? Since reciprocity in this sense of what is balanced or appropriate is difficult to determine, social Widerspiegelung is required: in this understanding, social Widerspiegelung is directed at the processes of giving, taking and reciprocating mentioned above. Is the relation right? This is the

---

[3] Gabriel in: Otto et al. (2008, p. 1288).

5 Social Widerspiegelung in Humans: Perspectives 153

central question with which social Widerspiegelung deals. Reciprocity thus not only refers to reciprocity in the social, but also focuses on reciprocity in the sense of a balance.

Adloff and Mau also deal with reciprocity. A partially critical view is to be directed towards them. Adloff and Mau regard reciprocity as "(…) die Logik des Gebens, Nehmens und Erwiderns (…)".[4] Reciprocity understood in this way is also based on the understanding of exchange. Taking up this idea, the disciplinary view of understandings of reciprocity oriented towards ethnography and sociology is to be directed in the following in order to grasp which understanding of reciprocity in social relations can be found there.

Adloff and Mau equate reciprocity with exchange.[5] Such explanations of reciprocity refer in turn to Mauss[6] and see reciprocity above all in the context of the exchange of gifts: "Der Gabentausch hat vor allem die Funktion, soziale Beziehungen aufzunehmen oder zu bekräftigen".[7] Thus, as Adloff and Mau see it, social relations are consummated in the act of gift-giving. Giving, receiving and reciprocating, as Adloff and Mau understand it, refers to the exchange of objects and is intended to help begin or continue social relationships. At this point, the authors emphasize that the aspect of reciprocation must be taken into account, because the giving of gifts always entails a reciprocation. The giving of gifts obliges to reciprocate with another gift: "Die Gegengabe erfolgt aus Angst vor der Repression des Gebers".[8]

Adloff and Mau's assessment that a counter-gift is given in order not to trigger repression on the part of the first gift-giver makes it clear that they are not thinking in terms of the situation surrounding a birthday or Christmas gift: Presumably, unrequited gifts are not likely to trigger joy there either and may also give rise to doubts as to whether the associated social relationships are in balance. Displeasure is to be expected, but probably not repression. This points to the background of the considerations of Adloff and Mau: These are ethnographic studies. The result of these studies is that gifts promote solidarity and have a binding and thus peacebuilding effect.[9] For a better understanding, these studies and their results should be briefly outlined.

---

[4] Adloff and Mau in: Adloff and Mau (2005b, p. 9).

[5] cf. Adloff and Mau in: Adloff and Mau (2005b, p. 14).

[6] cf. Mauss in: (Adloff and Mau 2005a, p. 61 ff.; first publication: 1923/24).

[7] Adloff and Mau in: Adloff and Mau (2005b, p. 13).

[8] Adloff and Mau in: Adloff and Mau (2005b, p. 14).

[9] cf. Adloff and Mau in: Adloff and Mau (2005b, p. 16).

154   5 Social Widerspiegelung in Humans: Perspectives

Mauss, whom Adloff and Mau use as a source for their argumentation, has carried out ethnographic and comparative studies on the distribution of economic benefits. In his investigations he has been able to identify – in his estimation – parts that "aus denen sich die so genannten primitiven Gesellschaften und auch jene Gesellschaften zusammensetzen, die wir archaische nennen können (…)".[10] To this it should be noted: The classification that societies are 'archaic' or 'primitive' is pejorative. With such statements, "(…) Eurozentrismus und Kolonialismus als immer noch aktuelle, inhärente Topoi des dominanten, westlichen Zivilisationsmodells (…)".[11] Societies that do not conform to this model of civilization are given pejorative attributes. For classification purposes, it should be said that Mauss wrote the cited text in the 1920s, i.e. in a significantly earlier historical period. Sahlins, to whom Adloff and Mau also refer, argues similarly to Mauss. Sahlins will be discussed later in this chapter. However, it should be noted in advance that Sahlins is also subject to criticism of a Eurocentric and colonialist view: in an essay from 1999 entitled *On the Sociology of Primitive Exchange,* Sahlins argues that this is an exchange of primitive humans under "(…) Bedingungen primitiver Gesellschaft (…)".[12] In key terms, forms of thought to be criticized become clear. Thus, in Mauss' and Sahlins' account, the term 'archaic' or 'primitive society' found in their texts is used in a distanced manner by the authorship of the present publication, made clear by single quotation marks.

After the preceding insertion, which has marked the critique of concepts and modes of argumentation, we must return to the presentation of Mauss's and Sahlins's results. To begin with Mauss: Mauss comes to the conclusion that in 'archaic societies', as he calls them, the gift received is always reciprocated or must be reciprocated: "In der skandinavischen und in vielen anderen Kulturen finden Austausch und Verträge in Form von Geschenken statt, die theoretisch freiwillig sind, in Wirklichkeit jedoch immer gegeben und erwidert werden *müssen*".[13] It should be noted that Mauss' assessments of Scandinavian culture refer to the Edda, which was written down in the twelfth and thirteenth centuries. Mauss mainly questions what the reason for the obligatory reciprocation of the gifts could be. He assumes that these 'reasons' will still operate in modern societies. Mauss notes that in the 'archaic societies' he has studied, which he has also found in Polynesia, humans did not primarily trade goods and commodities – in the sense of exchanging goods – but rather exchanged courtesies such as a feast or gifts. The emphasis here

---

[10] Mauss in: Adloff and Mau (2005a, p. 63).

[11] Melber in: Autrata et al. (1989, p. 29).

[12] Sahlins in: Adloff and Mau (2005a, p. 75).

[13] Mauss in: Adloff and Mau (2005a, p. 63); Herv. i. Orig.

5 Social Widerspiegelung in Humans: Perspectives 155

is on exchange, which takes place on a voluntary basis according to the principle of performance and reciprocity. Mauss names this principle as a "(…) *System der totalen Leistungen* (…)".[14] *The* characteristic of this system is that there is a clear obligation, firstly, to give a gift, secondly, to accept a gift, and thirdly, to reciprocate a gift. In this way, the gift becomes an object that is handed over, but which must also be returned, that is, reciprocated.

At this point it should be pointed out that this 'exchange' has always been from person to person: humans hand over gifts, humans accept these gifts and it is humans who return the gift. The 'exchange' of gifts thus takes place in the context of social relations; humans must know each other and be sure that their gift will be reciprocated. In 'archaic societies' – at least as authors such as Mauss describe it – this principle enabled survival and, moreover, peaceful social coexistence, which he describes as interrelated coexistence. It should be noted that in Mauss' usage, the social has the connotation of the pro-social: The social does not correspond to the definition of the term given in this paper.[15] For Mauss, the social is a system of social order that secures reciprocity: he states that all forms of determination for the exchange of gifts "(…) bringen nur *eine* Tatsache zum Ausdruck, *ein* soziales System, *eine* bestimmte Mentalität: dass nämlich alles (…) Gegenstand der Übergabe und der Rückgabe ist".[16]

We should now move on from Mauss to Sahlins. Sahlins follows Mauss in his argumentation and finds a vivid formulation: "Die Verbindung zwischen Güterströmen und sozialen Beziehungen ist reziprok. (…) Wenn Freunde Geschenke machen, so machen auch Geschenke Freunde".[17] Social relations are equated by Sahlins with friendly relations. Movens for the friendly relations are gifts. It should also be noted with respect to Sahlins that social relations are always thought of by him as friendly relations. It should be further noted that Sahlins sees social relations in the context of ethnographic research, that is, as contacts "(…) in der Wirklichkeit primitiver Gesellschaften".[18] The framing by the pejoratively apostrophized 'primitive societies' noted by Sahlins, often also assumed, comes to the inadmissibly generalizing conclusion that since gifts and presents always create and maintain friendships. The fact that gifts and presents can also be classified differently in their meaning is not taken into account: Gifts can initiate and consolidate

---

[14] Mauss in: Adloff and Mau (2005a, p. 67); Herv. i. Orig.
[15] cf. e.g. Sect. 3.2 in this volume.
[16] Mauss in: Adloff and Mau (2005a, p. 71); author's note.
[17] Sahlins in: Adloff and Mau (2005a, p. 75).
[18] Sahlins in: Adloff and Mau (2005a, p. 73).

156 5 Social Widerspiegelung in Humans: Perspectives

friendships, but they can also be merely material surrogates intended to replace the existence of a successful social relationship.

It should be noted, however, that there are methodological reservations about investigations in historically early or remote forms of society: The dignity of the results remains doubtful. It is questionable whether the exchange of gifts can always be seen as friendly. As a cross-check, it is worth recalling a historically uncertain, but at least frequently handed down example, that in the exchange of gifts, occasionally a gift of lesser value was exchanged for a good of much higher value. The Bible records that Jacob, the younger son of Isaac, once gave a plate of lentils as a gift to his older brother Esau when the latter returned home from hunting hungry and exhausted. In return, Jacob received the birthright. In this exchange, Jacob intentionally initiated a gift exchange that was decidedly disadvantageous to Esau. The birthright referred to is the legal position of primogeniture. This refers to an order of succession according to which only the firstborn and thus oldest child inherits and succeeds to the rights of a deceased person. Siblings are not considered in an order of succession according to the principle of primogeniture: Thus Jacob would have been left empty-handed after Isaac's death, but was able to rectify this by exchanging lentil dish for the birthright.[19] The described example of Jacob and Esau makes it clear that gifts and counter-gifts can also be underpinned by the declared intention to take advantage of others in the exchange of gifts. Scepticism is called for at least with regard to the exclusivity of the objectives that Mauss and Sahlins claim to have found as a result of their investigations into gift exchange: Why, in gift exchange of all things, should humans deal with each other only in a friendly and amicable manner? There is little doubt of this kind to be found in Mauss or Sahlins.

Sahlins continues: "Die Bewegung der Güter bestätigt die sozialen Beziehungen oder bringt sie erst in Bewegung".[20] Sahlins assumes the exchange of goods and the unfolding of social relations are closely related, at least for such 'primitive' forms of society. The exchange of goods can take place in two ways: "Hierbei handelt es sich um Prozesse des Zusammenlegens (Pooling) und der Umverteilung (Redistribution)".[21] The two forms of exchange differ in terms of their relational constellations: In the context of pooling, the exchange takes place within a group. In pooling, the exchange within a group, Sahlins assumes equality of interests. Redistribution, on the other hand, is based on differences in interests and different positions of groups that relate to each other reciprocally: "Reziprozität aber setzt

---

[19] cf. Württembergische Bibelanstalt (1964, p. 37 ff). (OT, Genesis 27).

[20] Sahlins in: Adloff and Mau (2005a, p. 75).

[21] Sahlins in: Adloff and Mau (2005a, p. 77).

5 Social Widerspiegelung in Humans: Perspectives

zwei Seiten voraus, zwei unterschiedliche sozioökonomische Interessen. Reziprozität kann zwar solidarische Beziehungen herstellen (…), aber der soziale Tatbestand der zwei Parteien ist unausweichlich".[22] The adjectival addition that the fact of the two parties is 'social' mainly provides an illustration of the quality of the social, but does not give any usable information.[23]

For 'primitive' societies, Sahlins found that the exchange of goods is closely related to social relationships. Goods are exchanged either within one's own group or family, that is, exchange takes place where humans are in cooperative relationship with each other. However, goods are also exchanged with other outside groups, which Sahlins calls reciprocal exchange. In the case of exchange between groups, this means that one group offers goods and the other group must respond to this offer by valuing the offer. The two groups may well have different interests, which must then be reconciled.

In Sahlins' sense, reciprocity means that goods are exchanged between two groups in the sense of giving and giving back and that there is a duality between these two groups in the sense of a difference of interests. Why, however, there should be no difference of interest within a group or family is not made clear. The biblical Jacob apparently saw socioeconomic differences of interest with his brother Esau enough to outmaneuver him in the exchange of lentil dish for birthright. More plausible than Sahlins' dichotomy between groups and families acting symbiotically within themselves versus exchanges between groups with party status seems to be that reciprocity – whether it involves the exchange of goods or social acts – always takes place between humans who, being subjects, exhibit differences of interest.

Although an understanding of subjectivity does not play a role in Sahlins' work, he does concede that even in the ethnographic observations differences in the expression of reciprocity became apparent: Thus "(…) wurde das *Kontinuum*, das Reziprozität ja ist, aufgedeckt: (…) Die Form des Austauschs pendelt von selbstloser Rücksichtnahme auf andere durch Gegenseitigkeit bis hin zum Eigennutz".[24] To what extent ethnographic observations or investigations in earlier or 'primitive' societies actually provide valid results or idyllizations may remain open: In substance, it can be stated that there is reciprocity between humans, but that the goals and interests pursued by humans vary.

Thus, Sahlins arrives at a distinction between different forms of reciprocity. This distinction classifies the aspect of return in the context of reciprocity of gifts.

---

[22] Sahlins in: Adloff and Mau (2005a, p. 77).

[23] See Scheu and Autrata (2018).

[24] Sahlins in: Adloff and Mau (2005a, p. 82).

158   5   Social Widerspiegelung in Humans: Perspectives

Sahlins names the first form with the term generalized reciprocity: "Der Empfang von Gütern beinhaltet die unbestimmte Verpflichtung, die Gabe zurückzuerstatten, wenn der Geber sie benötigt und/oder dies dem Empfänger möglich ist".[25] It should be emphasized in this somewhat ambiguous formulation that it is an indefinite obligation. Actually, no return is expected: "Ein praktischer Indikator für generalisierte Reziprozität ist ein dauernder einseitiger Fluss der Gaben".[26] Whether the designation as generalized reciprocity is meaningful remains to be seen. The second form is equilibrium reciprocity: gifts are returned within a short time: "Bei vollständigem Gleichgewicht wird der gebräuchliche Gegenwert des empfangenen Gegenstands getauscht und erfolgt ohne Verzögerung [sic]".[27] The third form is antisocial or negative reciprocity: an exchange takes place with the aim of obtaining the greatest benefit from the exchange. "'Negative Reziprozität' ist der Versuch, etwas umsonst und ungestraft zu bekommen".[28] Negative reciprocity for Sahlins includes theft. The exchange of Jacob's lentil dish for Esau's birthright would also probably be counted as negative or antisocial reciprocity. Once again, it should be noted that the use of the term antisocial reciprocity suggests that Sahlins connotes the social as prosocial.

It should also be noted that in Sahlins' account of reciprocity, the object of reciprocity is not clear: is reciprocity in Sahlins' sense about gifts and offerings or about the exchange of objects up to and including theft or robbery in order to gain possession of objects? Sahlins mixes the two without hesitation. For the exchange of objects, for example, it would have to be considered that such objects are usually produced specifically in order to be able to exchange them later. In Sahlins' statement that an exchange of such objects refers to a *customary value*, the distinction between a use value and the exchange value of an object enters, but without being explained.[29] Thus, commodity exchange would have to be considered as a component of the social economy under the influence of capitalism and to be distinguished from host gifts. Whether one can now classify theft or robbery as structurally identical and only formally different from gifts and the exchange of goods is doubtful. This is not to be pursued further here, but it is to be problematized in the respect that very different things are subsumed under the guiding concept of reciprocity.

Sahlins goes on to discuss the distribution of the forms of reciprocity he introduces. He notes – again drawing on ethnographic studies – that 'primitive' societies

---

[25] Sahlins in: Adloff and Mau (2005a, p. 82).

[26] Sahlins in: Adloff and Mau (2005a, p. 82).

[27] Sahlins in: Adloff and Mau (2005a, p. 82).

[28] Sahlins in: Adloff and Mau (2005a, p. 82).

[29] In detail on use-value and exchange-value: cf. Marx and Engels (1977, MEW 23, p. 49 ff.).

5 Social Widerspiegelung in Humans: Perspectives 159

were organized kinship-wise, that is, the humans living in them were in kinship relations with one another. Sahlins again relates this to the concept of social distance that he uses: "Die zwischen tauschenden Menschen bestehende soziale Distanz bedingt die Art und Weise des Tauschs".[30] Sahlins assumes that in such societies, which were strongly interwoven with kinship, there was little social distance between humans. Sahlins goes on to note that in groups with low social distance, exchange – Sahlins refers to this as reciprocity – is more of the generalized form, and in groups with further social distance, exchange tends to take on the 'antisocial' reciprocity. Social distance, in this usage in Sahlins, is an indicator of equality of interest among humans living in such societies. More precise and coherent would thus be the notion of a *social* distance. Whether the distribution of forms of reciprocity presented by Sahlins – in societies with low 'social' distance the generalised form dominates, in societies with high distance the 'antisocial' variant dominates – can be empirically proven remains questionable. Thus, Sahlins' considerations on reciprocity can only be noted, but are not shared by the authors. Perhaps Sahlins' results should at best only be regarded as food for thought and not as firm scientific conclusions? Sahlins himself relativizes that the conclusions derived from the ethnographic data "(...) abgeleiteten Schlüsse stellen eher ein Diskussionsangebot an die Ethnographie dar als einen Beitrag zur Theorie (...)".[31] Thus, it remains open whether the ethnographically collected connection between gifts and friendship can claim fundamental validity.

At least it should be noted that in contemporary societies the principle of giving gifts is no longer the exclusive strategy for ensuring survival: It is, however, still found, for example, in neoliberalism with its principle of demanding and promoting. But nevertheless the principle of 'exchange' has survived, even if not in the sense of a system of 'total benefits', as Mauss also described it. The principle of gifts and counter-gifts has survived in the case of Christmas, birthday or wedding presents: at Christmas humans give gifts to other humans, who accept the gift and return it immediately or on a suitable occasion. The basis for this is still interpersonal – i.e. social – relationships. Thus, it can be summarized that 'out-exchange' takes place on the basis of social relations on the one hand, but also that 'out-exchange' promotes social relations on the other hand. 'Out-exchange' is thus a reciprocal process. This can be stated in this way.

Thus, gifts and offerings and their reciprocity are anchored in social relations. It occasionally happens that gifts and presents are given to humans whom one does not know and with whom one therefore has no social relationship. This happens,

---

[30] Sahlins in: Adloff and Mau (2005a, p. 84).
[31] Sahlins in: Adloff and Mau (2005a, p. 73).

for example, in an election campaign: The question here would be whether the giving of gifts is not intended to suggest the existence of a social relationship. Since gifts are usually only given in close social relationships, humans who receive gifts would therefore have a close relationship with the givers. However, gifts and presents have no significance at all in the distribution of goods and commodities. Even the direct exchange – object for object – has had its day. Instead, goods and commodities are acquired against the payment of money. Also, as a rule, it is no longer the producers of goods and commodities who come into contact with those who demand them; the acquisition of goods and commodities is handled in sales outlets. Although one has to pay there, this has little to do with the reciprocity surrounding gifts. Reciprocity in connection with gifts and offerings remains tied to social relations. Admittedly, even and especially in social relations, the issue of how humans deal with reciprocity remains: If I give something to someone, do I expect a gift in return? Does the reciprocal gift have to be as large as the original gift? After what period of time should the reciprocal gift be given?

This raises the question of why humans do what is done around the reciprocity of gifts? Why do humans give gifts and why do they reciprocate the gift they receive? Mauss would answer this question this way: there is an obligation to do so. In other words, there is a norm according to which a gift must be reciprocated; if this is not done, a sanction would have to be expected. This consideration, based on Mauss or Sahlins, is not wrong, but it does not go far enough: it could perhaps also be stated for the present that a Christmas or birthday gift that is not reciprocated several times leads to disgruntlement on the part of the giver, perhaps even to a breakdown in the social relationship. However, this still does not clarify why humans started gift giving. One thing to think about in the context of the argument of this paper would be subjective quality of life. A gift can contribute to the recipient's subjective quality of life in two ways: first, the gift itself can be something that increases the recipient's subjective quality of life. Secondly, it can also be the gesture that someone chooses a suitable gift and hands it over; this makes it clear that one cares about the recipient's quality of life. It is also conceivable, however, that gifts are given for other motives: One's own quality of life is perhaps sought to be strengthened by giving more beautiful or more expensive gifts than the recipient. Giving and the quality of life that can be achieved through it becomes competitive.

Hillebrandt pursues a further approach to explaining reciprocity. He assumes that the exchange of objects, but also of information, "(…) nicht folgenlos für die Form der Reproduktion von Sozialität [ist, d. Verf.], weil durch Tauschprozesse soziale Beziehungen zwischen sozialen Akteuren entstehen und auf Dauer gestellt

5 Social Widerspiegelung in Humans: Perspectives 161

werden können, die neue Formen der Sozialität hervorbringen".[32] Hillebrandt speaks of humans as actors and subsequently also deals with the "(…) *Sozialdimension* der Tauschpraxis".[33] Hillebrandt assumes that humans with the same preferences, similar lifestyles and lifestyles meet each other more often. For example, they seek out the same leisure facilities or meet at the workplace. Only then can an exchange take place, which in turn can result in and consolidate social relationships, which is then the basis for reciprocity.

Thus, exchange practice, as Hillebrandt understands it, always involves humans. Hillebrandt concludes: "Damit soziale Praxisformen möglich werden, müssen nicht nur Formen der Habitualisierung von Sozialität abrufbar sein, die an Praxis beteiligten Akteure müssen zudem die anderen Akteure beobachten und diese mit praktischem Sinn ausstatten, damit sie zu Bezugspunkten der Praxis werden können".[34] For Hillebrandt, exchange and thus reciprocity is less significant from the point of view of what is exchanged and how. Hillebrandt assumes that in the process the participating actors reciprocally undergo the process of a social construction: The first actor constructs the second actor.

According to Hillebrandt, the practice of exchange – i.e. reciprocity – takes place between at least two humans who, on the one hand, have to recognize each other and, on the other hand, give each other a meaning. Reciprocal exchange can involve objects, but also information: Hillebrandt thus moves away from considerations of Mauss or Sahlins, who consider reciprocity only with regard to objects. Hillebrandt describes the forms of exchange he is referring to – entirely in the sense of symbolic interactionism – as meaning-giving or symbol-giving. It should be emphasized once again that the process of exchange is thereby subordinated: Reciprocity in Hillebrandt's terms denotes the process of other humans 'receiving meaning' in the context of exchange. One wonders: did humans have no meaning before the exchange?

The authors take a critical view of this – supposedly – meaning-giving process: Why do humans give other humans exactly the meaning they give them? Why do they use just that symbol and disregard another? Hillebrandt does not give an answer to this question. What is important is Hillebrandt's hint that in exchange and reciprocity not only objects are passed on. In the social, actions between humans are important. The assessment of whether reciprocity turns out as desired by the humans involved relates to this sphere of action between humans.

---

[32] Hillebrandt (2008, p. 9).

[33] Hillebrandt (2008, p. 180); Herv. i. Orig.

[34] Hillebrandt (2008, p. 181).

At this point it becomes clear that sociologically and ethnographically oriented explanations for reciprocity or reciprocal action are not sufficient and must be abandoned. The focus must be on humans and their subjectivity: It is a matter of clarifying the initial question of what role reciprocity plays in the context of the social as a whole and especially of social Widerspiegelung.

It has already been introduced and illustrated that reciprocity is a constitutive feature of social relations.[35] Widerspiegelung in humans in the context of the social needs other humans who also reflect; Widerspiegelung in the context of the social is based on reciprocity: social Widerspiegelung and social action are reciprocal, social Widerspiegelungen and social actions build on Widerspiegelungen and actions of others.

What needs to be made clear is that social acts are very often linked to expectations and ideas about what social act should be done by another person reciprocally to the first social act. This has already been considered for the area of gift giving: When one presents a gift, that is a social act. One may already hope for a countergift in order to see the reciprocity of the social relationship confirmed.

However, there are other social actions that are not linked to objects. For example, if one makes a declaration of love, one hopes for a reciprocal and concordant expression. This would establish reciprocity in terms of goals and subjective quality of life. If one reaps silence in response to the declaration of love addressed, reciprocity is questionable. Admittedly, silence could also be telling or – supported by a heartfelt smile – certainly be a signal of agreement.

In the context of the social, occasionally actions are ambiguous: one finds it difficult to clearly understand a social action as to what was meant by it. This is especially exhausting and perhaps stressful when, in the course of a certain expected reciprocity, one is uncertain whether the expressed social action of the other person or humans corresponds to what one expected. Reciprocity here captures the fit of one person's social actions to another person's ideas in the context of a social relationship.

On the one hand, this observation that reciprocity maps the fit of one person's social actions to another person's ideas leads to the question of how social actions between humans in social relationships take place or should take place: Social actions can hit just the 'right' thing and thus give rise to reciprocity. However, social actions can – quite the opposite – do exactly what they should not do or, sometimes even worse, do exactly what the other person imagines should not have been done under any circumstances.

---

[35] cf. Sect. 4.2 in this volume.

5 Social Widerspiegelung in Humans: Perspectives 163

At this point, however, the debate about reciprocity must focus on the other side of the social, namely on social Widerspiegelung. In the context of the social, processes of Widerspiegelung take place in that humans reflect other humans. That is, they perceive other humans, on the one hand, in their uniqueness and, on the other hand, with their choices. As a result of this Widerspiegelung process, humans seek to recognise their counterpart together with their intentionality, their wishes, needs, requirements and intentions. For this it is necessary that the counterpart (besides his own) also recognizes the intentionality of the other. The respective intentionalities must be recognized and compared with each other: A reciprocal recognition of the respective intentionalities must therefore be grasped.

Intentionality can hardly be reflected directly. Social Widerspiegelung must take the detour of filtering out the intentionality underlying a social action. In the course of establishing reciprocity of intentionalities, these must be extracted from social actions in a gnostic process of analysis.

That may sound theory-heavy. But if you imagine the situation that you – as a student or teacher – have given a lecture after meticulous preparation and with high commitment and then dead silence spreads in the hall, then perhaps the approach as well as the emotional state of the following social Widerspiegelung becomes clear: What is going on? Did one not recognize or reach the intentionality of the audience? One has expected a reaction that could have ranged from approving knocks to critical objections. This would have been within the range of an expected reciprocity of social action. Silence is difficult to capture through social Widerspiegelung. Is this perplexity or a concerted snub? But it could also be that the listeners are so reserved because reciprocity among themselves demands it: No one wants to rush forward in order not to be judged as chumming up by the others. Under certain circumstances, the social Widerspiegelung of facial expressions, gestures and body language provides clues for the breakdown of the situation.

Social Widerspiegelung in the horizon of reciprocity is an important, yet very complex and also error-prone process. For social relations it is indispensable to track whether the respective intentionalities of the participants match each other or not. However, it is not easy for social Widerspiegelung to come to a clear and unambiguous conclusion as to whether reciprocity exists in this respect.

In summary and by way of perspective, it can be said that reciprocity, as a desideratum that has or has not been achieved, is an essential benchmark of social relations. Above all, complaints about unsatisfactory social relations often refer to the stated lack of reciprocity. Of course, reciprocity is anything but an objective or objectifiable value: the provision of the existence of reciprocity is based on social Widerspiegelung of the social actions of other humans. In the process of social Widerspiegelung, the social actions are compared with one's own actions and,

164 5 Social Widerspiegelung in Humans: Perspectives

finally, a balance sheet is drawn up. Such provisions of reciprocity are based on the assumption that the social can be counted or calculated, although this is hardly ever the case.

Perspectives and development potentials for the social result from the fact that the social Widerspiegelung of reciprocity can detach itself from the proximity to the exchange of gifts or goods. The misunderstanding inherent in reciprocity is its classification in the vicinity of gift or commodity exchange. In fact, however, the reciprocal social relation is the connection of two subjects who, by their very subject status, exclude a direct comparison or even an offsetting of their social actions. Reciprocity is the mutual reference of subject-unique humans. The perspective and potential of reciprocity is thus to be thought dialectically in the way that a synthesis results from thesis and antithesis in the reciprocal social relationship. However, this in turn requires a social Widerspiegelung that does not aim at a difference calculation, but rather pursues intimating and incipient innovative potentials.

Of course, it would be nonsensical to prescribe or prescribe a normative goal for social Widerspiegelung: Social Widerspiegelung is inherently subjective; it makes no sense to standardize subjects. It should also be noted, however, that subjects are under the influence of social reality and forms of thought. If, on the other hand, social relations are to exploit the potential of what can be found in them, reciprocity must not be thought of as a levelling standard, but as a complementary relationship open to results. This is to be taken up as a question of the extent to which this can be implemented in and for social Widerspiegelung. Social Widerspiegelung is the key to how reciprocity develops in social relations. In social Widerspiegelung, ideas and concepts of the social as it is and as it should be are linked to what is received as a Widerspiegelung of a social relation.

5.2 Understanding

Social Widerspiegelung can generally be characterized as the attempt to adequately grasp other humans. One aspect that influences social Widerspiegelung, as already explained in the previous sub-chapter, is reciprocity: on the one hand, social Widerspiegelung is reciprocal in the sense of mutuality; on the other hand, social Widerspiegelung is reciprocal in the sense that, in the process of mutual Widerspiegelung, an attempt is made to ascertain the extent to which other humans's social actions correspond to one's own ideas and interests. The provision of reciprocity via social Widerspiegelung thus checks the balance or equilibrium in social relations.[36]

---

[36] cf. Sect. 4.2 in this volume.

5 Social Widerspiegelung in Humans: Perspectives

In a second respect – after reciprocity – the specificity of understanding for the shaping of social Widerspiegelung is to be explained. In order to delineate what is at stake here, the already familiar protagonists from the Greek mythological world should once again be consulted: Eurykleia recognized Odysseus when he returned to Ithaca. How she managed to do this despite adverse circumstances has already been described.[37] But did she also *understand why* Odysseus returned? The seemingly innocuous question raises some need for clarification.

From what is communicated in the saga, it is not clear whether Eurykleia understood why Odysseus returned. It is not even clear whether Eurykleia asked herself why Odysseus had arrived back home. Odysseus did not explain this further to Eurykleia either: heroes are often silent. We know from the saga, however, that Odysseus had to resist some temptations that would have made other perspectives conceivable: The beautiful goddess Calypso made Odysseus her lover, wanted to marry him, and additionally promised him immortality along with eternal youth. Nevertheless, Odysseus longed to return to his wife Penelope on Ithaca. After leaving Calypso, Odysseus met the equally beautiful and young king's daughter Nausikaa, who would not have been averse to marrying him. Odysseus resisted all these temptations and continued his adventurous journey home. However, he would obviously have had good reasons to continue his life as an immortal or as a royal successor at the side of Calypso or Nausikaa.

In fact, however – as far as the factual claims of sagas can be trusted – he did return to Ithaca. He must therefore have found a reason for himself why he wanted to expose himself to the dangers of returning home. But he did not communicate this rationale. Possibly it was of no further importance to Eurykleia why Odysseus had returned. What mattered was that he had done so, thus setting in motion the liberation of the court in Ithaca from Penelope's all-too-pushy suitors. Presumably, however, Calypso and Nausikaa had difficulty understanding why Odysseus had left them. Penelope may also have questioned why it took Odysseus so long to arrive home after the war against Troy: She found it hard to understand and may have doubted Odysseus' fidelity. This brings us back to the beginning. That Odysseus performed certain actions is obvious: he had to make a long and perilous journey to reach Ithaca. This action, that is, the accomplishment of the journey, was social in intention: Odysseus wanted to see his wife and son again. Odysseus has returned to Ithaca after years, and thus to his wife, his son, and various other humans he knew from earlier times: social Widerspiegelung of these humans was necessary in order to try to recognize Odysseus again and thus to state that he is back. But this did not mean that his actions were understood: Why has he returned, what are his

---

[37] cf. Chap. 1 in this volume.

166 5 Social Widerspiegelung in Humans: Perspectives

reasons? This is also part of social Widerspiegelung, but it requires a certain procedure of social Widerspiegelung: that is understanding.

Understanding does not come 'just like that'. One can look at Odysseus or another person for a long time without being able to understand his social actions. It should first be noted that understanding in this context of the social has two sides: First, this is the human being with his reasons, which may need to be understood. Secondly, it is another human being who understands the first human being and his reasons for acting socially in the way he did. So – referring to the first side of understanding – it is to be broken down how a person's reasons for acting socially in a certain way are formed. Further – related to the second side of understanding – it is to be broken down how another person's reasons for acting socially can be understood. For a better understanding, understanding a person's justification is to be distinguished from adopting or sharing this justification: whether one criticizes Odysseus' decision to return home after years to his wife and son Telemachos as conventional orientation or praises it as lived fidelity are evaluations. Understanding is the penetration of Odysseus' reasoning: whether one would act the same or differently in Odysseus' place is not important.

Understanding, then, is a thoroughly complex process in the spectrum of social Widerspiegelung that has several facets. But one can console oneself with the fact that understanding already appeared in Greek mythology as a task that had to be mastered. Understanding, then, exists in the practice of the social of humans: Admittedly, understanding as a parameter of social Widerspiegelung does not have the diffusion that reciprocity has, as presented in the previous subchapter. Social Widerspiegelung is – almost – always reciprocal. In contrast, many social actions are not understood; it is sometimes unnecessary, and sometimes impossible, to understand the justifications of social actions. That Odysseus left Kalypso and Nausikaa to arrive back in Ithaca later is an evidential social action. But did Calypso and Nausikaa understand why he did this? Did they even want to know?

Understanding is a special form of social Widerspiegelung, which deals with the social Widerspiegelung of the obvious with backgrounds and – more precisely – justifications of social action. It is not only a matter of establishing that someone has done something, but beyond that the question arises as to why this was done. Understanding, then, is a far-reaching engagement with another person, aimed at understanding the reasons for his or her actions. This in turn has an impact on the gnostic process of apprehending and evaluating that action: under the impression of understanding the motives that led to a social action, it may be evaluated differently. Thus, while understanding is not something that always and consistently occurs or must occur in the context of social Widerspiegelung, understanding is a process with high weighting for one's subsequent social actions. If one

5 Social Widerspiegelung in Humans: Perspectives 167

mentally seeks a connection to the experiences made by Odysseus and the women he encountered on his long journey back from Troy to Ithaca, the question arises: Is it not the case that, in the case of separations in partnership relationships, one tries with great energy to understand what reasons the partner has for his or her actions?

Understanding thus very much plays a role in the practice of the social of humans, but rarely is understanding analytically broken down in the context of the social. It is, of course, impossible to understand Odysseus with the Capabilities Approach as a yardstick: What Kalypso or later Nausikaa offer Odysseus as a standard of living arguably leaves nothing to be desired. Even the "lustvollen Erfahrungen"[38] demanded by Galamaga or Nussbaum in their catalogue should not have been lacking for Odysseus. The fact that Odysseus nevertheless longs to return home does not fit in with Galamaga's and Nussbaum's catalogue: he would have to be completely satisfied with the quality of life offered to him on Kalypso's island of Ogygia. Only with the subjective quality of life introduced in the present publication is the theoretical key given to conceiving a subjective reference for justifications of social action.

Before understanding, it must be analytically unfolded what can or should be understood in the context of the social. Understanding in the context of the social is a process within social Widerspiegelung. Understanding in the context of the social is thus structurally similar to recognition: Both are processes within social Widerspiegelung that lead to specific insights about another person. In recognition, other humans are recognized again, so one may find that one has met these humans before. In order for such recognition to be possible, social Widerspiegelung must be used to establish the presence of certain characteristics that can be remembered. This has already been explained.[39] The key to the success of recognition, then, is features, which includes Odysseus' scar, which was recognized by Eurykleia. But what does understanding refer to in the context of the social, what is understood there?

Understanding also refers to features, one can postulate in advance: They are not, however, such obvious features as a scar. What humans do in the social sphere is sometimes cryptic and not easy to decipher. Again, however, it must be assumed that humans also have good reasons in the social for doing one thing and not doing another. Understanding must therefore make it possible to comprehend this.

This comprehension refers to three dimensions: These are conditions, meanings and ultimately justifications. Later, reference will be made to subjectivity and the

---

[38] Galamaga (2014, p. 60); cf. also: Sect. 2.5 in this volume.
[39] cf. Chap. 1 in this volume.

subjective quality of life. So that readers do not lose the overview at this point, two things should be pointed out: Firstly, the social aspects of humans, when broken down analytically, reveal quite complex interrelationships; secondly, however, these interrelationships must in turn also be grasped and processed by humans in their everyday lives. If humans can cope with the demands of the social in their everyday lives, this must also and especially be feasible for an analysis of the social.

First of all, an exclusion has to be made when thinking about conditions and meanings as dimensions of understanding: This is not to say that all of a sudden understanding as well as social Widerspiegelung as a whole can or should be regarded as determined by conditions and meanings. On the other hand, it is not the case that humans choose what they do socially at random: Odysseus did not let the dice decide whether or not to travel on. Nor is it random how humans conduct social relations: Rather, social actions are justified. The reasons, in turn, for why a particular social action is chosen or a social relation is conducted in a particular way are fed by the social Widerspiegelung of the realm of conditions and meanings. Therefore, the comprehension of justifications depends on the breakdown of conditions and meanings. The goal of the social Widerspiegelung of justifications and their anchoring in conditions and meanings is in turn the understanding of what another person does or has already done.

The aim of this subchapter is to work out the connection between the preconditions of social action in social relations and the action actually selected and realised: These presuppositions are established via understanding. From the point of view of the human being as a subject, it can be stated that the social action selected in each case must be more suitable than all other possible actions: from the subject's point of view, i.e. on the basis of the comparison of possible actions with the requirements of the subjective quality of life, it must have advantages over other actions. Actions of humans are, it can be stated so generally, subjectively justified. Humans compress their own Widerspiegelung of the situation, which in the gnostic process carries out the comparison of possibilities with their own preferences, into a subjective justification: Odysseus thus had to grasp his situation on the island of Ogygia and his life with Calypso, as well as make the comparison with the return to Ithaca to Penelope, in order to derive from this the justification for precisely one action to be chosen. Actions are – again generally speaking – subjectively justified, the subjective justification is the result of one's own Widerspiegelung of the given and the resulting selection of an action.

Thus, on the side of the socially acting humans there is the connection of conditions and meanings to the shaping of subjective justification of actions. If, on the other hand, humans want to understand why they act socially in this way and not in

5 Social Widerspiegelung in Humans: Perspectives 169

a different way, and how this subjective justification relates to conditions and meanings, understanding must be achieved through social Widerspiegelung.

The end point is thus the subjective justification that marks the decision for a certain action. Before this end point, there is the confrontation with the space of possibilities, which takes place primarily through social Widerspiegelung. However, this in turn must be broken down and differentiated to the effect that knowledge and experience enter into the Widerspiegelung: Humans can gnostically unravel realities and structurings of the social, which are established via Widerspiegelung, on the basis of their knowledge in this regard.

What this means and how it turns out can be illustrated by examples of how social Widerspiegelung of conditions and meanings unfolds. Reference should be made to social relations, since the social Widerspiegelung of conditions and meanings is of particular importance in this context. In the context of – one-off – social action, the social Widerspiegelung of conditions and meanings is only possible to a limited extent: conditions and meanings are usually not revealed 'at first glance'; more contacts are needed for this. If one assumes that social relations already exist, that is, that one is in a context of reciprocal social action as well as reciprocal Widerspiegelung with humans and that these are known to other humans as individuals, then these are structures with a social connotation: they are, for example, social relations in a professional context or in the context of an education, in a family, in a club or a driving school. Social relations unfold in such contexts vis-à-vis their respective given preconditions, which in turn can be differentiated into conditions and meanings.

First of all, other humans are an indispensable condition of social relations: One can only enter into social relations with other humans, so the presence of other humans is a condition for social relations to become possible at all. This continues in that the specificity of each person shapes the conditions for social relations: Humans are men, women, or occupy a type of the third sex and have an age; furthermore, humans have undergone an education and occupy a social position – of whatever kind. This is only an exemplary list, which is meant to emphasize that humans are a condition for social relations: The so-being of humans is given and presupposed for action in the social relation. At the same time, although the 'so-ness' of humans is given as a condition, it is by no means unchangeable: humans age and die at the end of life, but they also develop and change. From the point of view of the subject, these humans are and remain a condition of social relations, and are thus a prerequisite for social action and social Widerspiegelung. Hypothetically speaking, if someone were to live in a place in the world where there are no other humans, social relations would be excluded. Of course, this is only conceivable temporarily, but it should make clear that humans are also to be understood as a condition, as a manifestation of the given.

In addition to the provision that humans are the condition of social relations, there is the further provision that they also have a meaning. The meaning side is to be differentiated to the effect that they have both an objective and a subjective meaning.

What has not yet been grasped is how it is possible to grasp such conditions and meanings through social Widerspiegelung. It has been established, however, that humans, in that they are the object of social Widerspiegelung, carry characteristics in themselves that can be grasped and broken down through social Widerspiegelung. This, however, is in turn known and familiar as knowledge to the humans who, as subjects, reflect socially. Social Widerspiegelung in the sense that other humans are thereby grasped as conditions and meanings would not be possible if there were no such knowledge about conditions and meanings. To illustrate: one must know that there are colours; only when one knows this can one attempt to distinguish colours.

For a better understanding of how the connection of conditions and meanings to social Widerspiegelung is to be seen, non-social Widerspiegelung and non-social action will be presented in a recapitulatory excursus. In contrast to non-social Widerspiegelung and action, the aim of this intermediate step is to make it easier to understand what constitutes the specificity of social Widerspiegelung and action with the related specification of conditions and meanings.

Non-social Widerspiegelung and action refers to a socially given space of possibility. This socially given space of possibility can in turn be broken down into conditions and meanings. Thus, for the possibility space, it is the conditions that are the reference point of Widerspiegelung and action. One can simply state that the givenness of conditions is a prerequisite for the existence of meanings: something that is not presupposed as a condition, that is, is not given, can have no meaning at all. At the same time, a condition need not necessarily be given in a representational or predominantly representational way: If one thinks of a text, for example, such a text may perhaps be preserved only in a person's memory or stored only digitally. One can imagine something similar for a piece of music that is not hand-written down or printed, but only preserved in tradition. Despite the hardly given concreteness, such texts or pieces of music are given as a condition and presupposed for a possible Widerspiegelung or action.

More evident is the conditional side for objects: they exist as objects, they can be looked at and touched. For hominization, the importance of tool making has been illustrated and elaborated.[40] In order for such tools to be used, they had to be

---

[40] cf. Sect. 2.3 in this volume.

5 Social Widerspiegelung in Humans: Perspectives 171

present as a condition. One cannot decide whether, for example, a hammer or an axe is the tool one needs until such tools exist, that is, are present as a condition. For life in the present, hammers and hatchets continue to be objects that one can actually and objectively access, but new conditions have arisen that one can now use: Tools in the present are generally machine-powered, so they are not usually driven by the force of one's own muscles. Nevertheless, the sequence remains that such objects must be present as a condition in order to be accessed in a reflecting and acting way. For Widerspiegelung said: One can only reflect an object that exists.

Conditions that are presupposed for humans, i.e. that already exist before a person deals with them, result to a large and for humans existentially very important part from the social process: humans lead their lives socially, their livelihood is based on the givenness of society. Conditions that humans face in the context of life in society are therefore to a very large extent the result of the social process. In turn, the possibility of gnostic apprehension of the environment as well as intentionality enter into the social process. In short, the production of a hammer, which is then socially given and passed on as a condition, is not a product of chance, but is linked to the generalized knowledge of what one can do with it. Only if an object – which is then available as a condition – carries a generalized object meaning in itself can it be used as an efficient possibility for action. If humans did not know about the connection between conditions and generalized meanings, the social process of securing existence would not be possible. Moreover, it must be possible to grasp the connection between conditions and generalized meanings via Widerspiegelung: Humans must be able to infer via Widerspiegelung what object they have in front of them and what one can do with such an object.

So you have to know what the meaning of something is: What can one do with a hammer or an axe, but also with a text or a piece of music? Humans must be able to recognize and deal with such meanings inherent in objects via Widerspiegelung. If one cannot read, a text would be inaccessible. If one does not know music, a piece of music that has been handed down is of little help. From the point of view of a human being, the connection and breakdown of the connection between condition and generalized meaning is indispensable: only if, firstly, something is present as a condition and, secondly, one knows about the meaning of this condition, can one refer to it by reflecting and acting – with a chance of success. If there is no hammer, the knowledge of its object meaning is only of limited use. If one has an axe but knows nothing about its inherent object meaning, one cannot handle it in a purposeful way. Both, the development of the conditional as well as the meaningful side of an object, need to be grasped through Widerspiegelung.

What has been explained so far is one side of the meanings, namely the side of the generalized and thus objective meanings: The exemplarily mentioned objects hammer, axe, text and piece of music have objective meanings, which is the same for all humans. A hammer is always an object which, because of its properties – long handle and heavy head – is suitable for transmitting specific energy impulses, for example for hammering in a nail. This meaning is objective and always given. The meaning of conditions, however, is also formed from the subject standpoint and is therefore called subjective meaning in distinction from objective meaning. The objective meaning thus remains unchanged: One can still do the same thing with a hammer. If one tries to use a hammer in the way that would be appropriate for a cooking pot, one will not achieve a useful result. Subjective meaning, then, is not the displacement of objective meaning into the arbitrary.

Rather, subjective meaning arises from its relation to subjectivity, that is, to the state of interest and the subjective quality of life. The subjective meaning of a hammer, hatchet, text or piece of music can vary: Some humans do not need a hammer or a hatchet, they do not perform manual activities. In this respect, a subjective meaning of these objects does not exist for them. This may possibly change when they undertake alterations or repairs to their house or apartment: In such situations, hand tools become important and their subjective significance is high. Humans may not have paid attention for years to whether a hammer or hatchet can be found in the basement: a more accurate Widerspiegelung of their tool inventory is only relevant when they need it. If these objects are missing in the situation in which one wants to realize planned projects, one misses them painfully. The subjective importance, it can be deduced, can also be temporary: For a certain task something is very important and has high subjective importance, but this can change again after the task has been completed. Of course, this does not affect the objective meaning, which always remains the same. The subjective importance can change temporarily, but can also remain the same for a long time: If something is the focus of one's attention for a long time because it is associated with interests and subjective quality of life, the subjective importance also remains high.

Conditions and objective and subjective meanings are presupposed for Widerspiegelung and action: When an intention presents itself, it is examined what conditions and meanings are present. The gnostic process further considers the subject standpoint with the formation of a subjective quality of life. On the basis of the Widerspiegelung of the given and the implications of the subject standpoint, humans make the decision for a certain action which – again from the subject standpoint – seems best suited to ensure the maintenance or increase of one's own subjective quality of life in relation to the conditions. Humans thus have good reasons for acting in each case in this way and not in a different way. This leads into

5 Social Widerspiegelung in Humans: Perspectives 173

the justification for a chosen action: Behind every action there is a justification for action, which summarizes the Widerspiegelung of conditions, meanings as well as the reference to the subject standpoint as justification for an action derived from it.

The fact that human action is and must be justified results from the fact that humans always have decision-making possibilities, i.e. they can choose between alternatives for their actions, and can also secure this choice externally and internally through the process of Widerspiegelung.[41] Via justification, the action that is performed is fitted into the preconditions of the action, i.e. conditions, meanings and subjective quality of life. This matching of the fit as well as the formation of a justification of the chosen action is carried out by each person for himself, thus subjectively.

If one states that actions are subjectively justified, this must be backed up by two things: First, the justification of the action is essentially conceived in relation to the subject's point of view. What constitutes quality of life for a person and what interests he pursues on this basis is his very own subjective point of view. Other humans may have quite different interests: In this respect, the subjective justification of actions is given for all humans, but the subjective justifications of other humans's actions, which in turn are drawn from their interests, are by no means always evident.

Second, the formation of a subjective justification may be gnostically subjective. It may be that the weighting or composition of the components that go into the subjective justification seems pertinent to the person forming the justification. To another person it may not be immediately apparent. In some circumstances, the subjective justification of an action is based on fallacies or errors. One may, by way of example, have overlooked the hammer in one's own cellar and thus come to the conclusion that it is necessary to borrow one from the neighbor next door. A family member, upon hearing the subjective reasoning that one thought it necessary to borrow a hammer from the neighbor, will ask with astonishment, Why, we have a hammer ourselves? The example points to a simple and easily clarifiable error in the subjective justification of action. However, it is easy to imagine that subjective reasons for action can cause more irritation. Analytically, one can only state that actions have and must have a subjective justification. That it is a matter of a justification, even if a subjective one, is stated by the fact that there must be a comprehensible connection between preconditions and action: A justification is not found by rolling the dice, but arises as the intellectually consistent linking of the objective and subjective presuppositions. The subjective justification is the proof that an action has been subjectively assessed as correct and appropriate.

---

[41] cf. Sect. 2.4 in this volume.

If one sums up the consideration of conditions, meanings and justifications for non-social Widerspiegelung and action, one can state that although difficulties in comprehension become apparent, a high proportion of them are hard facts: Conditions like objective meanings are given. Conditions like objective meanings are indeed subject to social change: this can be illustrated by changes in mobility or telecommunications. Objects in themselves cannot change: A car remains a car, a telephone a telephone. Thus, important preconditions of Widerspiegelung and action are subject to the process of social change, but since they are objects, they cannot intentionally intervene in the process of change. Subjective meanings as well as reasons for action are also subject-bound in non-social reflecting and acting: If one wants to comprehend the subjective meanings as well as the subjective justifications of actions, one has to break down the corresponding subject standpoint in an understanding way for this purpose. Overall, however, the fact remains that essential preconditions of action – conditions and objective meanings – do not actively intervene in Widerspiegelung and action. In non-social reflecting and acting, a person becomes active towards preconditions that do not themselves become active, i.e. remain unchanged by themselves. This concludes the excursus on conditions and meanings in the non-social realm: The account turns again to the social in human beings.

In the context of the social, there are also conditions, meanings and ultimately justifications. However, one essential fact changes: in the social, the counterpart is also a human being. This means that the second human being can also reflect and act, and presumably will also reflect and act. But this further means that, since it is human beings to whom the social refers, the conditions and objective meanings of the social are essentially incorporated in human beings. It has already been argued that conditions and objective meanings for the social can also be found outside humans: For example, a bus stop, the existence of which is a condition for young humans to meet at it, that is, in the subjective meaning it is a meeting place for young humans, is in the objective meaning a place where humans get on or off buses. Young humans therefore need the bus stop as a meeting place, i.e. as a prerequisite for their social action. However, social Widerspiegelung and social action are not directed at the bus stop, but at the other young humans who are there.

Thus, for the social, conditions are to a large extent to be found in humans. It bears repeating that conditions are given, but are not to be regarded as determinative. Further, it may seem somewhat strange to speak of humans as conditions; likewise, it may be doubted that humans have objective meaning. Both, however, are true for the social and are to be explained in more detail in its provisions.

That other humans are present and can be reached is a prerequisite for social action. The presence of other humans is therefore a condition for the social being

5 Social Widerspiegelung in Humans: Perspectives 175

possible. Now, however, the other humans in turn have that in their hands, whether they want to be present or stay: They are capable of locomotion, so they can move away. A hammer could not: it remains where someone has put it down, and thus remains as a condition for possible action. For a one-time social encounter, one could still assume that the presence of humans is often accidental: meeting a stranger at the door to a public building is presumably an unplanned encounter on both sides. In contrast, in social relationships, it is part of the fabric to know when and where you will encounter certain humans. You can control that, too: If one wants to avoid social contact with and towards a person, one evades it by being absent. The prerequisite for the social is thus withdrawn: The necessary condition for social, namely presence, is withdrawn, which can go as far as breaking off or ending the social relationship. This is exactly what Odysseus, the hero from ancient Greece, did: he left Calypso and thus ended the social relation with her. The condition for the continuation of the social relation, namely the presence of the two acting persons, was thus no longer given.

But humans can also shape their presence as a condition for social action in such a way that they intensify their presence and perhaps also shape their locomotion in such a way that they assume greater proximity to the other person. The humans remain the same and unchanged; the change in the conditional structure concerns presence in general as a basic condition for social action, as well as the proximity or distance of presence. It should only be noted that, again, it is not always easy for the other person(s) to recognize via social Widerspiegelung whether the presence or non-presence is intentionally controlled or accidental. The same applies to proximity and distance: if changes in this respect are intentional, parallel changes in the dimension of meaning are to be assumed.

So far, it has been analytically assumed that humans do not change, but only the dimension of presence as well as proximity and distance changes the conditional structure. In fact, humans change in the course of their lives, which in turn changes the conditions for social action. Processes such as maturation and development or aging come to mind. Social action towards an infant takes into account the conditions of infancy. Towards the same person who has grown 30 years older, social action is likely to be created quite differently. If the same person should suffer from dementia at an advanced age, social action towards him or her would have to be designed in a completely new way. These are just a few examples. However, the dimension of humans as a condition for social action also includes processes intentionally controlled by humans: development does not only take place through external influences, but also through one's own efforts. This should make it clear that humans are subject to changes in their being like this. They are the same humans, but they are by no means constant in their physical appearance and their

176   5   Social Widerspiegelung in Humans: Perspectives

mental capacity. This has already been outlined under the aspect of individualiza-tion, which also has to deal with constancy and change.[42] This can now be contin-ued for the dimension of conditions for the social: humans are a condition for so-cial action, i.e. presupposed. Humans as a condition are subject to change, but they also actively make changes to themselves. These can be, for example, forms of learning and education, but also – if one thinks of changes in physical potential – training. Humans, then, do not remain constant and always the same given condi-tion of social action. Rather, first, other humans have to adjust to changes in hu-mans as changes in the conditional structure of social action. Secondly, in the gnostic Widerspiegelung of themselves, humans must also deal with the fact that they themselves are subject to changes as well as actively bring about changes in themselves, i.e. that they present themselves differently to other humans as a condi-tion for their action. However, this places new demands on social Widerspiegelung: social Widerspiegelung is still relatively clear as to whether someone is present or not. Admittedly, Odysseus already succeeded in camouflaging his presence by dis-guising himself as a beggar. It is even more difficult to determine why someone is present in a certain place. That the presence in a place is borne by the intention to meet someone can only be broken down by social Widerspiegelung with the coef-ficient of understanding.

After the debate on the dimension that humans are the condition for social Widerspiegelung, we need to continue with meanings: Humans have objective meaning for the social. The provision of what is the objective meaning of humans for the social continues the provision of what has been carried out for the general-ized or objective meaning of objects: The generalized meaning or objective mean-ing is inherent in the object and results from the social process of the object. A hammer, in its objective meaning, is not a hammer by chance, but because it has been so produced purposefully and on the background of the socially handed-down knowledge of the generalized meaning of the hammer. Such traditional knowledge of objective meanings also enters into the social careers of humans: Humans reach the objective meaning of, for example, a teacher or a policeman after a socially prescribed course of training and development. The training and development path can be long or short, formalised or informal: Differences result from socially deter-mined knowledge, but also from social assessments. Thus, such objective meanings are linked to different social valences: For example, housewife is an objective meaning based on a more informal career associated with traditional familial ideas; from the social structure of remuneration for work, however, the objective meaning of housewife is excluded. Objective meanings are always accompanied by the

---

[42] cf. Sect. 3.5 in the appendix

5 Social Widerspiegelung in Humans: Perspectives

adoption of societal knowledge: on the way to an objective meaning, corresponding societal knowledge must always be adopted in order to be able to fill out the objective meaning.

However, it must also be emphasized for the objective meaning of humans that the path to objective meaning has a subjective side. Humans have an objective meaning, but humans can, through their own actions and thus subjectivity, influence that and how they form themselves as a condition and with an objective meaning. A hammer cannot decide whether to become a hammer or a book; a human being, on the other hand, is involved in the process of genesis of itself as a condition with objective meaning. This points to the relation of possibility of human beings to the world: human beings can choose between possibilities. Whether all possibilities or exactly those that correspond to the ideas of subjective quality of life were available at the time of the decision is an open question. But it is always the case that the path to attaining objective meaning as a human being is accompanied by decisions between possibilities.

When humans have achieved objective meaning, it should be noted that this provides an important precondition for corresponding social action. Social action in social relations takes into account the objective meaning of another human being especially on the background that such social actions are often performed by humans with relational objective meanings.[43] For example, it is students who act socially towards teachers and vice versa. Humans with relational objective meaning know about the nature of other objective meaning or at least have to acquire such knowledge. The objective meaning of a person is also determinant for social action insofar as the objective meaning entails legal or other normative specifications: teachers can act socially with students within the corridor of their objective meaning. If they leave this corridor and intensify social relations with – individual – pupils, this could lead to professional difficulties.

Non-social and social action have the difference, with respect to reference to objective meanings, that non-social action can often be undertaken with more certainty about objective meaning: A hammer is usually recognizable as such by sight, and its inherent object meaning identifiable. In contrast, the objective meaning of humans is more complex and requires more disaggregation, primarily because objective meaning interacts with subjective meanings in two ways.

In addition to the objective meaning that a person has in the context of social relations, there are subjective meanings of two different origins: firstly, the respective person himself can attach a subjective meaning to his objective meaning and to himself. Secondly, the other person, who acts socially towards the first person, can

---

[43] Objective meanings are based on societal knowledge: Cf. Sect. 2.3 in this volume.

likewise form a subjective meaning for the first person. It should be noted with regard to the dimension of subjective meanings that these derive from subjectivity, and thus accordingly also carry the diversity of the subjective within them. Subjective meanings can have quite different emphases than what is represented in the objective meanings. For example, someone is a teacher in his objective meaning, but sees himself in the subjective meaning as a painter or poet or in a mixture of both.

A distinction must therefore be made between the subjective meaning for and in social relations that one sees for oneself and the subjective meaning attributed by another person. If one starts with the subjective meaning that one sees for oneself, this often relates to the objective meaning: it is possible, for example, that the objective meaning is 'underpinned' with the subjective meaning. One adopts the objective meaning and becomes absorbed in the subjective meaning attribution: Such a coincidence of objective and subjective meaning is found, for example, in the proverbial version of the teacher 'with body and soul'. This has the advantage that for the social action of other humans different objective and subjective meanings do not have to be dealt with, i.e. a high unambiguity of the structure of meaning is given. However, it should not be overlooked that the independence of the subjective becomes questionable in the process: A perhaps necessary independence or distance of the subject standpoint from the objective meaning is not given. But it is also possible that objective and subjective meaning fall apart: one has a position with an objective meaning, but sees oneself quite differently in the subjective meaning. This at least shows that the subject standpoint intervenes with power in the shaping of the subjective meaning. For others, however, such a divergence of objective and subjective meaning is difficult to handle: should the social relation unfold vis-à-vis the objective or the subjective meaning, how can social action respond in a fitting way to the contradictions of its presuppositions?

The subjective meaning can also become detached from the objective meaning one has for a social relationship. The starting point would then be that one is no longer satisfied with the objective meaning and no longer wants to fill it. Thus, one first seeks a subjective meaning that corresponds more to one's own subjective point of view. Subsequently, one may also seek a new objective meaning: To do this, it is usually necessary to go through a further course of development or training. From the subject standpoint, this is an adequate and necessary change. For other humans with whom one is in a social relationship, however, this gives rise to problems of attribution: What is the current status of objective and subjective meaning, what results from this for social action?

Subjective meaning in social relations is conferred not only from one's own subject standpoint, but also from that of other humans. Various relations or lines of

5 Social Widerspiegelung in Humans: Perspectives 179

development are also possible for this. The subjective meaning of a person seen by other humans can be closely related to the objective meaning: Someone is a teacher in the objective meaning. This can lead to the fact that of someone who has little affinity to school, the subjective importance of this person is low: One perhaps tries to limit social relations as much as possible. It is also possible that an attempt is made to sound out which values and shades the objective meaning has: social relations and social action then have a test character. In contrast, the subjective importance of such a teacher is high for students who want to achieve educational success: they may try to gain special attention in order to achieve an appreciation of their own achievements.

These remarks on the relationship between humans as conditions, objective and subjective meanings for social relations should make it clear that the preconditions for social action are complex. However, by stating that the conditions for one's social action are complex, one cannot pause: The situation demands a decision for social action. This implies that the complex preconditions are met with an action as well as the associated justification. This in turn requires that the preconditions of social action be reflected. Widerspiegelung is also to be understood metaphorically: A mirror reflects something; that which the mirror reflects is thus actually there and present. For the Widerspiegelung, however, the position of the mirror is important: depending on how the mirror is held, some things are seen better, others remain in the background or are perhaps obscured. If you turn the mirror differently or change your own position to the mirror, you get different Widerspiegelung results. Again, however, one needs the result of the Widerspiegelung as a basis for action. The differentiation into conditions and objective as well as subjective meanings is not familiar as such for humans who stand and act in social relations. It serves at this point to improve the scientific understanding of the conditions of social relations. As a rule, humans acting in everyday life do not have such a set of instruments, but they still have to arrive at assessments and justifications that are as reliable as possible to guide their actions.

Acting in social relations – like acting in general – is justified. The assessment of the preconditions in social relations, under consideration of one's own interests and the idea of subjective quality of life, establishes a subjective justification for a certain action. This subjective justification draws the conclusion from all considerations and results in action. The action that is chosen seems conclusive and most appropriate.

This fixes what needs to be understood if one wants to understand the social actions of other humans: It is the justifications for action. Apodictically, one can state that there must be such a justification. No matter how nonsensical social action may seem, for the person acting it results from a subjective justification. This justification must be comprehended if the subjective meaning of the action is to be understood. If one – looking at our ancient hero – only considers that Odysseus leaves the beautiful Calypso, who promises him marriage, immortality and eternal youth, one may doubt his judgment. But if one knows the subjective reason for this action, namely that Odysseus wants to return home to his wife Penelope and his son Telemachos, one probably revises the first judgement. It is necessary, however, to learn and understand the subjective reason.

It was explained that and how a person positions himself in relation to preconditions, which can be fanned out into conditions and meanings, and as a consequence, and taking into account his subject standpoint, arrives at a justified action. In the context of social relations, humans now meet each other and have to cope with actions of other humans: Actions of one human being are – in the context of a social relation – preconditions for the actions of another human being. It should be added that the justifications and the understanding of these justifications are also prerequisites for social action. Calypso might have been snubbed and hurt if she had not known and understood the rationale for Odysseus leaving her. However, once she has understood the reasoning, she may be able to understand Odysseus. Understanding the social action and its justifications of other humans creates new conditions for one's own social action.

This in turn brings with it requirements for social Widerspiegelung. How can one deal with the actions of other humans with whom one may live in a close social relationship? The unravelling of one person's subjective justification by another must take this into account. One can understand subjective justifications by breaking down their internal logic: This involves analytically breaking them down into their constituent parts and reference points. Of course, one will not be able to understand subjective justifications if one applies external, supposedly objective standards to them.

The comprehension of subjective justifications requires a specific form of Widerspiegelung: this is understanding, which attempts to approach the subject's point of view. It is known with certainty that there must be a subjective justification of actions; how the justification is actually situated, on the other hand, must first be discovered. This happens through understanding.

Understanding is to be delimited and classified. Understanding is not limited to the social. The development of objects and object meanings also requires understanding. In an earlier publication it was formulated: "Verstehen ist die Form, über die Gegenstandsbedeutungen in den Wissensbestand von Menschen überführt werden".[44] Understanding as an important area of Widerspiegelung deals with

---

[44] Autrata and Scheu (2015, p. 116).

5 Social Widerspiegelung in Humans: Perspectives 181

conditions and meanings. The task and goal of understanding is a transfer of knowledge: existing knowledge from the stock of societal knowledge is transferred into a person's stock of knowledge. This is based on the specificity of human beings and their possibility of entering into a gnostic relationship with the world and themselves. Understanding, however, is not only the comprehension of knowledge, but the embedding of this knowledge in one's own subjectivity: "Verstehen schöpft seine Energie aus der angenommenen Relevanz des zu verstehenden Gegenstands für die subjektive Lebensqualität".[45]

This provision can be transferred to understanding in the context of the social: understanding the reasons for social action can be of extremely high relevance for one's own subjective quality of life. One's own social actions and thus the continuation of a social relationship are constituted in a completely different way in relation to the understanding or non-understanding of reasons for action. This has undeniable relevance for one's own subjective quality of life. Thus, if the relevance of understanding in the context of the social for a particular person is recognized, a great deal of energy is likely to be invested in this. Admittedly, it should be said as a precautionary measure: High energy does not always guarantee success. Understanding in the context of the social can suffer or fail because of the meticulous search for whether the social actions and their justifications of other humans correspond to one's own intentions and interests: however, this is not understanding in the sense of comprehending the subject standpoint of another person, but rather checking whether the subject standpoint of another person coincides with one's own. Understanding in the context of the social is the comprehension of the subject standpoint that can be discerned behind the social actions of another person; whether one approves of this subject standpoint and the actions resulting from it is quite another question.

Basically, one can say that understanding is the goal of the Widerspiegelung of objects. But understanding is also a component of social Widerspiegelung. The components of understanding are preserved, so the grasping of conditions, meanings and justifications as well as the comparison with one's own subjective quality of life is also given for the social. Understanding makes clear the potential of social Widerspiegelung that goes beyond empathy: it is also true for social Widerspiegelung that conditions, meanings and justifications are to be grasped and processed in the gnostic process.

If one wants to reflect on action in social relations or initiate and accompany Widerspiegelung on it, the subjective justification is the starting point. It is not possible to determine from the outside whether an action in social relations is right or

---

[45] Autrata and Scheu (2015, p. 120).

wrong. But one can help to check whether the justification for the action is conclusive, has adequately reflected the preconditions and has also taken into account one's own subjective quality of life. This in turn creates points of reference for new considerations.

In summary and by way of perspective, it can be said that understanding in the context of social relations can be characterized as the comprehension of the subject standpoint of another person. The comprehension of this subject standpoint is made possible by the postulate that every human action, and thus also social actions, are subjectively justified. By understanding the subjective reasons behind social actions, it is possible to understand them.

Understanding a person's subject standpoint, which has led to a social action via subjective reasoning, is different from adopting this subject standpoint. If one takes subjectivity and the resulting subject standpoint seriously, the adoption of another subject standpoint is not possible: every person is a subject and thus unique; another point of view cannot fit one's own subjectivity, since this very subjectivity is a different one. Notions such as the perspective-taking found in Walter, for example, do not work, since one cannot simply duplicate another person's perspective.[46] The subjective justification of social action is valid for one person, it necessarily does not fit the subjectivity of another person.

The effort to understand can contribute to the further development of the social. Social Widerspiegelung does not remain attached to the surface, social Widerspiegelung penetrates via gnostic-understanding processes to the level of subjective justifications. Whether on this basis something like an understanding on common goals occurs or can occur is an open question. But at least the possibility of intersubjective understanding is opened, which in turn is indispensable for the dimension of social action that wants to reach beyond the limits of given possibilities. This will be discussed in more detail in the next subchapter.

5.3   Directional Provisions

Social Widerspiegelung is a mental process: Social Widerspiegelung in all its parts – sensory perception, active control, gnostic process including comparison with knowledge as well as comparison with one's own subjectivity and ultimately the creation of an image – is realized in the psyche of a human being, i.e. it is not visible to the outside. What is visible, on the other hand, are the resulting social actions, which are ascertainable in their form: When someone raises his hand in

---

[46] cf. e.g. Walter (2014, p. 51) as well as Sect. 3.1 in the present report.

5 Social Widerspiegelung in Humans: Perspectives

greeting, addresses the word to another person, kisses or slaps the other person, these are all social acts. Social actions are therefore more amenable to empirical recording than social Widerspiegelungen. Social Widerspiegelungen are accessible via subsequent social actions: One would not raise one's hand in greeting unless someone entered the room. Similarly, it can be assumed that a kiss or a slap is given after social Widerspiegelung: From sensory perception and active control via gnostic apprehension involving the subject's point of view, an image is generated. After the social Widerspiegelung, one knows which of the two forms of expression are appropriate for the respective addressee.

Thus, conclusions about social Widerspiegelung are plausible from the observation of social actions: social Widerspiegelung and social action usually belong together, they form a unity. However, it should always be borne in mind that humans are also capable of tactical manoeuvres. For example, *false kisses* appear in various idioms or proverbs. There are, then, to be understood, kisses which, as a social action, do not express what would be found in the corresponding social Widerspiegelung. Social actions, then, can also deceive or disguise, and in any case are not in every case indubitable indicators of the image created in the social Widerspiegelung. A deception of the social Widerspiegelung about what a social action stands for can thus occur coincident with the goal of the social action: The social Widerspiegelung has thus fallen for the deception. However, a deception in the social Widerspiegelung can also occur as an erroneous result that was not intended in this way: a social action was misunderstood without this being the intention of the actor.

The dimension of deceptions and concealments is even more strongly reflected in the directional provisions that the social can take as an interplay of Widerspiegelungen and actions. Even if one can determine social actions, one cannot always discern from them the subjectivity that lies behind them. What subjective purpose a social action serves is not necessarily apparent from it. For example, a *false kiss* whose purpose was not the expression of closeness or affection is found in the Bible: Judas kissed Jesus in order to give a sign to the arriving henchmen who is the one they are looking for.[47] After this incident such kisses with a double bottom are also called Judas kisses.

Thus, in the following account of the provision of direction within the framework of the social, social Widerspiegelung is not considered in isolation, so as not to fall into the realm of unprovable speculation: social actions are more manifest than social Widerspiegelung, they are consulted as an important supplement. Further, even this is not sufficient to achieve freedom from doubt: Social actions

---

[47] cf. Württembergische Bibelanstalt (1964, p. 43) (NT, Mt 26:48 ff.).

are manifest, but with regard to their subjective backgrounds they are often deceptive. It has to be taken into account that from an external point of view, no clear and reliable results can be gained about the directionality of what humans do. Only the humans themselves know about their – partly hidden – subjectivity. But this does not make the directionality of the social obsolete: there are such directional provisions, as can be deduced from the comparison of the social with its possibility structure. It must be made clear that the observation of social actions is a means to an end: a provision of direction can hardly be seen in social Widerspiegelung or grasped through other forms of sensory perception. Whether one kisses or slaps someone expresses in each case a direction that the social takes or should take in the process. This is not beyond doubt, since the action can also be tactical. This is exactly what was exemplified with the *false kisses*: a kiss is commonly the social action that expresses closeness and affection. However, it is possible to perform this seemingly explicit social act with the intention of deception. Such a *false kiss,* but actually given with the intention of deception, is nevertheless justified. Admittedly, it is difficult to reflect socially the directionality of such an act: Is it affection or deceit that is being encountered? Nevertheless, the act remains an important anchor that can be used to break down the directionality of the social. From there, with an experiential background, one can ask how a provision of direction is obtained via social Widerspiegelung, which is, after all, the subjective means of clarifying the situation.

It is therefore a matter of recording in which direction the social – and thus also the social Widerspiegelung – unfolds and to which results this leads. This cannot be done here for individual cases and traced in relation to experience. The point is to work out the possible constellations that the social can take on in relation to others. This means, in continuation, that these constellations are provisions of the direction in which the social moves. At the same time, it is to be expected that these are ideal-typical provisions of direction, which – when applied to empirically found social things – are not to be found in the exclusivity in which they are introduced: Under experiential conditions, the two still-to-be-introduced directional provisions mix.

The directional provision of social action and social Widerspiegelung results from the relationship to the respective space of possibility: humans can be satisfied with the given space of possibility, settle down in it and act within the limits of the space of possibility. Here, too, the 'double' possibility is found, here now as "doppelte Beziehungsmöglichkeit".[48] The 'double relational possibility' means that humans can enter into relationships in different forms; they can enter into

---

[48] Holzkamp (1985, p. 375).

5 Social Widerspiegelung in Humans: Perspectives 185

relationships in order to jointly achieve a realisation of interests (generalised form of social action) or they can enter into relationships which, under certain circumstances, also contribute to a realisation of interests, but this time at the expense of others (restrictive form of social action).

Social action in humans is characterised by the fact that it is firstly oriented towards the life interests of the individual, secondly takes place in the context of possibilities for action and thirdly involves the shaping of living conditions. Humans thus act firstly according to their life interests, i.e. according to their respective intentions. In other words, they act on the basis of their intentions and interests. In terms of social action, this then means that the individual humans who relate to each other in action must act according to their own intentionality and interests and, in addition, recognise and understand the intentionality and interests of their counterpart. The recognition and understanding of intentionalities and interests – both one's own and those of the other – means that the socially mediated meanings inherent in the respective intentionalities are recognized. It is therefore necessary to recognize the societal knowledge inherent in the intentionalities; it is necessary to grasp the social framing of the intentionalities. Socially acting subjects build up a gnostic relationship to the intentionalities and interests of the counterpart: social action thus takes place in the context of reciprocal intentionality; in other words, social action involves a process of Widerspiegelung that captures one's own intentionality and interests as well as those of the counterpart.

Furthermore, the establishment of a gnostic relationship is not a deterministic process (in the sense of stimulus-response), but an active – cognitive – process that subjects enter into on the basis of their own intentionality and interests. Thus, whether subjects relate to other subjects in a social-acting way also depends on whether they are able to realize their own interests in life or their own intentionalities. Thus, the decision whether to enter into a gnostic process of recognizing and understanding the intentionalities as well as interests of the counterpart is also subject to choice. Social Widerspiegelung as a process of gnostic apprehension is thus an active process of the subject.

The distinction between directional provisions must also be observed specifically for social action: Social action can be restrictive or generalized, that is, it can remain within existing boundaries or seek to overcome them.[49] This distinction should be taken up and adapted for social relations. The distinction between restrictive and generalized in reflecting and acting is basically conclusive and stringent: reflecting and acting remain in the restrictive provision of direction within a given space of possibilities, which can also be restrictive and limiting. If one does

---

[49] cf. Sect. 4.1 in this volume.

186   5   Social Widerspiegelung in Humans: Perspectives

not want to accept the constrictions and limitations, one must try to expand or change the possibility space in order to be able to realize the generalized provision of direction.

It is important to emphasize the role of Widerspiegelung in the process of the social. Widerspiegelung is not as evident and visible as action, but it is an important instance for determining the direction in the social. Widerspiegelung creates the orientation that is then implemented in action. If possibilities are overlooked or if the aspect of limiting the space of possibilities for subjectivity is not recognized, subsequent action remains consistently restrictive. Widerspiegelung, however, is not only a Widerspiegelung of the given, but also creates a broadening of perspective on the potential. It should be remembered that social Widerspiegelung is more than sensory perception: social Widerspiegelung is also a gnostic process and establishes comparison with the subject's point of view, which ultimately leads to an image. The image as a result, however, is not a photograph of the other person as she or he faces you, but also an expression of the possible perspectives associated with that person. Social Widerspiegelung thus captures not only the factual, but also the potential. A person's possibility space, which arises for the social through other humans, is thus reflected not only as it is, but also as it could or should be. Only by reflecting that and how the space of possibility – i.e. living together with other humans – could be expanded can generalized action be set in motion.

The combination of social Widerspiegelung with the point of view of its directionality is to be focused on the situation in social relations: To the distinction between the two provisions of direction, formulated first from the point of view of an individual, is added the consideration of what these orientations do to other humans. If one accepts the limitations of the space of possibility and remains restrictive in such circumstances, the consequence is that one participates in the fact that spaces of possibility are also limited for other humans and continue to be so. If one positions oneself in the sense of the generalized provision of direction, this is on the one hand the effort to expand one's own possibility space, but on the other hand also the effort to change other humans's possibility spaces to their advantage. The generalized provision of direction does not only want to realize one's own subjective quality of life, the generalized provision of direction wants – in a perspective open to all humans and in solidarity – the realization of subjective quality of life for all.

So far, however, this definition of the direction between restrictive and generalized has not taken into account the fact that the humans involved know each other and relate to each other in their actions: In order to impair the subjective quality of life of other humans, it is also not absolutely necessary that humans know each other. Rather, the acceptance of restrictive possibilities with the negative

5 Social Widerspiegelung in Humans: Perspectives 187

consequences for other humans can be carried out anonymously: One knows nothing, or at least little, about other humans's subjective quality of life, nor does one need to be particularly concerned with it. The restrictive provision of direction is narrowed to one's own perspective, which in turn is defensive and narrow.

The generalized provision of direction includes the view of the perspective of other humans, is indeed designed in such a way that the realization of subjective quality of life also becomes possible for other humans. It is indeed conceivable in principle that a generalized perspective is included by humans in Widerspiegelung and action without knowing the other humans and knowing about their subjective quality of life, for which the generalized perspective also wants to create an expansion of possibilities. Given the diversity of conceptions of subjective quality of life and the implied need to coordinate such conceptions between humans, the question arises as to the limits of the generalized perspective between humans who remain anonymous to each other: Humans do not live solitarily, but are connected to each other through society as well as social things. Thus, one's own realization of subjective quality of life is in close proximity to that of one or more other humans: processes of coordination are accordingly necessary. This does not mean that subjective quality of life should be levelled or standardised. But it is precisely the generalised perspective, which seeks to shift the boundaries and limitations of possible spaces, that requires the element of communication with other humans. Understanding is to be understood as mutual understanding between humans. Understanding can be one-sided in the sense that one person has comprehended the subjective reasonableness of another person's perspective; the other person – vice versa – has not attempted to do so or has not succeeded. When understanding is reciprocal, so that the humans concerned can understand each other's perspectives, we speak of understanding.

Understanding in the sense of mutual understanding between humans occurs essentially through social Widerspiegelung and social action. Both elements, social Widerspiegelung and social action, enter into understanding: Understanding is a process of clarifying the intersubjective fit between ideas of subjective quality of life. The question here is: does what another person does fit my intentions and interests? If the question can be answered in the affirmative, which in turn becomes apparent after the sequences of action and Widerspiegelung, then understanding is given. Even in processes of understanding that are strongly legally sheathed, as in contracting, contract terms are negotiated, that is, established at meetings and through social Widerspiegelung and social action. This is to plausibilize that the dimension of referring to subjective quality of life of others requires the social: How else is one to know what another person's subjective quality of life is like?

188 5 Social Widerspiegelung in Humans: Perspectives

This brings us back to the two poles of directionality. The restrictive perspective is also possible between humans who remain anonymous to each other. In this case, i.e. the restrictive perspective without knowledge of the other person(s), a reference to the subjective quality of life of other humans is not necessary: In realizing one's own subjective quality of life, it is accepted that the subjective quality of life of other humans will be affected by it. But exactly how this happens is not pursued further in the process.

But the restrictive perspective can also be realized in the social between humans. This can be fanned out even further: The restrictive perspective in the social exists between humans who do not know and recognize each other, i.e. cannot individualize each other. This again presupposes that it remains with the one-time or at least at most occasional social Widerspiegelung and social action: With more frequent social Widerspiegelung and social action between the same humans, mutual individualization is almost inevitable. Such a restrictive, but limited to the framework of the unique or occasional social Widerspiegelung and social action can perhaps be imagined as an example in the search for a parking space: A car driver has managed to get a parking space by quickly reflecting that another car driver is manoeuvring carefully and by aggressively pushing ahead; he/she waves ironically and smilingly at the other car driver who has been left behind. They don't know each other, but the intention of the first driver is clear: they want to gain an advantage for themselves and are happy to accept that this is disadvantageous for another driver.

In the brief encounter of two humans in a parking lot described above, the preconditions are such that the two humans do not know each other, i.e. individualization is not possible. In this respect, social Widerspiegelung and action cannot be based on additional knowledge about the other person: Thus, one does not know whether the other person needs the parking space in order to subsequently pursue his or her occupation; it is also possible that the parking space is sought for a subsequent walk. Thus, the maneuver to deprive the other person of the parking space is admittedly to the other person's disadvantage. However, the extent to which this manoeuvre is really detrimental to the other person's subjective quality of life can hardly be determined by social Widerspiegelung: whether someone misses an important appointment or is merely able to start his walk 5 minutes later cannot be anticipated by social Widerspiegelung in the situation described. The restrictive directionality – one wants to gain an advantage at the expense of another person – is, however, inherent in this. Further, the restrictiveness is ultimately realized in action, i.e. in pushing ahead when entering the parking lot. This is prepared by social Widerspiegelung, which is thus also an important element of restrictiveness. Social Widerspiegelung builds up the chance to act restrictively socially in the

5 Social Widerspiegelung in Humans: Perspectives 189

situation described; the other person's driving movements are reflected, the given spaces and one's own acceleration potential are assessed. Restrictive orientation thus ends with social action, but it begins with social Widerspiegelung.

More frequent and lasting than the one-time contacts outlined above is the restrictive perspective between humans who know and can individualize each other. Since individualization results from social relations, this individualized restrictive perspective of the social is realized in the context of social relations. Thus, information from earlier social Widerspiegelungen about the respective other person is available; reciprocal social actions have also taken place earlier. With the beginning of social relations, information about the nature of the subjective quality of life in the respective other person also comes into play. So when one reflects socially in social relations and acts socially, this happens on the basis of – more or less well developed – information about the subjective quality of life of the other humans involved in it. One can therefore assess – more or less well – what is beneficial or detrimental to the subjective quality of life of the other humans. That is why in social relationships it is quite possible to reflect and act on the subjective quality of life of the other person, often with the added value of tactics. For example, social Widerspiegelung can focus on the weaknesses of the other humans involved and try to exploit these weaknesses to one's own advantage. In such cases, social Widerspiegelung is used as a tool that provides useful information. Simplistically, one could say that such knowledge about the other person's subjective quality of life is exploited to enforce advantages for one's own quality of life.

Again, it must be remembered that longitudinal social relationships are not possible without the cooperation of both humans involved: If one person were to take the restrictive perspective in the social relationship and thus assert his own quality of life at the expense of the other person or humans involved, this could result in the break-up or end of the social relationship. Only if the second person also sees advantages for himself or herself and his or her subjective quality of life, and thus pursues the reciprocity of the social,[50] does the social relationship remain intact. The dimension of self-enmity[51] should be recalled: by participating in the social relation led by one person via the restrictive perspective, the second person becomes an enemy to himself insofar as he 'actually' harms his subjective quality of life and becomes active against his own interests. Admittedly, this is not always apparent and is obscured primarily by the tactical reference to one's own subjective quality of life. But the perspective in social relations that is characterized as self-enmity is restrictive: one settles into the given and accepts its limitations. It should

---

[50] cf. Sect. 5.1 in this volume.
[51] cf. Sect. 4.1 in this volume.

be emphasized, however, that for such maneuvers of tactical concealment as well as of self-enmity, knowledge of the subjective quality of life of the other person towards whom one acts socially must be present. This knowledge results from social Widerspiegelung. The restrictive perspective in social relations between humans who know each other and are individualized for each other is based on mutual knowledge about the respective subjective quality of life and carries this knowledge over into the shaping of the social relation.

On the other side of the directionality is the generalized perspective. The generalized perspective is designed in such a way that it is not only a matter of expanding the space of possibilities for one person, but of advancing the expansion of the space of possibilities in solidarity for many, if possible even for all humans.[52]

When considering the direction of the generalized for social relations, distinctions of the circumstances are again to be made and considered. The first step is to look at one's own subjective quality of life and the subjective quality of life of another person. Above all, it is the non-own subjective quality of life that is to be taken into account. Widerspiegelung and action with the direction of the generalized is given with regard to the expansion of one's own possibilities: One's own subjective quality of life is thereby the yardstick for what is pursued. If limitations are recognizable or perceptible, one can work on overcoming them. For example, if one wants to read a book, but the book cannot be found or is not available, this would be a restriction of the possibility space. If one does not accept this restriction, one looks for starting points for overcoming the restriction: one campaigns for a higher library budget, procures money for one's own book purchase or obtains access to the sought-after book as an e-book. What remains open in the example is how a generalized perspective with a solidarity component could be applied: One does not know which subjective quality of life is pursued by other humans. Do other humans also want to read the book they are looking for, or do they have completely different preferences? One could, for example, try to clarify the book needs of other humans by means of a notice. But if one wants to pursue this more seriously, a transition to the social is probably inevitable: One would then have to get in touch with other humans via social Widerspiegelung and social actions such as meetings or conversations.

Thus, if one moves on to the social, a contact to other humans is established: There are thus means of access to the subjective quality of life of other humans via social Widerspiegelungen and social actions. Again, however, the range of the social must be taken into account: When you meet a person for the first time, look at him and greet him, you probably still know nothing about whether he reads at all, and if

---

[52] cf. Secti. 4.1 in this volume.

5 Social Widerspiegelung in Humans: Perspectives 191

so, what books he reads. You can put it this way: Without the social, access to other humans's subjective quality of life is impossible. This is of great importance, since it is of central importance for the formation of a perspective: without individualisation, information on subjective quality of life cannot be assigned to a specific person. If, without individualisation, the intention is to generalise social Widerspiegelungen and social actions in such a way that they are also designed to improve the realisation of the subjective quality of life of other humans, this has to cope with the disadvantage that this cannot be goal-oriented and is correspondingly prone to error: since one does not know what the subjective quality of life of other humans is like, one can possibly do more harm than good through one's own activities. In reversal, the perspective that emerges is that in order to understand the quality of life of other humans, it is essential to seek access via social Widerspiegelung.

These are – and above all from the outside, i.e. not from an internal perspective – considerations that are based on plausibility and probability: Already for a human being himself it is fraught with difficulties to grasp gnostically his own subjective quality of life in an inner process of Widerspiegelung; deceptions and distortions are possible. For a human being the access to the subjective quality of life of another human being is already difficult by the fact that it must fail indirectly: One must attempt to draw conclusions about other humans's subjective quality of life from the Widerspiegelung of their actions. The social in humans must therefore also deal with such presuppositions and must come to a conclusion that is cogent enough to select and implement one possibility among several for oneself: The social in humans must deal with ambiguities and imponderables insofar as it depends on reciprocity with other humans. If one wants to relate to the subjective quality of life of another via social Widerspiegelung and social action, one must develop an idea of what this subjective quality of life is like and how one could possibly position oneself adequately in relation to it.

From this, two things can be deduced for the generalized perspective in the social: The generalized perspective in the social is more or less inevitably dependent on intersubjectivity and social relations. Since the generalized perspective in the social also includes solidarity and cooperation, i.e. it should not only benefit the expansion of one's own possibilities and thus the expanded realization of one's own subjective quality of life, but also work for the realization of other humans's subjective quality of life, the subjective quality of life of other humans – or at least parts of it – must be known: One can hardly do anything for another person's subjective quality of life through Widerspiegelung and action if one does not know what it is like. If the generalized perspective in the social is not to rely solely on chance, it must achieve a resilient contingency between one's own subjective quality of life and the subjective quality of life of others.

A second aspect makes it necessary for the generalized perspective in the social to clarify the subjective quality of life of the other humans who are involved in the process of the social: This is the question of whether and to what extent the subjective qualities of life of those involved might touch each other, might perhaps also come into conflict with each other. If it is not a question of the social, a juxtaposition is conceivable: the expansion of subjective quality of life for one person is fulfilled, for example, by gaining the freedom to read the books he has long wanted to read but has not been able to; the expansion of quality of life for another person is perhaps to exercise more or to do sport more intensively. The person who focuses on reading and the person who focuses on exercise and sports do not come into conflict with this for the time being. If, on the other hand, the two humans are in a context of reciprocal social Widerspiegelung and action, this can become more difficult: One person may want to tell the other about his new reading experience, while the other person favors climbing a mountain together. Of course, it is possible to imagine solutions for such different interests: But the starting point for this is always the clarification of the respective subjective quality of life and the implications that arise from it. To put it somewhat apodictically: a generalized perspective of the social from a distance, towards humans one knows little or not at all, is unlikely to be crowned with success. It is possible in principle, but difficult to imagine: How is one to advocate for the subjective quality of life of others if one does not know them? How is one supposed to achieve a fit between one's own subjective quality of life and the subjective quality of life of others in the social sphere and at the same time strive for an expansion of one's disposal over restrictive possibilities without carrying out intensive coordination processes?

This leads back to the already mentioned intersubjectivity and its location in social relations. If we consider the given possibilities of social Widerspiegelung and social action, we come to the conclusion that the generalized overcoming of their limitations and restrictions cannot be achieved by one person alone. This induces the necessity of intersubjective understanding about respective ideas of subjective quality of life as well as about perspectives for its extended realization. Both the intersubjective clarification of the different ideas and the process of expanding possibilities are only conceivable as a joint procedure within the framework of social relations. One could also put it this way: The provision of the direction of the generalized in the social characterizes both the goal and the path of such a process.

What is meant by this is that generalized social Widerspiegelung and social action represent the directional provision of the social, which triggers the overcoming of boundaries that stem from the social. If one considers that such boundaries

5 Social Widerspiegelung in Humans: Perspectives

can be very constricting and oppressive, it becomes clear that overcoming them is linked to a high degree, and to the point of existential threat, to the subjective quality of life. Formulated as a suggestion for personal Widerspiegelung: Close social relationships such as neighbourhood relationships, a friendship, a love relationship or one's own family can – in everyday language – enrich and make happy; scientifically speaking, the hope is placed in them that they contribute to the realisation of one's own subjective quality of life. However, it can also be ascertained that such close social relationships can also have exactly the opposite effect, as well as actually doing so: Humans suffer from such close social relationships and cannot find a way out of them. It is evident that a generalized perspective that overcomes the obstacles to further development for oneself as well as for others involved would be helpful. However, it is often difficult to find precisely this further and generalized perspective.

It should be noted that the provision of the direction of the generalized, i.e. the overcoming of limitations of subjective quality of life, for the social is dependent on processes of intersubjectivity within social relations. On the operational level, this involves processes of knowledge and negotiation: what constitutes subjective quality of life for the other person in each case must therefore firstly be attempted to be fathomed; secondly, attempts must be made to achieve a balance or understanding between different conceptions of subjective quality of life. It should be remembered that quality of life in the social is achieved through reciprocal Widerspiegelung and social action: That is, two or more humans participate in bringing about such a quality of life under certain circumstances. One person alone can only realize a generalized perspective in the social to a very limited extent: The generalized perspective in the social, through its interwoven nature with intersubjectivity and its embeddedness in social relations, is something that can only be achieved through the participation of two or more humans.

To summarize and to form a perspective, it can be said that a generalized perspective in the social can only be achieved if humans jointly contribute to its realization. For the realisation of a generalised perspective in the social, reciprocity in the described understanding of a dialectical development of social relations is indispensable.[53] Likewise, understanding in the sense of intersubjective understanding is a prerequisite for the unfolding of a generalized perspective.

Essential to the generalized perspective in the social is social Widerspiegelung: social Widerspiegelung with a generalized perspective must recognize the given possibility space that arises through other humans and at the same time determine

---

[53] cf. Sect. 5.1 in this volume.

its limitations. However, this does not end the realization of the generalized perspective of Widerspiegelung in the social. Via social Widerspiegelung, first, it must be established situationally that there is the basic possibility of expanding or changing a limiting possibility space; second, via social Widerspiegelung, steps must be grasped that one can take in order to be able to overcome these limiting possibilities. Thirdly, social Widerspiegelung must also provide anticipations of how the generalized perspective could be approached in view of the specific situation together with other humans – taking into account the subjective quality of life of these humans as well. In this case, social Widerspiegelung is by no means only the capture of the given; social Widerspiegelung is also the capture of the potential and utopian.

Social Widerspiegelung and Social Work

6

In the previous presentation, Widerspiegelung was introduced and explained as the conception of matter. This was continued to define social Widerspiegelung, which is – in general – the Widerspiegelung of other living beings of the same species and – specifically – the Widerspiegelung of other human beings. With regard to the social Widerspiegelung of human beings, the basics, forms and perspectives were presented.

In this penultimate chapter of the present publication, classifications are to be made for further scientific work on social Widerspiegelung. It is therefore a question of clarifying the status, which on the one hand is to secure the results, and on the other hand is to provide orientation for further work. In doing so, it must be clarified how the responsibility and competence for the scientific work on social Widerspiegelung is to be seen and distributed. Thus, the debate on the disciplinary affiliation of social Widerspiegelung as an object of scientific research must be conducted. It is also clear from the course of argumentation in this paper that scientific research on social Widerspiegelung must be fundamental research: The instrument with which social Widerspiegelung can be elucidated is theory.

The second part of the clarification is aimed at defining how social work as a profession can and should address the issue of social Widerspiegelung. Social work as a profession has special knowledge about the nature of social Widerspiegelung, which in turn comes from social work as a discipline. For professional social work, therefore, there is the dual task of working on problems of social Widerspiegelung through processes of accompaniment and support and of exploiting the potential of social Widerspiegelung. On the one hand, respect for humans's own responsibility for the processes of social Widerspiegelung they carry out must be taken into account; on the other hand, innovative possibilities can be realized through

© The Author(s), under exclusive license to Springer Fachmedien
Wiesbaden GmbH, part of Springer Nature 2023
O. Autrata, B. Scheu, *Subjective quality of life and social work*,
https://doi.org/10.1007/978-3-658-40400-0_6

accompaniment and support, which stem from the expertise of professional social work. A balance must be found between these two sides, i.e. respect for personal responsibility and the introduction of innovative possibilities.

6.1 Social Widerspiegelung in the Context of the Discipline

If one assumes that social Widerspiegelung has been researched and clarified in principle with the present publication, a reference to the validity of research results is nevertheless necessary: There can be no final and conclusive research into an object – be it social Widerspiegelung or something else. It should be recalled that motion is the mode of existence of matter[1]: Since matter never comes to rest, but remains in motion, research, which is always concerned with matter, must take this into account and update its results. By its very nature, therefore, there is no standstill for matter and, as a consequence, no standstill for research that elucidates the so-being of matter or of a part of matter.

The obligation for research and science to deal with objects that are in motion and evolving becomes particularly clear when it comes to humans and society. Changes can also be observed in inanimate nature, some of which proceed slowly, while others unfold with enormous dynamism: Mountains, for example, erode over comparatively long periods of time. In contrast, a volcanic eruption occurs in a very short time. If one thinks, for example, of global warming and its consequences, one realizes that there are changes in the world that began slowly and have since increased in speed. All these movements and changes of matter must be followed by science.

On the one hand, humans face matter and grasp matter through consciousness. On the other hand, humans themselves are also part of matter, which is grasped by other humans through social Widerspiegelung. Thus, the determination that motion is the mode of existence of matter penetrates into the scientific apprehension of social Widerspiegelung. Humans as a part of matter are subject to development and change, at the same time social Widerspiegelung does the same. This is particularly evident in the part of gnostic processing of impressions obtained from sensory perception: Gnostic processing must take into account the societal framing of social Widerspiegelung. Scientific research into social Widerspiegelung must also

---

[1] cf. para. 2.1 in this volume. as well as Marx and Engels (1962a, MEW 20).

6   Social Widerspiegelung and Social Work   197

take this into account. When social circumstances change, and with them the spaces of possibility in and vis-à-vis which humans move, scientific research must be able to detect this.

The first point of view of continuing scientific research is thus due to the effort to keep pace with the development and movement immanent in the respective objects of research: If the object of research – as part of matter – is in motion, research on that object cannot pause either.

The second point of view, from which further research becomes meaningful and necessary, is the examination of whether the state of research achieved with the results obtained does justice to the object to be elucidated. Klaus et al. find the following formulation for this – with recourse to the concept of Widerspiegelung: "Das Gegenteil von Wahrheit ist Falschheit, die Nichtübereinstimmung der Erkenntnis mit dem widergespiegelten Sachverhalt".[2] The state of research reached is thus to be examined, this can be read out as a procedural rule, to see whether it becomes adequate to the object it covers. If an explanation of the object succeeds which corresponds to the object, then the explanation is to be recorded as true. In the contrary case, that is, if the cognition is not adequate to the object, the cognition is to be marked as false and consequently rejected.

So in the case that research results could not find an adequate explanation for their subject matter, these results are simply wrong. So it would make no sense, if starting from the wrong results, one tries to trace developments of the object from the point of view of the moving matter: One does not turn false results into true knowledge by extrapolating them. If the results were wrong in principle, they remain wrong also in the adaptation to changes of the object.

However, there is another aspect to be examined: if it is taken for granted that scientific findings have been obtained that provide adequate results for the object to be explained, then it must be clarified whether the object has been grasped in its entirety. The demand that science must grasp an object in its entirety is already found in Kant, who writes: Science must be a "(…) nach Prinzipien geordnetes Ganzes der Erkenntnis sein (…)".[3] The aim of scientific knowledge is therefore to explain an object in its entirety. It is not enough to correctly grasp partial aspects, but not to be able to determine at which point of the whole object they have their place.

This point of view, that an object is to be grasped scientifically in its entirety, combined with the observation that matter is constantly in motion, i.e. that the ob-

---

[2] Klaus and Buhr (1976b, vol. 2, p. 1272); see also Autrata and Scheu (2015, p. 211 ff.).

[3] Kant (2014, p. 4) (first published: 1786); see also Poser (2012) and Scheu and Autrata (2018).

jects of scientific knowledge are not static but dynamic, justifies the classification of scientific knowledge as only provisionally final. This results in the permanent requirement to update scientific knowledge. It is open whether the updating of scientific knowledge will show that an object has changed completely, i.e. a new object has emerged, or whether the given and already explained object has changed only in parts. But even if an object has changed only in parts, the necessity remains to grasp the object in its entirety: One must therefore scientifically grasp which parts have changed and how, and what effect the change of the parts has on the whole.

From these fundamental requirements, which apply to science as a whole, it follows that the scientific findings on social Widerspiegelung presented in this publication can only be provisionally definitive. Research into social Widerspiegelung does not end there once and for all. The results presented in the present publication must, in the sense of the scientific-theoretical criterion of truth testing, satisfy the requirement of providing true findings on the subject of social Widerspiegelung. Of course, truth testing is not to be carried out in the form of verification and falsification, which is often seen as the only possible form of truth testing: That would be abbreviating and would not do justice to the subject matter.[4]

The introduction of results for social Widerspiegelung into scientific discourse must furthermore also take place in a comprehensible and verifiable argumentative structure. Poser thinks that such a conception of results "(…) eine *argumentative Struktur* haben muss; eben dies ist mit der These Kants gemeint, es müsse sich um ein 'nach Prinzipien geordnetes Ganzes' der Erkenntnis handeln".[5] Scientific knowledge is thus not an assertion, but results from a derivation. On the one hand, such a derivation is to be gained in a process of scientific analysis; on the other hand, this scientific analysis is to be presented as an argumentation to justify the results obtained. Results and their justification are a unity that constitutes the scientificity of these results.

It is to be formulated as a task that from the achieved state of scientific results social Widerspiegelung must be further researched: Matter is always in motion, society and humans are no exception to this determination. On the contrary, it must be stated that humans can influence their development through the possibility of voluntary action given to them. A stone or other components of inanimate nature are also subject to the law of matter, that matter is always in motion and development. However, the stone itself cannot influence this: It cannot initiate a development, it cannot influence the direction of a development, and it cannot accelerate or

---

[4] For detailed information on the truth test, see Autrata and Scheu (2015, p. 211 ff.).

[5] Poser (2012, p. 24); orig. cit.

6   Social Widerspiegelung and Social Work   199

decelerate the speed of such a development at its own discretion. Humans can do all this, which in turn means for phenomena that belong to the life of humans that they are subject to a high development dynamic that is difficult to predict. In order to keep pace with this developmental dynamic, ongoing research that accompanies this dynamic is necessary.

The dynamics of the development is to be emphasized exemplarily and in detail for the area of the ways and media of social Widerspiegelung. It can be assumed that social Widerspiegelung in humans will continue to follow the principles described[6] and will also build on the foundations introduced[7]: Social Widerspiegelung will therefore continue to include sensory perception, active control and gnostic processes as well as subjectivity and will ultimately lead to an image. Likewise, recognition and recognition will take place in social Widerspiegelung, which will continue to lead to individualisation.

On the other hand, the ways and media in which and through which social Widerspiegelung is carried out are subject to processes of change and development. The change and development of the paths and media through which social Widerspiegelung takes place is also ultimately based on human action: It was humans who invented such ways and media and implemented them in the social situation.

Social Widerspiegelung is always the recording of other humans. Of course, if one considers *how* humans carry out such a capture, striking developments can be observed. Social Widerspiegelung was and is possible in the direct presence of the participants, who stand face to face. But social Widerspiegelung is also possible via video conferencing, as current developments show. Likewise, forms of social Widerspiegelung based on the use of the Internet, computers and mobile phones are currently gaining considerable space. This can only be stated analytically at this point: Whether social Widerspiegelung thus becomes more incomplete or is subject to other impairments remains an open question. What speaks for the use of such ways of social Widerspiegelung is that contacts over long distances are no longer a problem. Perhaps – thinking anachronistically – Penelope would have been pleased to receive news and a photo of Odysseus during his long absence via social media?

The ways of social Widerspiegelung can therefore be subject to change: When you have contact with someone in the present, you do not always and exclusively talk face to face. This kind of thing existed in the past, too: you could make a phone call from home via the landline and, if you already had your own connection. If you

---

[6] cf. Chap. 2 in this volume.

[7] cf. Chap. 3 in this volume.

200 6 Social Widerspiegelung and Social Work

were not technically well equipped, you had to go to a telephone box. Even before that, you could send letters and keep in touch. In all these ways – video conferencing, messaging via social media, landline telephony, letters or meeting in person – it was and is possible to conduct social Widerspiegelung. There is also no hierarchization or normativity per se: The Corona pandemic showed that, under its conditions, face-to-face encounters are not always possible. Alternative ways of social Widerspiegelung, which can take place from a distance, offer considerable opportunities. It is, of course, not yet possible to assess what the consequences would be if social Widerspiegelung were to take place predominantly at a distance in terms of space and personnel: Social Widerspiegelung also takes place in an online conference or via video telephony, but not within direct sight, reach and hearing distance of other humans. Whether social Widerspiegelung is enriched by the outlined new ways or has to accept a loss must be pursued by scientific research.

Blanket condemnations, such as those made by Spitzer, will not be of any help in future scientific research into social Widerspiegelung. Spitzer makes polemical outbursts against the use of digital media and, in a book entitled "Digitale Demenz",[8] complains about the consequences of media use, which in his opinion arise from the use of computers or mobile phones. Spitzer says: "Wer möchte, dass aus seinen Kindern Mathematiker oder Spezialisten für Informationstechnik werden, der sorge für Fingerspiele statt für Laptops in den Kindergärten. Und wer die Schriftsprache ernst nimmt, der sollte eher für Bleistifte als für Tastaturen plädieren".[9] He does not provide evidence for his thesis that the use of computers by children and young humans could cause something like dementia, which he suggests with his book title.[10] Impairments of social Widerspiegelung are well conceivable, but certainly not linearly attributable to the – early – use of computers: reciprocity or understanding in social relationships may fail.[11] However, this can also be observed for the social relations of non-computer users. The causality claimed by Spitzer between early computer use and the resulting psychological damage to humans is an assumption and not the result of reliable scientific research.

If, therefore, the argumentation introduced, that further and permanent scientific research is indicated in view of the processes of development and change of social Widerspiegelung, is considered conclusive, the question arises as to who

---

[8] Book title by Spitzer (2012).

[9] Spitzer (2012, p. 203).

[10] cf. Spitzer (2012).

[11] cf. Sects. 5.1 and 5.2 in this volume

6 Social Widerspiegelung and Social Work 201

could be responsible for this. Since it is supposed to be a matter of scientific research, divisions of science come into consideration: Such divisions are the disciplines, i.e. the sub-areas of science.[12]

In order to clarify the question of which scientific discipline is suitable for ensuring further research into social Widerspiegelung, we must return to the definition that a scientific discipline is characterised by its ability to grasp an object in its entirety. Which scientific discipline, then, is capable of grasping social Widerspiegelung in its entirety, and in such a way that the insights gained in the process become adequate to the object?

In the present publication, results on the recording of social Widerspiegelung from different disciplines have already been introduced. This should be recapitulated and linked to the question of the extent to which this has made it possible to capture social Widerspiegelung in its entirety. We should start with the research direction that can be found as neurophysiology, neurobiology, neuroscience or brain research. This line of research belongs – strictly speaking – to different scientific disciplines: These are medicine, psychology and biology. The aforementioned Manfred Spitzer is a psychiatrist, i.e. he is located in the field of medicine. Hans Förstl is himself also a psychiatrist and psychotherapist. Förstl, however, as the subtitle of an important publication indicates, counts Theory of Mind with its investigation of neuronal connections to neurobiology and psychology.[13]

Neurophysiological explanations of psychological processes receive a lot of attention. Spitzer is less self-critical and considers his views, which call for abstinence from computer use among children and adolescents, to be proven. Förstl, on the other hand, admits that the results of neuroscience are far from being proven findings, but are currently still in the realm of speculation.[14] The lack of evidence for the results of neuroscience stands in striking contrast to their broad reception, especially by popular science.

It should also be noted that neuroscience has serious gaps in its theorising at crucial points: Neuroscience aims solely at the recording of neuronal and thus physiological processes. What humans think when their mirror or spindle neurons 'fire', however, cannot be grasped by neuroscience. If one relates this to social Widerspiegelung, one must come to the conclusion that neuroscience can currently at best only capture aspects of it. It has already been noted that objects such as subjectivity or society cannot be grasped by neuroscience. If neurons 'fire', is this

---

[12] cf. Scheu and Autrata (2018, p. 132 ff.).

[13] cf. Sect. 3.1 in this volume and Förstl (2012).

[14] cf. Walther/Förstl in: Förstl (2012, p. 103 ff.) as well as Sect. 3.1 in this volume.

the exact same process for every human being and in relation to all possible social conditions, leading to the same result? Here neuroscience falls far short of the entirety of social Widerspiegelung and – at least for the time being – is not a discipline that can be considered for the scientific elucidation of social Widerspiegelung.

Similarly to the concerns expressed about neuroscience's ability to scientifically grasp social Widerspiegelung in its entirety, the same applies to research on empathy: In this research, too, reference is often made to the notion of a Theory of Mind, that is, to the question of how humans conceptualize for themselves the process of humans apprehending other humans. This research is to be found within the framework of cognitive psychology, and thus stands overall within the disciplinary framework of psychology. It has already been pointed out that such approaches fall short and are normatively preformed: Humans can grasp what other humans do. If, however, this is reduced ex ante to the idea that it is only a matter of empathy or perspective-taking, the entirety of human possibilities and the subject matter is missed. Humans are not only guided by compassion in its social Widerspiegelung. The concept of perspective-taking makes it completely clear that subjectivity is not taken into account. A subject cannot adopt the perspective of another subject, because the subjectivity of the other person excludes this. Figuratively speaking, one cannot see through the eyes of another person, one is solely dependent on one's own eyes. Thus, it should also be critically noted for cognitive psychology that it does not do justice to the entirety of social Widerspiegelung in its work.

Thus, there are approaches within the discipline of psychology to capture social Widerspiegelung. Of course, it has to be said that neither the social nor Widerspiegelung are used as concepts. It can be stated for the presented approaches from cognitive psychology that empathy, perspective taking or theory of mind correspond in parts to what is defined by the authors of the present publication as the social in humans: It is about the apprehension and activities of and towards other humans. However, in the presented approaches from cognitive psychology, a recourse to the social in its entirety is not made: It remains with individual aspects such as empathy. But whether empathy belongs to a larger whole is not pursued in cognitive psychology.

Another – not only conceptual – difference to a large part of psychology as a discipline is to be noted: In psychology, humans's grasp of the world is not understood as Widerspiegelung, but as perception. Thus, Rohracher defines perception as "(…) komplexe, aus Sinnesempfindungen und Erfahrungskomponenten bestehende psychische Erscheinung, deren Inhalt im Raum lokalisiert wird und dadurch zur Auffassung von Gegenständen der Außenwelt führt".[15] Perception determined

---

[15] Rohracher (1960, p. 107).

6 Social Widerspiegelung and Social Work

in this way is an important field of work in psychology: "Die Wahrnehmung und die Wahrnehmungsfunktionen (…) bilden ein zentrales Forschungsfeld der Allgemeinen Psychologie, die in ihrem Teilgebiet, der Wahrnehmungspsychologie, praktische wie auch in speziellen Ansätzen theoretische Ergebnisse im Verlauf ihrer Entwicklung aufweisen kann".[16] Perceptual psychology is therefore a subfield of psychology and deals with the perception of humans.

Within the psychology of perception there are again different directions that conceptualize human perception on the background of their basic theoretical understanding. Not in or from all schools of psychology there are conceptions of a psychology of perception: Thus, from psychoanalysis and behaviorism perception is not thematized. In contrast, ideas of a psychology of perception can be found on the background of cognitive psychology.[17]

Perception, however, remains a rather unspecific term used by different schools of psychology for the study of the connection between sensations and the conception of the external world. It would go too far at this point to introduce and discuss different conceptions of perception against each other. Abels sceptically states: "Gerade im zentralen Forschungsbereich der Psychologie, dem der Wahrnehmung, wird signifikant, welche Vielfalt von Schulen und Richtungen (…) die Psychologie bestimmen, so daß von einer Einheitlichkeit dieser Wissenschaft, wenn überhaupt, nur im Sinne eines Desiderats die Rede sein kann".[18]

However, perception is to be distinguished from Widerspiegelung. Perceptual psychology looks at the connection between sensory perceptions and the external world. The perceiving humans appear predominantly as passive-receptive, who take in impressions and process them internally. The dimension of activity, which is central to Widerspiegelung, is not found in perceptual psychology. Widerspiegelung belongs to an active person who can obtain a different Widerspiegelung result just by changing his or her position. Widerspiegelung further incorporates subjecthood, which is not found in perceptual psychology. The dimension of the societality of humans's lives is also not pursued by the psychology of perception.

Widerspiegelung as an object and concept can be found in one school of thought in psychology, namely the Cultural-Historical School with authors such as Wygotski and Leontjew, as well as in the continuation in subject science, represented by Holzkamp.[19] Considerations of these authors have been included in the

---

[16] Abels in: Rexilius and Grubitzsch (1986, p. 317).
[17] cf. Goldstein (2002).
[18] Abels in: Rexilius and Grubitzsch (1986, p. 318).
[19] cf. Chap. 2 in this volume.

argumentation of the present publication. However, neither the cultural-historical school nor subject science specifies Widerspiegelung in terms of the social: The fact that there is a Widerspiegelung precisely in the social, i.e. towards other humans, is not addressed there. The theoretical grasp of social Widerspiegelung by authorship thus takes up considerations from the cultural-historical school and subject science – thus psychology – but is originally at home in social work.

When considering which scientific discipline might be predestined for the recording of social Widerspiegelung, sociology still needs to be taken into account. It has already been pointed out that the aspect of reciprocity has a special significance for sociological research.[20] Reciprocity has a double meaning: from the point of view of sociological authors, reciprocity refers to the exchange of things, but reciprocity is also a constituent of relationships. Thus it is pointed out that in the context of reciprocity "(…) zwischen Akteuren immer mehr getauscht wird als der rein ökonomische Vorgang andeutet. Mit dem 'mehr' ist die Beziehungsdimension gemeint: Mit jedem Austauschvorgang ist gleichzeitig ein Beziehungsvorgang verbunden. (…) Das Ausbleiben der Reziprozitätsleistung gefährdet die Beziehung".[21] Reciprocity thus stands – from a sociological point of view – as a significant process in the middle of relationships: Relationships of humans constitute and regulate themselves through the exchange of things. If a relationship does not succeed in bringing the exchange of things into a balanced relationship, the relationship is endangered.

This view of reciprocity is also found in the Latin proverb: Do ut des (I give so that you give). The reciprocity established by authors from sociology can therefore claim plausibility for itself. Stegbauer goes even further, he states that reciprocity is "(…) für den Zusammenhalt in der Gesellschaft verantwortlich (…)".[22] However, this exaggerates the scope and importance of reciprocity. In the coexistence of humans, there is certainly the aspect of the exchange of things and services, which can succeed or be disrupted by one-sidedness. At the societal level, however, it is probably reductive and inadmissibly simplistic to want to reduce everything to the simple principle of reciprocity.

Such sociological explanations of social relations, however, lack the necessary determination that reciprocity has social Widerspiegelung processes as its basis. Without social Widerspiegelung, reciprocity would not be possible: reciprocity needs social Widerspiegelung. Of course, without reciprocity the establishment

---

[20] cf. Sect. 5.1 in this volume.

[21] Stegbauer (2011, p. 129 f.).

[22] Stegbauer (2011, p. 129).

6 Social Widerspiegelung and Social Work

and maintenance of social relations is impossible. Social relations need reciprocal Widerspiegelung. This connection can be taken even further: Reciprocal Widerspiegelung and social relations are indispensable for the social life of humans together.

Thus, however, it can also be stated for explanatory approaches from sociology as a discipline that they take a look at significant aspects of social Widerspiegelung in partial areas. However, it is again not possible to capture social Widerspiegelung in its entirety. Thus, subjectivity is once again missing as a decisive factor for why humans realize reciprocity in one situation but not in another. Sociology is therefore not the right place for future research into social Widerspiegelung.

The authorship of the present publication proposes to locate the study of social Widerspiegelung in social work. This has two backgrounds to be mentioned: First, the authorship sees social work as an independent scientific discipline alongside other scientific disciplines. Social work is therefore not only application-oriented and draws its knowledge from reference disciplines. Rather, social work is an independent scientific discipline with its own subject matter. This requires that social work, as such a discipline, provides fundamental research services on its subject matter.[23]

Second, the object of social work must be clearly delineated so that it can, as a discipline, conduct its fundamental research. Lambers takes up the authors' position in this regard: He recapitulates the view of the authorship of the present publication in this way, that "(…) *Soziale* insgesamt soll Gegenstand der Sozialen Arbeit als Wissenschaft werden. Überraschend einfach ist zunächst der Ausgangspunkt ihrer Theoriebildung. Sie stellen fest, dass die wissenschaftliche Soziale Arbeit bis heute keine Klarheit darüber erlangt hat, was das sogenannte *Soziale* ist (…)".[24] It is the social, as determined in the authors' 2018 publication,[25] that constitutes the object of social work as a discipline.

It is therefore social work as a discipline that should scientifically work on the social as a whole and thus also on social Widerspiegelung. This is a specification made by the authors of the present publication and, at least in its reception, understood in this way by some authors. It remains to be seen whether the broad range of scholars in social work will subscribe to this view.

In favour of the proposal that social work as a discipline should assume responsibility for the social and social Widerspiegelung is the fact that several relevant publications have already been presented by the authorship of the present publication,

---

[23] cf. Scheu and Autrata (2018, p. 254 ff.).

[24] Lambers (2020, p. 220 f.).

[25] See Scheu and Autrata (2018).

who come from the field of social work. It is therefore not the case that it is only a requirement yet to be fulfilled to research the social and social Widerspiegelung from the context of social work: Results of such fundamental research already exist.[26] The demand is to be understood in such a way that social work as a discipline should commit itself thematically to the study of the social and social Widerspiegelung.

This clarifies the question of responsibility for the scientific study of social Widerspiegelung. At the same time, however, the question arises as to what this means for professional social work? Should there not also be a professional occupation with social Widerspiegelung and what would be its tasks?

Two aspects are to be named, which will be outlined in more detail in the next subchapter. The first aspect is that social Widerspiegelung repeatedly fails and thus causes problems and challenges. The starting point for dealing with social Widerspiegelung is thus – in reverse – the perspective of reducing or completely eliminating such problems. Of course, in dealing with the problems of social Widerspiegelung, it must not be forgotten that social Widerspiegelung also brings with it important potentials that often remain unused. Social Widerspiegelung is therefore not only a source of misunderstanding or misinterpretation, social Widerspiegelung also brings opportunities. The aspect to be pursued in the next subchapter is that of identifying problems and potentials of social Widerspiegelung and thus finding starting points for accompaniment and support. Accompaniment and support of social Widerspiegelung is in turn to be institutionally located in professional social work.

6.2 Social Widerspiegelung as Framing for the Profession

Social Widerspiegelung is a complex process, the outcome of which can vary. It is worth recalling the social Widerspiegelung through which Eurykleia recognized Odysseus, who had returned home. In contrast to Eurykleia, Penelope, Odysseus' wife, did not recognize her husband: Penelope likewise saw the supposed beggar who had arrived at her court, but could not recognize Odysseus in him. For Eurykleia, it was through recognizing the scar on her thigh that she was able to recognize Odysseus as Odysseus. When comparing the social Widerspiegelung of Eurykleia and Penelope, one finds that they both reflected the same person, Odysseus. One of the two women, Penelope, comes to the conclusion in her social

---

[26] See Scheu and Autrata (2011, 2013, and 2018).

6 Social Widerspiegelung and Social Work 207

Widerspiegelung that the person reflected is a beggar unknown to her; the other woman, Eurykleia, recognizes in the person the long-absent Odysseus.

Social Widerspiegelung involves recognizing or recognizing other humans by their specific characteristics and peculiarities. This can be illustrated for the present in this way: A person meets another person and recognizes him: 'Ah, that is Franz'. Franz is recognised on the basis of his specific features, such as grey hair, glasses and pale skin. But if Franz has dyed his hair, wears contact lenses and regularly visits a solarium, the process of recognition is made more difficult, but it is by no means cancelled, because the personal specificity of a person also includes unchangeable features (or features that can only be changed with great difficulty by external influences) and these too can be recognised: Ah, that is Franz with the big ears. However, the uniqueness of a person can also be socially framed. One might think here of Franz wearing a police uniform. Franz could also be recognized from this. However, the recognition of the latter feature, the uniform, presupposes societal knowledge in humans, in the form that police officers usually wear a uniform. Again, it is possible that Franz, the policeman, is not so easily recognized in casual clothing: Features that are otherwise considered specific are then missing.

Social Widerspiegelung was reduced to the aspect of recognition via the examples in the previous section: even this shows that social Widerspiegelung of the same person can lead to different results. This does not even take into account the really complex interactions of subjectivity and intersubjectivity on social Widerspiegelung: The image that emerges as a result of social Widerspiegelung is partly to be grasped in a mode of yes or no. Is it Ulysses or is he not? Once a conclusion has been reached, however, this by no means settles everything: what have 20 years of absence done to Odysseus would also have to be addressed via social Widerspiegelung. Equally, however, it is also a question of what the 20 years of absence have done to the subjects reflecting him. Can we mutually understand what has happened to the other person in the meantime? In this context, there are serious difficulties and hurdles for a successful social Widerspiegelung.

Recapitulating what has been said so far, one can conclude: Social Widerspiegelung is fundamental for the construction and maintenance of the social and especially of social relations.[27] Thus social Widerspiegelung is of high importance for humans (of course also for other living beings, but the focus of these remarks is on humans). Human life takes place – apart from a few exceptions – in the social, i.e. with and in relation to other humans. The way in which this relationship to one another takes shape is essentially guided by processes of social Widerspiegelung. For human coexistence, this aspect must not be neglected.

---

[27] cf. Chap. 4 in this volume.

The process of reciprocal Widerspiegelung in humans provides the basis for social relations. However, this does not mean that it is always a matter of successful social Widerspiegelung and successful social relations. A look into everyday life and the practice of social work shows that social relations in many cases have to do with problems and challenges, that they sometimes fail: An unclear and conflictual situation as a scenario of intersubjectivity in social relations is a frequently occurring case in professional social work. Usually, in the Widerspiegelung segment of sensory perception, one can only rely on the recording of facial expressions or vocal expression: The recording of the subjectivity of the counterpart must subsequently make do with assumptions and conjectures. When subjectivity of clients becomes apparent, for example through a verbalized position or even a demand, such a version of subjective quality of life can be quite contrary to the subjectivity of other humans: Problems and challenges for professional social work thus often arise from scenarios of intersubjectivity. The starting point for deciding between conceivable alternatives for action in the context of professional social work are essentially processes of social Widerspiegelung.

Social Widerspiegelung is therefore essential for professional social work: it can be a problem, but also an opportunity. This can become problematic if the reciprocal Widerspiegelung processes are subject to deception. One can recognize a person or not, one can also misrecognize humans. For example, the person might not recognize his or her counterpart in the 'right' form, thus deceiving himself or herself: The other person may not be as friendly as was assumed in advance. Such a deception can also occur in the process of reciprocity: a person develops an assessment of what another person thinks about him from the social Widerspiegelung. He then acts according to this assessment. However, it is possible that a misjudgement results in an action, which in turn is misjudged, since the reasons for the action cannot be understood.[28]

The possible range of results of social Widerspiegelung should be pointed out. Social Widerspiegelung can determine exactly what has been reflected in the image. But is there such a thing at all? Firstly, social Widerspiegelung is always carried out from the subject standpoint; secondly, the socially reflected humans are also subjects who can act while being reflected by other humans. Thus, a Widerspiegelung as a result of social Widerspiegelung is always influenced by subjects: the standard of a 'right' or 'wrong' social Widerspiegelung is thus not objectifiable. Nevertheless, in the sense of a possible range of results of social Widerspiegelung, it can be assumed on the one hand that social Widerspiegelung can succeed less well, i.e. is subject to deceptions or errors. The result is problems

---

[28] This aspect is by no means to be understood in the sense of constructivism.

6 Social Widerspiegelung and Social Work 209

stemming from such faulty social Widerspiegelung. On the other side of the range of possible outcomes is the possibility that something is socially reflected that does not yet exist or does not exist completely: Social Widerspiegelung is not only something like a measuring instrument for what is given, but also a sensorium to recognize a potential. Social Widerspiegelung on this side of the scale thus captures not less, but more than the objectively already given reality. For an approach to social Widerspiegelung by professional social work, this spectrum needs to be considered. Concentrating on mistakes and – as a consequence – problems and challenges would be abbreviating and would not do justice to the object, namely social Widerspiegelung and its range.

So there are many possible causes that can make social Widerspiegelung a problem, a challenge, a task or an opportunity. Before thinking about this for professional work, a central premise of social Widerspiegelung must be emphasized: The outcome of social Widerspiegelung is accurate from the subjective perspective of those being reflected. The process of social Widerspiegelung via sensory perception, active control, gnostic classification and ultimately to form an image takes place in relation to the respective subjectivity: from a subjective point of view, the respective result is 'correct'. This result enters the subsequent action via a subjective justification: Eurykleia recognizes Odysseus and subsequently welcomes him as her returned ruler; Penelope does not recognize Odysseus and invites the supposed beggar to stay at her court and eat something. In this example, it would be conceivable that Penelope's identifiable social Widerspiegelung problem would be remedied by an additional piece of information. But: had Eurykleia rushed to Penelope in jubilation to tell her that Odysseus had returned, would Penelope have believed it? As the saga progresses, it becomes apparent that Penelope remained skeptical as to whether the beggar, who seemed unknown to her, was really Odysseus: She demanded additional proof from him after he had identified himself as Odysseus. He had to know about the special construction of the common marriage bed, which was known only to Odysseus, who had built the bed on the trunk of an olive tree.

This makes it clear that subjective results of social Widerspiegelung are 'right' for the reflectors in the first place. Additional information can help to correct problems or fallacies. However, it is not always possible for humans to rush in 'from behind the scenes' to provide the information to correct the errors of social Widerspiegelung.

What is to be questioned anyway is what is to be classified as error or mistake with regard to social Widerspiegelung. One could still label the dichotomous decision whether the man arriving at the court of Ithaca was Odysseus or not as 'right' or 'wrong'. But what would be said from Penelope's point of view to the following question: is the man returning home still the Odysseus she last saw 20 years ago? In between are years of participation in an extremely violent war for Troy, adventures on the return journey that took Odysseus to the underworld, and love affairs with various women. Of course, one may object that these are just incidents that happened to a legendary hero. But is 'real' life so much quieter? There, too, the necessity arises to grasp humans and their actions by means of social Widerspiegelung. There is no such thing as 'right' or 'wrong'. However, the requirement for social Widerspiegelung to provide subjective reasons for social action remains. The image of another human being obtained through social Widerspiegelung enters into social relations in a way that triggers action.

The tension remains that social Widerspiegelung has to deal with a complex initial situation and diverse information that has to be condensed in such a way that a subjectively justified action can be derived from it. Even if one – supposedly – does not act, this is ultimately also an action: there is no standstill in the lives of humans. Even if one does nothing, one favours developments that take place. Through the reciprocity of the social, one is always involved in what is happening. Other humans reflect what one does oneself and draw their conclusions from it. The process of the social thus continues.

The demand for social Widerspiegelung is therefore not small: humans must constantly engage with other humans through social Widerspiegelung. Moreover, what other humans do is not always easy to grasp. It has already been shown under the guiding concept of understanding that social Widerspiegelung is not only directed at the surface, i.e. the sensory perception of other humans's actions, but also at the rationales behind them.[29] For example, if a person leaves another person, i.e. ends a social relationship with that person, this may be classified very differently in social Widerspiegelung: If one can grasp and thus understand the associated subjective justifications, this may lead to a different Widerspiegelung of the person than if no effort is made to understand these subjective justifications at all. The action remains the same, but by breaking down the reasons via understanding, other possibilities of classification and evaluation arise.

Understanding in itself is the attempt to grasp the subjective reasons of another person. Understanding as an important form of social Widerspiegelung is thus the approach to the subject standpoint of another person, whom one wants to comprehend in his being-so. In itself, understanding is the engagement with another person's subject standpoint. Understanding can thus be an important step for social relations: social action can appear in a different light if one arrives at an understanding of the subjective justifications of another person via social Widerspiegelung. If the social actions of other humans remain misunderstood, there is indeed a reciprocal

---

[29] cf. Sect. 5.2 in this volume.

6 Social Widerspiegelung and Social Work
211

reaction to them: However, the component of the justifications that one could not or did not want to make oneself understood is missing.

Based on the guiding concept of understanding, it was thus made explicit that social Widerspiegelung does not always achieve what it could. Subjective reasons of other humans are by no means always understood, often no attempt is even made to realize such an understanding. Apparently this leads to constrictions and misunderstandings in social relations: What the other person's reasons are or were for doing something does not appear, the reciprocal action must be based on assumptions. The resulting problems can be imagined.

Social Widerspiegelung is not limited to a specific and separate area of humans's lives. Social Widerspiegelung is therefore not only to be found in the segment that is called private life: This includes constellations such as family, the upbringing of children or social relationships in a circle of friends or a club. Social Widerspiegelung can also be found in education and in professional life. One could list many more segments in which social Widerspiegelung plays an essential role. However, there is no area of humans's lives in which social Widerspiegelung cannot be found. Accordingly, the consideration must be continued that problems and challenges of social Widerspiegelung also run through the entire life horizon of humans. In addition, these are often problems that can have an existentially detrimental effect, if not even threaten one's existence.

Such problem situations and challenges, which result from social Widerspiegelung, can also be identified in the fields of social work: The clients of social work reflect other humans and draw conclusions for their actions. Here, too, misunderstandings and deceptions can be identified. At this point it would lead too far to look at individual cases and their processing. What needs to be addressed, however, is the structural situation of problems of social Widerspiegelung and the question of how this can be worked on professionally with the aim of accompanying such problem situations and challenges.

On the one hand, it would fall short of the mark to take up problems of social Widerspiegelung normatively and to refer them back to the responsibility of individual humans as weaknesses or failures. Of course, it is individual humans who realize social Widerspiegelung and thereby also bring their own subjectivity and intentionality to bear. Does one want, for example, it would have to be asked, to understand the subjective reasons of other humans in every case? Is it not functional in the sense of restrictive orientation to pursue one's own advantage by means of a corresponding utilization of social Widerspiegelung and thereby to accept that the quality of life of other humans suffers as a result?[30] That there are problems

---

[30] cf. Sect. 5.3 in this volume.

stemming from social Widerspiegelung is an analytical consideration, not an attribution of blame. Work on tasks related to social Widerspiegelung must analyse and take note of the functional contexts in which humans live. Humans are not determined by the circumstances in which they live: they always have choices between which they can choose.[31] This is also true when dealing with social Widerspiegelung. However, it is neither appropriate nor sufficient to say that humans deal with the possibilities of social Widerspiegelung in a wrong way. There remains a field of tension in dealing with possibilities, towards which it is necessary to think about how it can be changed.

Just as it is insufficient to refer problems of social Widerspiegelung to the responsibility of humans alone, it is not appropriate to try to solve problems of social Widerspiegelung from the perspective of the audience. It is not expedient to shout or whisper to someone that he/she has overlooked this or that, should correct his/her evaluation. It should be remembered that at the end of a social Widerspiegelung there is a subjective justification for action. Thus, what is done is justified from a subjective point of view. A subjective justification cannot be undermined by declaring it false: Penelope was convinced that the presumably unattractive beggar could not be her husband, who had departed as a radiant hero. Even when Odysseus came forward to correct Penelope's attitude, she demanded further proof. This proves that a subjective view resulting from social Widerspiegelung is not easily changed.

It should be noted in this context that there is no real tradition and institutionalization in the work on tasks stemming from social Widerspiegelung. It would probably hardly be possible to seriously deny that such tasks exist. Nevertheless, there is no, or at most little, anchoring of work on such tasks. This was already debated in the previous chapter for the area of the scientific processing of social Widerspiegelung: social Widerspiegelung in its entirety is not covered by other disciplines, only from social work is this gap filled – by the authors and a few other authors.[32] Attention to the issue of the social and its promotion raised by authorship can be found, for example, in Ortmann et al., who also belong to social work: "Unter Verwendung der von Scheu und Autrata (2011) formulierten Sozialbeziehungstheorie als Grundlage Sozialer Arbeit (…) wären somit belastende Sozialbeziehungen abzubauen, förderliche soziale Unterstützungsleistungen von Netzwerken und Sozialbeziehungen zu stärken, um auf diesem Weg die Lebensführungsoptionen von Betroffenen zu erweitern und zwar insbesondere mit dem Ziel, ihre Lebensqualität zu verbessern".[33] Although a social relationship the-

---

[31] cf. Sect. 2.3 in this volume.

[32] cf. Sect. 6.1 in this volume.

[33] Ortmann et al. in: Lammel et al. (2017, p. 39).

6 Social Widerspiegelung and Social Work

ory was not presented by the authors or at least not named as such, it can be read from the formulation of Ortmann et al. that they consider the work on social relationships and thus on subjective quality of life to be significant for social work.

A prerequisite for the professional promotion of subjective quality of life, however, is a corresponding theory of the subject in its entirety. This leads to an understanding of the contribution of social Widerspiegelung to subjective quality of life. If one does not have a basic theory of social Widerspiegelung, a professional approach to solving problems and tasks arising from social Widerspiegelung can only be partial. A verdict against the use of computers and mobile phones or the promotion of empathy are too much guided by normative and too little by analytical ideas. The analytical breadth of the breakdown of social Widerspiegelung must be preserved when considering how to address related problems and tasks. Thus, it is not appropriate to ignore the subject-bound nature of social Widerspiegelung: Who, for example, would allow herself/himself to be told that her/his Widerspiegelung of another person is simply wrong or at least flawed? Presumably, an intervention presented in this way would hardly be able to contribute successfully to solving actually existing problems of social Widerspiegelung.

As a result, the question arises as to how professional work on social Widerspiegelung could be more successful. If nothing is done, problems of social Widerspiegelung will hardly disappear by themselves. It is not discernible that humans will suddenly be able to shape social Widerspiegelung better or differently. Thus, the potentials of social Widerspiegelung remain buried and unused.

Humans must not be accused of deficient social Widerspiegelung in a generalized way. Furthermore, it is not appropriate to subordinate social Widerspiegelung to a scientific control body that evaluates and uncovers deficiencies in this regard. Social Widerspiegelung is realized by subjects and is therefore the responsibility of humans as subjects. But: There is a field of tension between subjective responsibility and nevertheless arising problems. The fact that social Widerspiegelung is subjectively bound back and responsible does not mean that it is beyond all doubt and always leads to 'correct' results.

By way of explanation of these considerations, reference should be made to the concept of self-hostility that has been introduced[34]: This concept states that humans can become an enemy to themselves through restrictive orientations, thus harming their own subjective quality of life. In doing so, one aligns oneself with given possibilities and thus actively adopts the structure of the given. This also applies to the social and social relations. One accepts the constrictions in some social relations: Social Widerspiegelung is only Widerspiegelung of the *given*, not of what is

---

[34] cf. Sect. 4.1 in this volume.

possible beyond it.[35] Social Widerspiegelung is thereby subjectively bound back and answered for, but it also reproduces a given structure of possibility. It would not be appropriate to discredit this as deficient. Social Widerspiegelung is, after all, also appropriate and pertinent: it arrives at an image that adequately captures the other person(s). It merely remains outside the perspective that another approach would also be possible. The area of tension here is how the perspectives of humans as subjects, which they have realized in their forms of social Widerspiegelung, can be mediated with possible other perspectives.

In order to classify how easy or how difficult it is to envisage such a broadening of perspective for one's own social Widerspiegelung, it is necessary to question whether one is so sure oneself that one will never settle or have settled in restrictive social relationships. The threat scenario is characterized in such a way that existing social relations could break up or change in their structuring in such a way that one experiences disadvantages from them. If one reflects the given in social relations in an open-ended way, changes are conceivable. It is not a foregone conclusion that changes will always take exactly the course one hopes for. Losses or even greater constrictions can also be the result. The consequence of such conjectures is not infrequently the observance of a proverb: A bird in the hand is worth two in the bush. One then makes do with what one has. The fact that what one 'has' in some social relationships is detrimental to one's own quality of life – at least in the long term – is lost sight of.

Thus, on the one hand, there are problems that result from social Widerspiegelung; on the other hand, the processing of such problems of social Widerspiegelung cannot be thought of as a simple process in which one arrives at the result by the shortest route. What needs to be taken into account is the involvement of humans's subjectivity in their social Widerspiegelung, the results they achieve in the process, and the options for action they derive from it. Furthermore, the self-determination of humans who are responsible for what they do must be taken into account: No one can dictate from the outside what the 'right' outcome of social Widerspiegelung is or should be. Ultimately, one cannot live life for other humans: The decision for or against a certain option in the social is up to humans themselves.

However, if one leaves social Widerspiegelung as it is – with consideration for subjective responsibility – the problems also remain unchanged. It is thus a balancing act between the idea of wanting to remedy problems of social Widerspiegelung and the necessary consideration of the subjective responsibility of social Widerspiegelung as well as of the social as a whole.

---

[35] cf. Sect. 5.3 in this volume.

6 Social Widerspiegelung and Social Work

If one links this idea of wanting to work on problems of social Widerspiegelung, taking into account subjective responsibility, with the considerations in the previous sub-chapter, it becomes clear that this is a continuation of the disciplinary tasks for social work: The scientific-fundamental research of social Widerspiegelung radiates out into the application in the profession. Social Widerspiegelung must be researched in its entirety, as was the postulate in the previous chapter, and social work as a discipline should take on this task.[36] However, this is not the end of the task for social work: it should continue to realise the transition from fundamental research to application in the profession for social Widerspiegelung as an object. The guiding question for the segment of tasks resulting from social Widerspiegelung is: How can a treatment of such tasks turn out that does justice to the specificity of social Widerspiegelung? Particular consideration must be given to the question of how external influence can be combined with respect for subjective responsibility.

Thus, one cannot work on and solve problems of social Widerspiegelung without knowledge about the nature of social Widerspiegelung. Knowledge about social Widerspiegelung is a prerequisite for working on problems and challenges in this regard, but it is not enough: knowledge about social Widerspiegelung must be embedded in ideas about how such processes of working on problems and challenges of social Widerspiegelung could be designed. It should be made clear that this is a plea for disciplinary and professional unity. Social work as a whole should link fundamental research and its application. Results from fundamental research on social Widerspiegelung are the basis from which considerations on the implementation of these results are made.

Two advantages would be associated with the realization of such an idea: First, it would be associated with a stringent theory formation for social work that breaks down an object – namely the social and social Widerspiegelung – from fundamental research to application orientation in a stringent theory. In fact, as Lambers sceptically judges, "(…) stehen wir vor einer Ansammlung von unterschiedlichen Theorien, Theorieentwürfen oder Theoriefragmenten, bei denen Anzeichen für das Zustandekommen eines konvergierenden, mehr oder weniger in sich geschlossenen Theoriegebäudes Sozialer Arbeit vordergründig nicht in Sicht ist".[37] For social work, then, fragmentation into divergent approaches and theoretical designs could be overcome. Moreover, the body of scientific knowledge that guides social work as a profession is composed of very different sources: Basic knowledge is drawn from knowledge that comes from so-called reference disciplines.[38] It is to be

---

[36] cf. Sect. 6.1 in this volume.

[37] Lambers (2020, p. 3).

[38] cf. Scheu and Autrata (2018, p. 132 ff.).

criticized that social work theory drafts refer eclectically to reference disciplines and formulate approaches that are usually not systematically presented and derived. In their application to the profession, completely different schools of thought are often drawn upon. In short – and with Lambers – it can be said: Social work as a discipline has so far "(…) nicht gelungen, eine für ihre Profession einheits- und identitätsstiftende Theorie zu entwickeln (…)".[39] The present publication contrasts these weaknesses of social work with a consistent theory that refers to the social and social Widerspiegelung as an object.

The second advantage would be to be able to form social Widerspiegelung as an object from fundamental research to application orientation into a self-contained theory. The specificity of social Widerspiegelung requires that its components be adequately captured: This applies to fundamental research as well as to the layout of efforts to remedy problems of social Widerspiegelung. This is what is to be achieved for social Widerspiegelung: An adoption of fundamental research findings in the design of efforts to reduce problems of social Widerspiegelung. But this can only succeed if work on problems of social Widerspiegelung is not trivialized. For example, it would not be adequate to try to deal with problems of social Widerspiegelung by means of advice or tips.

Work on problems of social Widerspiegelung must rather begin with understanding in the social. This in turn derives from the fundamentally explained constitution of social Widerspiegelung: social Widerspiegelung is carried out from the subject's point of view. Social Widerspiegelung therefore does not always lead to the same results, but to results that vary from person to person. Thus, problems of social Widerspiegelung are also essentially induced by the subject standpoint. Problems of social Widerspiegelung must therefore first be understood in their specifics so that they can be reduced or eliminated altogether. The essential starting point for working on problems of social Widerspiegelung is thus understanding.

Understanding in the context of the profession is indeed also understanding, as it is part of social Widerspiegelung between humans as the comprehension of subjective reasons.[40] However, understanding also belongs to the context of science and a profession, namely social work, as an intended component of the formation of a theory of how problems of social Widerspiegelung can be dealt with. Understanding is therefore always linked to humans, but in this case it is seen specifically as a component of scientific – and from this derived professional – considerations of how work on problems of social Widerspiegelung is to be approached. Understanding thus does not arise unplanned and by chance in humans's lives, but

---

[39] cf. Sect. 6.1 in this volume.

[40] cf. Sect. 5.2 in this volume.

6 Social Widerspiegelung and Social Work 217

is anticipated specifically and scientifically in the context of working on problems of social Widerspiegelung. The results of social Widerspiegelung in humans's lives are by no means universally understood, nor is there always an attempt to understand them. In order to deal with problems of social Widerspiegelung, it is, of course, essential to understand how the subject's point of view has entered into the Widerspiegelung.

The element of understanding in the context of the profession is the starting point for dealing with problems of social Widerspiegelung. Apodictically it can be stated: If one cannot understand the background of such problems, one cannot work on them in a goal-oriented way. Understanding is a milestone that must be passed. When understanding has been reached as a milestone, the further path can be planned.

Work on problems of social Widerspiegelung is to be differentiated as work with individual humans, as work on social relations and as a preoccupation with social constellations. This is to be sketched out for the three areas mentioned in order to make clear what is meant by this. It is obvious that further clarifications and adaptations are still necessary. At this point, however, it is first of all a matter of marking out the path along which social work should continue fundamental research on social Widerspiegelung towards an orientation towards application.

Social Widerspiegelung belongs directly to the concerns of an individual person. Thus, problems of such Widerspiegelung are also within the sphere of influence of humans as individuals. Humans are capable of working out problems of social Widerspiegelung for themselves: Penelope had not initially recognized Odysseus, which is clearly a problem of social Widerspiegelung. For herself, in order to get clarity, she developed a strategy: Odysseus was subjected to a test by Penelope, which he was able to pass. This at least solved the problem of non-recognition: however, noticeable reservations still remained with Penelope.

Admittedly, it is not always so easy, quick and possible to deal with problems of social Widerspiegelung on one's own. For this reason, the possibilities for support that have arisen from the existence of science with its division into disciplines must be taken into account: It has already been pointed out that it is social work as a discipline that is supposed to fan out fundamental research on social Widerspiegelung into an application-oriented use for remedying problems of social Widerspiegelung. This signals that knowledge about the nature of social Widerspiegelung should be usefully introduced into the treatment of problems.

In this first segment, the processing of problems of social Widerspiegelung is to be considered from the horizon of individual humans with the inclusion of the support possibilities through social work as a profession: What do individual humans contribute to the emergence of such problems, where and how can they start to remedy them? This is again to be thought of on the background of understanding. Problems of social Widerspiegelung are, on the one hand, man-made problems, since social Widerspiegelung is performed by humans. Thus, such problems cannot be solved without the intervention of the same humans. It can, however, be important and further-reaching if social work gives supporting and accompanying impulses as to where and how to start. This has to happen in the tension between immanence and innovation: Approaches to a solution of problems of social Widerspiegelung must result from the immanent comprehension of the associated subject standpoint. This, however, must be followed by an impulse for change and innovation, otherwise the status quo will remain. The impulse for innovation in turn results from the knowledge of how social Widerspiegelung is constituted.

In order to be able to imagine the problems of social Widerspiegelung that can arise from the horizon of a single person, we will mention a typical one: A typical set of problems is that around constancy and change of a person who is socially reflected.[41] Of course, it should be noted immediately that there are also other such problems, and that a view of the individual person is short-sighted. Nevertheless, it should be explained what problems can arise around the Widerspiegelung of constancy and change of another person: Social Widerspiegelung, in order to achieve an adequate Widerspiegelung, should keep pace with what is currently happening in another person, but often does not. This may be due to the fact that, from the point of view of the subject of the reflecting person, changes in the reflected person do not appear desirable, and the – supposedly – still given constant is seen as the achieved result of social Widerspiegelung. Distortions are the consequence, the correction of which can be triggered by support from outside.

Social Widerspiegelung is always bound to individual humans who reflect other humans. Social Widerspiegelung as the Widerspiegelung of other humans thus takes place in the context of social relations, if it is not performed once, but repeatedly or even regularly. This also covers the second area in which problems of social Widerspiegelung can occur. At the same time, this is the second area – after starting with individual humans – in which one can think about starting to remedy problems and challenges of social Widerspiegelung. What remains is that social Widerspiegelung is always realized by a human being: Thus, it is equally always necessary to consider what individual humans do in social Widerspiegelung and what problems and challenges this may trigger. However, a promising way to work on these problems – beyond dealing with individual humans – is to start with certain constellations of social relations.

---

[41] Societal knowledge, which is processed in the gnostic process, plays an important role in this: cf. Sect. 4.2 in this volume.

6 Social Widerspiegelung and Social Work 219

A typical problem area in this segment is reciprocity or – more precisely – the identification of a lack of reciprocity. This means that an imbalance is found in the comparison of one's own social actions with those of one or more other humans involved: One's own social actions are summed up in terms of the effort required to do them or their effectiveness and placed in a ratio to the social actions of other humans with whom one is in a social relationship. The result is usually in favour of one's own actions and to the disadvantage of other humans in this social relationship. Vice versa, the other humans in the social relationship often make similar considerations and come to the opposite conclusion: in their view, it is they who suffer from a lack of reciprocity in the sense of balance of social actions.[42]

In this typical constellation of social Widerspiegelung, too, the problems catch the eye. It is obvious that in view of the problems that arise, it makes sense not to start with individual humans alone. One person alone can hardly free himself or herself from this reciprocity trap: No matter what he or she does, there is a high probability that it will be judged as too little by the others involved. In addition, the person who has made an effort to develop will probably be disappointed by the lack of appreciation, which will lead to renewed complaints about the lack of reciprocity.

It is recognizable that innovative impulses from outside can make an important contribution to solving problems of social Widerspiegelung in such and other constellations of social relations. The analytical external view is not involved in the web of mutual – expressed or unspoken – reproaches. If individuals become proactive in working through the problems exemplified, they are caught up in the immanence of the situation. If the humans who form the social relationship with the described Widerspiegelung problems of the stated lack of reciprocity want to achieve a change, they would have to communicate about it: This is precisely what they have failed to do so far. In this respect, it becomes clear that accompaniment and support by social work, which adopts an external point of view not bound up in the situation and has special knowledge of social Widerspiegelung, can take on an important role. It should be emphasized once again that such an external point of view of social work is based on understanding on the one hand, but on the other hand it must also intend innovation and initiate development and change.

A third area through and in which problems of social Widerspiegelung can arise is societal framing. Social Widerspiegelung always stands in a societal framing. Via the gnostic processes that belong to social Widerspiegelung, reference is made to societal knowledge, but also to social forms of thought. This is constitutive for the specifically human form of Widerspiegelung, since knowledge stocks can be used via the reference to societality.

---

[42] cf. Sect. 5.1 in this volume.

However, the reference to societality can also lead to problems. Not everything that comes from the stock of societal knowledge and thought is secure. There are also, what is relevant for social Widerspiegelung, distortions that have led to common forms of thinking. A typical problem of social Widerspiegelung that results from the segment of social integration are attributions that are made for migrants, for example. There, a supposed knowledge about the being like this of migrants is imported via gnostic processes and seen as the actual result of social Widerspiegelung. The characteristics and above all weaknesses of migrants that are determined as the result of social Widerspiegelung are thus often based on adopted forms of thinking that have nothing to do with actual sensory perceptions. Such problems of social Widerspiegelung obscure the view of other humans.

Obviously, an approach to problems of social Widerspiegelung that stem from the societal framing is too short-sighted for individual humans or social relations alone. Both, the approach to individual humans and social relations, can also be appropriate, since problems of social Widerspiegelung are often multidimensional, i.e. they are also located in individual humans and humans in social relations. However, problems of social Widerspiegelung that stem from the social framework must also be addressed in relation to this framework. The aim must be to highlight the connection between social Widerspiegelung and societal framing and to put social forms of thinking to the test. Of course, this is easier said than done, but it is important as an indication of the connection between the identification of the causes of problems of social Widerspiegelung and their corresponding need for treatment.

Also for this third segment, from which problems of social Widerspiegelung can originate, namely the societal framing, it is promising to think of an accompaniment and support by social work. The connection between societal framing and social Widerspiegelung must first be established in order to be able to work on it. Furthermore, dealing with problems within the social horizon is not an easy undertaking: To name starting points and perspectives is the task to be accomplished from the point of view of professional social societal framingwork.

Outlook

7

The outlook of what is to be deduced for the future from the results of the present publication starts with the persons mentioned for the starting point of the argument, namely Penelope and Odysseus[1]: The two met again after 20 years of separation. Thus, after a long interruption, their mutual social Widerspiegelung resumed. Bierl writes about this: "Die ἀναγνώρισις der beiden über zwanzig Jahre getrennten Eheleute Penelope und Odysseus, auf die die Erzählung der Odyssee wie auf ein τέλος und einen Höhepunkt hin zugespitzt ist, hat erwartungsgemäß zahlreiche Behandlungen erfahren. (…) Als zentrales Problem galt immer, das kühl distanzierte, nahezu abweisende Verhalten der Gattin verständlich zu machen (…)".[2] Whether Penelope really did not recognize Odysseus or whether she first wanted to clarify and understand for herself what circumstances and reasons had led Odysseus back home after such a long time remains open in the Odyssey. It is striking that Penelope shows great reserve towards Odysseus. This suggests that she still has reservations about continuing her social relationship with Odysseus without further ado, as if nothing had happened.

There are thus problems between Penelope and Odysseus that stem from the long interruption of their mutual social Widerspiegelung. It is quite conceivable that in the mutual gnostic process they reflect on what may have happened in the meantime: has the heroic Odysseus met other women and how did that turn out,

---

[1] cf. Chap. 1 in this volume.

[2] Bierl in: Bierl et al. (2004, p. 103). ἀναγνώρισις (anagnorisis) is to be translated as recognition, τέλος (telos) as goal.

© The Author(s), under exclusive license to Springer Fachmedien Wiesbaden GmbH, part of Springer Nature 2023
O. Autrata, B. Scheu, *Subjective quality of life and social work*,
https://doi.org/10.1007/978-3-658-40400-0_7

Penelope may have asked herself. Likewise, Odysseus may be in doubt as to whether or not the beautiful Penelope has succumbed to the advances of the suitors at her court.

In the Odyssey, Penelope and Odysseus overcome such problems of social Widerspiegelung. A reconciliation takes place: "In inniger Verschlingung vergessen sie die Zeit, und Athene veranlaßt, daß die Nacht verlängert wird ".[3] Penelope and Odysseus thus succeed in getting closer again by their own efforts. Of course, in Athena, the Greek goddess of wisdom, they have an energetic supporter: Athena is even able to prolong the night so that the couple can spend more time together undisturbed.

With the reconciliation, however, by no means all problems of social Widerspiegelung are eliminated: obviously, at the moment between Penelope and Odysseus there is again an interpersonal attraction. Still open, however, is the time when they were separated: This long past has created a gap in their mutual social Widerspiegelung, which they must now fill. Bierl describes this as follows: "Es beginnt Penelope mit ihrer Schilderung der Ereignisse, die eigentlich eher einen ausgedehnten Zustand des Leids darstellen und kaum in eine narrative Abfolge gebracht werden können (…). Dann gibt Odyssseus [sic!] einen Bericht über seine Abenteuer (…). Erst jetzt haben sie sich ganz wieder und können sich dem Schlummer hingeben (…)".[4]

Penelope and Odysseus have thus achieved intersubjectivity and mutual understanding, realizing the aspiration to increase their respective subjective quality of life.[5] They have been able to eliminate their problems of social Widerspiegelung through their own efforts. This is to be noted and adopted as a guideline: Social Widerspiegelung is something that is the responsibility of humans. Humans are subjects of their lives and lead their lives at their own discretion in accordance with their subjective quality of life. Whether others see this as admirable or react to it with disapproval does not change the fact of subjectivity and personal responsibility. What becomes clear in the reconciliation between Penelope and Odysseus is that social Widerspiegelung contains parts that are not intended for any kind of public. This underlines that support and accompaniment of social Widerspiegelung is dependent on the discretion of humans: humans can decide where and for what they would like to have support and where support is not desired.

---

[3] Bierl in: Bierl et al. (2004, p. 121).
[4] Bierl in: Bierl et al. (2004, p. 122).
[5] cf. Sects. 5.1 and 5.2 in this volume.

7 Outlook

Penelope and Odysseus had in the goddess Athena a supporter in working through their problems of social Widerspiegelung. This fact is also indicative: sometimes it can be very helpful to have support and guidance in shaping social Widerspiegelung. Athena, of course, did not have to stay within the boundaries of ordinary mortals when providing support: she could change conditions if she felt it was necessary. If the night was too short for reconciliation and understanding, Athena simply made it longer.

Also for the present and the future it seems appropriate that the design of social Widerspiegelung finds the best possible support. Whether one should rely on the appearance of Greek goddesses for this, however, is questionable. Moreover, the Greek goddesses are notoriously capricious: they sometimes show their favor, but also quickly withdraw it. In this case, the support in the design of social Widerspiegelung from another side is more reliable, since it is institutionally secured.

What is meant is social work. Social work cannot change conditions by winking. But it can take up something that was to be found in Athena: Athena was the goddess of wisdom. Wisdom and above all knowledge is what social work can contribute through support and accompaniment to enable the shaping of social Widerspiegelung.

Social work could take on the task of shaping social Widerspiegelung in such a way that the potential of social Widerspiegelung is brought to bear and its weaknesses are eliminated. It can bring its knowledge of the nature of social Widerspiegelung to this task. Social Widerspiegelung remains the subjective responsibility of humans, but receives qualified support from social work in its shaping.

References

Abels, J.G.: Wahrnehmung. In: Rexilius, G., Grubitzsch, S. (Hrsg.) Psychologie. Theorien – Methoden – Arbeitsfelder, S. 313–331. Reinbek (1986)

Adloff, F., Mau, S. (Hrsg.): Vom Geben und Nehmen. Zur Soziologie der Reziprozität. Frankfurt a. M. (2005a)

Adloff, F., Mau, S.: Zur Theorie der Gabe und Reziprozität. In: Adloff, F., Mau, S. (Hrsg.) Vom Geben und Nehmen. Zur Soziologie der Reziprozität, S. 9–57. Frankfurt a. M. (2005b)

Ainsworth, M.: Muster von Bindungsverhalten, die vom Kind in der Interaktion mit seiner Mutter gezeitigt werden. In: Grossmann, K.E., Grossmann, K. (Hrsg.) Bindung und menschliche Entwicklung. John Bowlby, Mary Ainsworth und die Grundlagen der Bindungstheorie, S. 102–111. Stuttgart (2003)

Autrata, O.: Was ist das Soziale? Kritische Betrachtung und neue Theorie. Sozial Extra. 5(6), 42–45 (2011)

Autrata, O., Scheu, B.: Theorie Sozialer Arbeit verstehen. Ein Vademecum, Wiesbaden (2015)

Autrata, O., Scheu, B.: Metatheoretische Rahmung von Theorie Sozialer Arbeit. Normativität als Chance. In: Krieger, W., Kraus, B. (Hrsg.) Normativität in der Wissenschaft der Sozialen Arbeit. Zur Kritik normativer Dimensionen in Theorie, Wissenschaft und Praxis der Sozialen Arbeit, S. 236–258. Weinheim (2018)

Beck, U.: Risikogesellschaft. Frankfurt a. M. (1986)

Begemann, V., Heckmann, F., Weber, D. (Hrsg.): Soziale Arbeit als angewandte Ethik. Stuttgart (2016)

Bierl, A.: Die Wiedererkennung von Odysseus und seiner treuen Gattin Penelope. Das Ablegen der Maske – Zwischen traditioneller Erzählkunst, Metanarration und psychologischer Vertiefung. In: Bierl, A., Schmitt, A., Willi, A. (Hrsg.) Antike Literatur in neuer Deutung, S. 103–126. Berlin (2004)

Bischof-Köhler, D.: Spiegelbild und Empathie. Die Anfänge der sozialen Kognition. Bern (1989)

© The Author(s), under exclusive license to Springer Fachmedien
Wiesbaden GmbH, part of Springer Nature 2023
O. Autrata, B. Scheu, *Subjective quality of life and social work*,
https://doi.org/10.1007/978-3-658-40400-0

226 References

Bischof-Köhler, D.: Soziale Entwicklung in Kindheit und Jugend. Bindung, Empathie Theory of Mind. Stuttgart (2011)

Braun, K.-H.: Kritik des Freudomarxismus. Köln (1979)

Brommer, F.: Odysseus. Die Taten und Leiden des Helden in antiker Kunst und Literatur. Darmstadt (1983)

Brun, G., Hirsch Hadorn, G.: Textanalyse in den Wissenschaften Inhalte und Argumente analysieren und verstehen. Zürich (2009)

Buldt, B.: Genus proximum. In: Mittelstraß, J. (Hrsg.) *Enzyklopädie Philosophie und Wissenschaftstheorie*, Bd. 3, S. 85–86, 2. Aufl. Stuttgart (2008)

Deutscher Berufsverband für Soziale Arbeit: Definition der Sozialen Arbeit. Deutsche Fassung. https://www.dbsh.de/profession/definition-der-sozialen-arbeit/deutsche-fassung.html. Accessed on: 12. Oktober 2020

Dilthey, W.: Die geistige Welt. Einleitung in die Philosophie des Lebesn. Erste Hälfte, Gesammelte Schriften, V. Band, 8. unveränderte Auflage. Stuttgart (1990)

Förstl, H.: Theory of Mind. Anfänge und Ausläufer. In: Förstl, H. (Hrsg.) Theory of Mind. Neurobiologie und Psychologie sozialen Verhaltens, 2. Aufl., S. 3–11. Berlin (2012)

Fuhrmann, M. (Hrsg.): Aristoteles Poetik Griechisch/deutsch Bibliografisch ergänzte Ausgabe. Stuttgart (1994)

Gabriel, K.: Religionen und Soziale Arbeit. In: Otto, H.-U., Thiersch, H. (Hrsg.) Handbuch Soziale Arbeit, 6. Aufl., S. 1287–1324. München (2008)

Galamaga, A.: Philosophie der Menschenrechte nach Martha C. Nussbaum. Eine Einführung in den Capabilities Approach, Marburg (2014)

Glasersfeld, E.V.: Konstruktion der Wirklichkeit und des Begriffs der Objektivität. In: Foerster, H.V., Glasersfeld, E.V., Hejl, P.M. (Hrsg.) Einführung in den Konstruktivismus, S. 9–40. München (1992)

Goldstein, E.B.: Wahrnehmungspsychologie. Heidelberg (2002)

Henke, W., Rothe, H.: Menschwerdung. Frankfurt a. M (2003)

Hillebrandt, F.: Praktiken des Tauschens. Zur Soziologie symbolischer Formen der Reziprozität, Wiesbaden (2008)

Holz, H.H.: Widerspiegelung. Bielefeld (2003)

Holzkamp, K.: Sinnliche Erkenntnis. Historischer Ursprung und gesellschaftliche Funktion der Wahrnehmung, 4., rev. Aufl. Königstein (1978)

Holzkamp, K.: Grundlegung der Psychologie. Frankfurt a. M. (1985, Studienausgabe)

Holzkamp, K.: Handeln. In: Rexilius, G., Grubitzsch, S. (Hrsg.) Psychologie. Theorien – Methoden – Arbeitsfelder, S. 381–402. Reinbek (1986)

Holzkamp, K.: Schriften II. Theorie und Experiment in der Psychologie. Eine grundlagenkritische Untersuchung. Hamburg (2005)

International Association of Schools of Social Work: Globale Definition von Sozialarbeit. https://www.iassw-aiets.org/de/global-definition-of-social-work-review-of-the-global-definition. Accessed on 12. Oktober 2020

Kant, I.: Metaphysische Anfangsgründe der Naturwissenschaft, 3. Aufl. Berlin (2014)

Klaus, G., Buhr, M.: Philosophisches Wörterbuch, Bd. 1, 12., gegenüber der 10. neubearb. Aufl. Berlin (1976a)

Klaus, G., Buhr, M.: Philosophisches Wörterbuch, Bd. 2, 12., gegenüber der 10. neubearb. Aufl. Berlin (1976b)

Lambers, H.: Theorien der Sozialen Arbeit. Ein Kompendium und Vergleich, 5., überarb. Aufl. Opladen (2020)

References

Latacz, J.: Homer. Der erste Dichter des Abendlands, 4. Aufl. Düsseldorf (2003)

Lawick-Goodall, J.V.: Wilde Schimpansen. 10 Jahre Verhaltensforschung am Gombe-Strom. Reinbek (1971)

Leontjew, A. N.: Probleme der Entwicklung des Psychischen, 3. Aufl. Königstein (1980)

Leontjew, A.N.: Tätigkeit, Bewußtsein, Persönlichkeit. Studien zur Kritischen Psychologie. Köln (1982)

Leupold, M.: Gelingendes Leben unter Berücksichtigung sozialräumlichen Handelns. In: Begemann, V., Heckmann, F., Weber, D. (Hrsg.) Soziale Arbeit als angewandte Ethik, S. 56–72. Stuttgart (2016)

Marx, K., Engels, F.: MEW 20. Berlin (1962a)

Marx, K., Engels, F.: MEW 21. Springer, Berlin (1962b)

Marx, K., Engels, F.: MEW 23, 4. Aufl. Berlin (1977)

Mauss, M.: Die Gabe. In: Adloff, F., Mau, S. (Hrsg.) Vom Geben und Nehmen Zur Soziologie der Reziprozität, S. 61–72. Frankfurt a. M. (2005)

Melber, H.: Rassismus und eurozentrisches Zivilisationsmodell. Zur Entwicklungsgeschichte des kolonialen Blicks. In: Autrata, O., Kaschuba, G., Leiprecht, R., Wolf, C. (Hrsg.) Theorien über Rassismus. Eine Tübinger Veranstaltungsreihe, S. 29–62. Hamburg (1989)

Nohl, H.: Aufgaben und Wege der Sozialpädagogik. Vorträge und Aufsätze von Herman Nohl, Weinheim (1965)

Nussbaum, M.: Aristotelian Social Democracy. In: Douglass, R.B., Mara, G.N., Richardson, H.S. (Hrsg.) Liberalism and the Good, S. 203–252. New York (1990)

Ortmann, K., Röh, D., Ansen, H.: Sozialtherapie als Handlungskonzept der Klinischen Sozialarbeit. In: Lammel, U.A., Pauls, H. (Hrsg.) Sozialtherapie: Sozialtherapeutische Interventionen als dritte Säule der Gesundheitsversorgung, S. 27–46. Dortmund (2017)

Poser, H.: Wissenschaftstheorie Eine philosophische Einführung, 2., überarb. u. erw. Aufl. Stuttgart (2012)

Premack, D., Woodruff, G.: Does a chimpanzee have a theory of mind? Behav. Brain Sci. **1**, 515–526 (1978)

Rohracher, H.: Einführung in die Psychologie, Wien (1960)

Roth, W.-M.: The Mathematics of mathematics, thinking with the late, spinozist vygotsky, Rotterdam (2017)

Roth, W.-M.: Translation and its consequences in qualitative social research: On distinguishing "the Social" from "the Societal" [45 paragraphs]. Forum Qualitative Sozialforschung/ Forum: Qualitative Social Research **19**(1), Art. 12. https://doi.org/10.17169/fqs19.1.2988 (2018)

Rubinstein, S.L.: Sein und Bewußtsein, 6. Aufl. erlin (1972)

Rückert, N.: Quality of Life – reloaded. In: Begemann, V., Heckmann, F., Weber, D. (Hrsg.) Soziale Arbeit als angewandte Ethik, S. 90–103. Stuttgart (2016)

Sahlins, M.: Zur Soziologie des primitiven Tauschs. In: Adloff, F., Mau, S. (Hrsg.) Vom Geben und Nehmen. Zur Soziologie der Reziprozität, S. 73–91. Frankfurt a. M. (2005)

Scheu, B.: Das Soziale und die Soziale Arbeit. Gestaltung des Sozialen als Grundlegung. Sozial Extra. **5–6**, 46–49 (2011)

Scheu, B., Autrata, O.: Theorie Sozialer Arbeit. Gestaltung des Sozialen als Grundlage. Wiesbaden (2011)

Scheu, B., Autrata, O.: Partizipation und Soziale Arbeit. Einflussnahme auf das subjektiv Ganze. Wiesbaden (2013)

Scheu, B., Autrata, O.: Das Subjekt als Instanz der Kritik. Entscheidungen gegenüber Möglichkeitsräumen. In: Krieger, W., Sierra Bierra, S. (Hrsg.) Systemisch – kritisch? Zur Kritischen Systemtheorie und zur systemisch-kritischen Praxis der Sozialen Arbeit, S. 257–273. Stuttgart (2017)

Scheu, B., Autrata, O.: Das Soziale. Gegenstand der Sozialen Arbeit, Wiesbaden (2018)

Scheu, B.: Demenz. Eine Herausforderung für die Soziale Arbeit. Sozial Extra. **4**, 24–27 (2014)

Schrenk, F.: Paläoanthropologie. In: Bohlken, E., Thies, C. (Hrsg.) Handbuch Anthropologie. Der Mensch zwischen Natur, Kultur und Technik, S. 197–207. Stuttgart (2009)

Schurig, V.: Naturgeschichte des Psychischen 1. Psychogenese und elementare Formen der Tierkommunikation. Frankfurt a. M. (1975)

Seligman, M.: Der Glücks-Faktor. Warum Optimisten länger leben. Lübbe (2005)

Simonow, P.W.: Widerspiegelungstheorie und Psychophysiologie der Emotionen. Berlin (1975)

Sommer, M., Döhnel, K., Schuwerk, T., Hajak, G.: Funktionell-neuroanatomische Grundlagen der Theory of Mind. In: Förstl, H. (Hrsg.) Theory of Mind. Neurobiologie und Psychologie sozialen Verhaltens, 2. Aufl., S. 89–102. Berlin (2012)

Spitzer, M.: Digitale Demenz. Wie wir uns und unsere Kinder um den Verstand bringen. München (2012)

Stegbauer, C.: Reziprozität. Einführung in soziale Formen der Gegenseitigkeit, 2. Aufl. Wiesbaden (2011)

Suddendorf, T.: Der Unterschied. Was den Mensch zum Menschen macht, 2. Aufl. Berlin (2014)

Tönnies, F.: Gemeinschaft und Gesellschaft. Grundbegriffe der reinen Soziologie, Nachdr. der 8. Aufl. Darmstadt (1963)

Verlag Herder (Hg.): Lexikon der Biologie, Heidelberg (1994)

Vollmer, G.: Wieso können wir die Welt erkennen? : neue Beiträge zur Wissenschaftstheorie, Stuttgart (2003)

Waal, F.: de: Das Prinzip Empathie. Was wir von der Natur für eine bessere Gesellschaft lernen können. München (2009)

Walter, N.T.: Die biologischen Grundlagen menschlichen Sozialverhaltens. Die Neurobiologie der Empathie und des prosozialen Verhaltens und Evidenz einer molekulargenetischen Grundlage. Hamburg (2014)

Walther, A., Förstl, H.: Zelluläre Korrelate der Theory of Mind. Spiegelneurone, Von-Economo-Neurone, parvo- und magnozelluläre Neurone. In: Förstl, H. (Hrsg.) Theory of Mind. Neurobiologie und Psychologie sozialen Verhaltens, 2. Aufl., S. 103–110. Berlin (2012)

Wickler, W., Seibt, U.: Das Prinzip Eigennutz. Ursachen und Grenzen sozialen Verhaltens. München (1981)

Wieland, W.: Die aristotelische Physik, 2., durchges. Aufl. Göttingen (1970)

Wilson, E.O.: Die soziale Eroberung der Erde. Eine biologische Geschichte des Menschen. München (2013)

Württembergische Bibelanstalt: Die Bibel oder die ganze Heilige Schrift des Alten und Neuen Testaments. Nach der deutschen Übersetzung Martin Luthers. Stuttgart (1964)

Wygotski, L.: Ausgewählte Schriften, Bd. 1. Köln (1985)

Zahn-Waxler, C., Radke-Yarrow, M., King, R.A.: Child rearing and children's prosocial initiations toward victims of distress. Child Dev. 50, 319–330 (1979)

Printed in the United States
by Baker & Taylor Publisher Services